Timbuktu

Also by Marq de Villiers and Sheila Hirtle

Sable Island: The Strange Origins and Curious History of a Dune Adrift in the Atlantic

Sahara: The Extraordinary History of the World's Largest Desert

By Marq de Villiers

Windswept: The Story of Wind and Weather

Timbuktu

The Sahara's Fabled
City of Gold

Marq de Villiers and Sheila Hirtle

Walker & Company
New York

Published by Walker Publishing Company, Inc., New York
Distributed to the trade by Holtzbrinck Publishers

All papers used by Walker & Company are natural, recyclable products made from
wood grown in well-managed forests. The manufacturing processes conform
to the environmental regulations of the country of origin.

Maps on pages ix, x, and xi by Dereck Day.

LIBRARY OF CONGRESS CATALOGING-IN-PUBLICATION DATA HAS BEEN APPLIED FOR.

ISBN-10: 0-8027-1497-8
ISBN-13: 978-0-8027-1497-8

Visit Walker & Company's Web site at www.walkerbooks.com

First U.S. edition 2007

1   3   5   7   9   10   8   6   4   2

Typeset by Westchester Book Group
Printed in the United States of America by Quebecor World Fairfield

Salt comes from the north, gold from the south, and silver from the country

of the white men, but the word of God and the treasures of

wisdom are only to be found in Timbuktu.

—*West African proverb*

If I were a cassowary

On the plains of Timbuctoo,

I would eat a missionary,

Cassock, band, and hymn-book too.

—*Impromptu verse, ascribed to Bishop Samuel*

Wilberforce 1805–1873

O City! O latest Throne! Where I was rais'd

To be a mystery of loveliness

Unto all eyes, the time is well-nigh come

When I must render up this glorious home

To keen Discovery: soon yon brilliant towers

Shall darken with the waving of her wand;

Darken, and shrink and shiver into huts,

Black specks amid a waste of dreary sand,

Low-built, mud-wall'd, Barbarian settlements.

How chang'd from this fair City!

—*Alfred, Lord Tennyson,* Timbuctoo

Contents

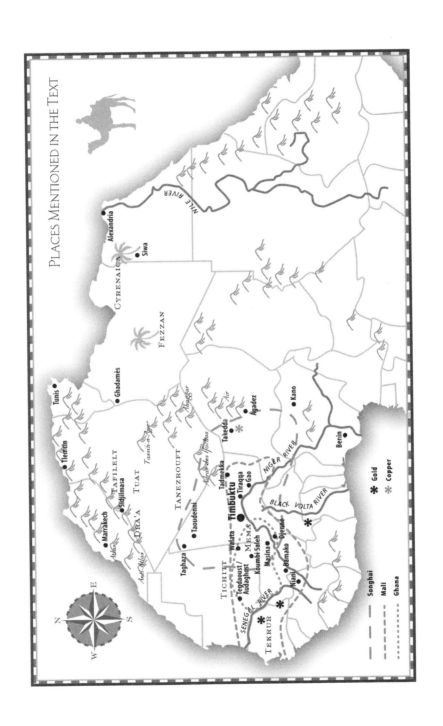

PLACES MENTIONED IN THE TEXT

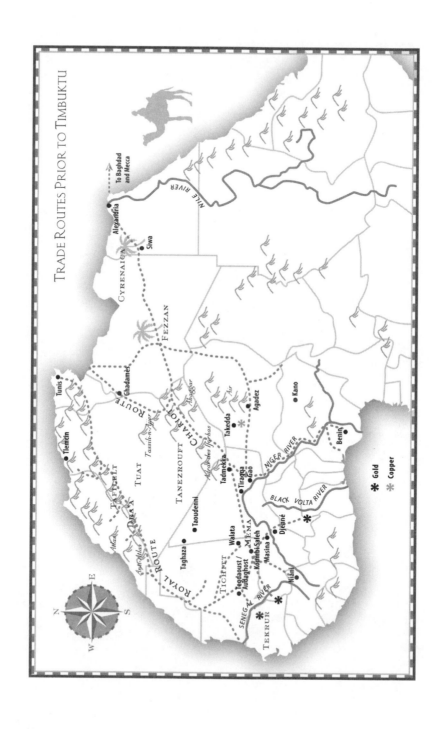

TRADE ROUTES PRIOR TO TIMBUKTU

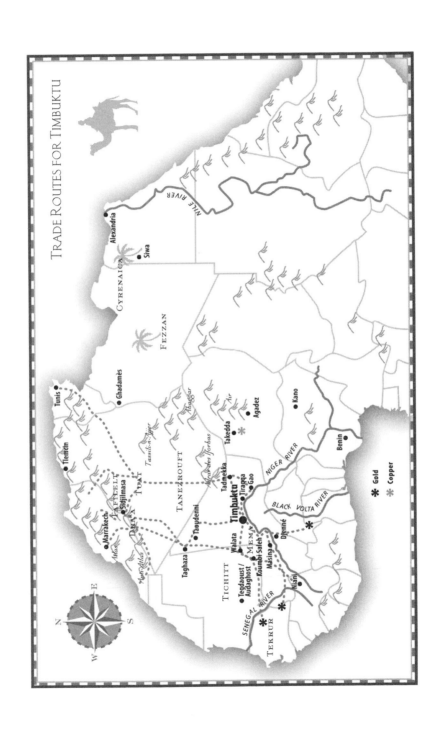

TRADE ROUTES FOR TIMBUKTU

ↁ

Acknowledgments

MANY PEOPLE HELPED us along the way, and we are grateful for their hospitality and their willingness to share their knowledge. Particular gratitude must go to Sidi Salem Ould Elhadj, *chevalier de l'ordre nationale* of Mali, a man steeped in history, with a wonderfully infectious love of his ancient city. A few years ago Sidi Salem gave a lecture to a university audience in Washington, D.C., on the golden age of Timbuktu but found to his chagrin that his listeners wanted only to know his views on Islamic fanaticism. He was not discouraged and is still willing to share his deep knowledge of Timbuktu's traditions and legends. Important also was Abdel Kader Haïdara, proprietor and manager of the Mamma Haïdara Library of ancient documents, and a key member of the Conflict Resolution Group, which was set up in homage to Timbuktu's traditions of tolerance and peace. We are grateful for the hospitality he extended us and for the glimpse he gave us of his extraordinary inheritance. We are grateful also to the Tuareg Halis, more properly known as Mohamed al-Hassan al-Ag Moctar *dit* Halis, and to Shindouk, or Shindouk Mohamed Lamine Ould Najim, chief of a Bérabiche tribe, both of whom know the desert intimately but are also comfortable in the universe of the World Wide Web; to Miranda Dodd, who has adopted Timbuktu as her home and whose character reminded us once again why the Peace Corps was such a good idea; to Sidi Mohamed Ould Youbba, director general of the Ahmed Baba Center, and to Djibril Doucouré, the center's director of conservation and restoration, both of whom were endlessly willing to share their knowledge; to Abderhamane Alpha Maïga, managing director of the Hendrina Khan Hotel in Timbuktu, who taught us much about the city's long traditions of tolerance; to the Dicko brothers, Litini and Malick, for their hospitality; to

Shamil Jeppe of the University of Cape Town, for telling us part of what the story is about; to Tahara Baby for her hospitality. And finally to John Hunwick, whom we have never met, but whose copious writing fills all the interstices of Timbuktu historiography, the kind of oversize presence that is greatly reassuring in these anti-intellectual and intolerant days.

Note to Readers

Alert readers will notice that sometimes the pronoun "I" appears in the text, although there are two authors. Unless otherwise specified, this "I" is Marq de Villiers. Two of us produced this book in equal measure. We both sojourned in Timbuktu. Otherwise, the travel into the archives, libraries, and technical journals was done mostly by Sheila Hirtle, the travel in the hinterlands of Timbuktu, and the consequent anecdotes and conversations, mostly by Marq de Villiers.

CHAPTER ONE

❧

Dreaming Spires of Gold, Under the Desert Sun

ABDEL KADER HAÏDARA'S Timbuktu home sprawls off an un-named sandy alley—they're all sandy in Timbuktu, and none of them are named—in the southeast quadrant of the city. We pulled up outside its walled courtyard late one winter afternoon; children were playing in the sand outside, building corrals out of twigs and dried goat dung, the source of the dung being tethered to a stake nearby. In the courtyard a graybeard sat companionably by, chewing rhythmically, and two women pulled and pounded at a laundry tub. Inside, the windowless main living room was sheltered from the sun, turquoise and cool, with carpets on the floor and red plush banquettes; the walls were lined with bookcases and cabinets and a hulking television set. Our host was there with an uncle and a friend; with us was a young Tuareg called Mohamed al-Hassan al-Ag Moctar *dit* Halis, usually just known by his nickname, Halis (which is an affectionate mother's "My Little Man" in Tamashek, the language of the Tuareg). It was Halis who introduced us. He was there as interpreter, though he was not needed; the urbane and ever-courteous Sidi Haïdara spoke fluent and effortless French, among many other languages. After the first pleasantries, the conversation ranged from the legends about the founding of Timbuktu, through the golden age of the city, to its gradual decline after the Moroccan invasions, some four hundred years ago. It's not too much to say that the city has been slowly declining ever since that invasion, for most of those four hundred years.

But, at least for the moment, we were less interested in the long decline, and the still active animus against the invaders, than in the city's days as a preeminent center of Islamic learning, as a locus of sophisticated scholarship that illumined and enlightened much of the civilized world. Eventually we fell to discussing Ahmed Baba, a scholar who died in the early 1600s but whose name is often still mentioned as though he were a favorite uncle who has just popped out for a quick prayer and will be back in a moment. Ahmed Baba's personal library contained some sixteen hundred volumes when he died, but he often remarked that his was one of the lesser collections among the eminent and worthy of his colleagues, and even among members of his family. We knew that our host, Sidi Abdel Kader, was a renowned expert on Timbuktu's literary heritage and was himself the head of the family that owned the Mamma Haïdara Library, one of the largest extant collections of ancient manuscripts left in the Saharan Sahel, a priceless link to the glorious past.

Could we see it?

Could we, indeed. The building that housed it was undergoing much-needed and expensive renovations, so he had, well, brought a good deal of it home . . . Where better to keep an eye on it? It was his, after all. Our host heaved himself to his feet and led us back into the outer courtyard. In one wall was a battered corrugated iron door, locked with an old-fashioned padlock. Sidi Abdel Kader fished a bunch of keys from his robe and opened the door, pushing it inward with a grinding sound. Inside a small room thus revealed, from floor to roof, were tottering piles of ancient manuscripts, some in loose bundles, some in battered tin trunks or leather portfolios, others simply piled higgledy-piggledy on the dusty floor.

I carefully lifted one from the top of a pile.* Its leather binding was scarred and felt brittle to the hand. It was in Arabic. Sidi Abdel Kader leaned over to look. "Arabic script but in the Bambara language," he said. It dated from somewhere around 1750 and was written here in Timbuktu, at a studio near the Sankoré mosque, by a scholar now forgotten. It had belonged to the Haïdara family during all that time. As we stared down at it, I noticed Halis hovering around in the background, looking smug, as though he had personally conjured up the whole collection.

"The oldest book we have," Sidi Abdel Kader said, gesturing at the jam-packed storeroom, "is a compilation of Islamic laws, written in 1204." Many manuscripts in the collection were imported from the Maghreb, from Fez and Tlemcen and the learned schools there, or from even farther abroad, from Cairo or the Holy Places themselves; some are histories that recount stories of

---

*See note to readers in the acknowledgments, page xiv.

Old Ghana and its now vanished capital, Koumbi Saleh, others date from the mansas of Mali, the most potent empire of Old Africa, still others from the time of the askias, who ruled their Songhai kingdom, and Timbuktu, from the Niger River port of Gao, until the Moroccans came and ruined everything.

✑

HE PULLED THE door closed and clapped on the padlock, not bothering to ram it closed, and we went back inside. But soon afterward we took our leave. Now that we'd seen Mamma Haïdara's astonishing library, in its equally astonishing closet, our minds were filled with the miracle of its survival after all these centuries, and we really had no more questions to ask. Or rather, the many questions we did have seemed banal by comparison, so we decided to leave them for another time. All those piles and piles of parchment and linen paper, all those hand-scribed histories and treatises and investigations and pious exhortations, all those glorious annotations and illustrations, were a powerful metaphor for the city as it once had been, in a golden age of scholarship, learning, piousness and tolerance. And the fact that all this astonishing intellectual history was just sitting there, in a sandy closet down a sandy street (no matter how sensible or temporary its life there) became another kind of metaphor—one that spoke to a glorious past turned to dust by invasion, conquest, jihad and the long, long, debilitating passage of time.

Buried in those tottering piles were all the great themes of Timbuktu's history, the very reasons it exerted such a hypnotic attraction on the Mediterranean world and especially the European imagination over so many centuries: its setting as the nexus of the trans-Saharan trade for more than five hundred years; the astonishing flowering of what started as a pasturing place for Tuareg nomads into a wealthy metropolis, a trading emporium that prospered on gold and salt and slaves, whose reputation loomed so large that it attracted the avaricious attention of the Venetian traders and then of the sultan of Morocco, who wanted the gold traffic for himself, to further his ambitions of supplanting the caliphs of Baghdad; and of Timbuktu as a center of learning, a preeminent locus of Islamic scholarship, luring the learned and the pious from Mecca, Alexandria, Baghdad, Tlemcen, Tripoli, Fez, Marrakech, Cordoba. In addition to all that, Timbuktu was a city of 333 saints, or marabouts, and its own proprietary demon, or so the elders said. The holy men, and the unmentionable other, had their place in the library too.

Real wealth, intellectual wealth and religious piety were intertwined all through the city's history. Only political wealth was missing: Timbuktu attracted the attention (and sometimes avarice) of many powerful sovereigns who wanted to control it, and sometimes did. But it never became the capital of any kingdom or empire or sultanate; it was the outlying commercial emporium first of the Malian kings, governing from the southwest, then the rulers of Songhai, governing from the east, then the sultans of Morocco, governing from across the sand seas, to the north. In between it was governed, mostly ineptly and fiercely, variously by Tuareg, Bambara or Fulani occupiers, but it had never run its own affairs.

Political power still eludes it. After fifty years of independence, the Malian state has yet to build a highway from the capital, Bamako, to Timbuktu. Timbuktu is a northern town, a Tuareg town, a frontier town. No one in the capital any longer cares. Timbuktu has . . . faded.

℘

SO WHY WAS it important, this now faded and dusty desert capital? In a curious way, the reputation, or reputations, that accreted to Timbuktu predate its actual founding by many years, perhaps by a millennium or more. Or put the other way, Timbuktu itself became a shorthand metaphor for a much greater body of stories and legends about other places altogether. Some of the images inserted into outside imaginations over the centuries were grafted onto the city in the days of its magnificence under the Malian king Mansa Musa. Some of these, in turn, were legends that enveloped the earliest of the Arab invaders, in the seventh and eighth centuries, which in their turn were based on folklore derived at least in part from hints and suggestions of travelers going back to earliest antiquity.

Europe and the Maghreb, or Christianity and Islam, always had differing views of Timbuktu. In both places the city's reputation shifted over time, and the various versions overlapped, but they were never the same.

It's true that in both places gold was at the heart of the matter, at least at first. Before the Arabs were routinely traversing the desert and seeing for themselves, their geographers had stitched together from obscure fragments of folktale and legend a dream of riches untold, of gold lying on the ground for the taking, of immense wealth just waiting for the intrepid. But that romantic notion had faded by the fourteenth century, for traders followed the stories, and traders had harder heads than the storytellers, and saw for themselves what was, rather than what should be. The renowned traveler Ibn Battuta and his medieval colleagues did report on the great wealth of the Malian Empire and its storehouses of gold, for the trade in that and other commodities was the city's reason for being, and Timbuktu really was very wealthy; but Timbuktu also took on a reputation among Muslims for its learning. Many of the Arab travelers remarked on the city's thirst for books, as well as its traffic in gold, and wrote commentaries on its savants as well as its opulence.

From the fourteenth century on, pilgrims from Timbuktu went to the Holy Places of Islam, sometimes in great numbers and in immense caravans, but scholars from Mecca and Medina also went to live and study in Timbuktu, where they found themselves (sometimes to their evident chagrin) not as eminent or as learned as they had supposed. The university at Fez and the University of Sankoré in Timbuktu were said to be equivalent; commentaries on the Qur'an produced at Sankoré were read in Jeddah and Cairo, and the eminent of both places corresponded over time and great distance, to the profit of both.

This Islamic combination of reputations, those of civilized affluence and scholarly erudition, were eventually fused in the mind of Moulay al-Mansur the Magnificent of Morocco, who in 1591 sent his armies across the desert hoping both to capture the gold trade and to extend his empire, and instead precipitated the city's gradual decay. The soldiers may have been emissaries from what they considered a high culture, but they killed or exiled most of the scholars, equating learning with disaffection, as conquerors are wont to do.

After that, the Arabs essentially lost interest, and for several dismal centuries the city was repeatedly besieged and sacked by a rolling roster of enemies—the Bambara, the Fulani jihadists and the Tuareg—until the French took it in 1893 and restored a semblance of order. Now the Bambara, who are in charge of Mali, are once again in charge of the city's destiny.

ও

IN EUROPE, WHERE they knew and understood much less, the legend of Timbuktu took on a different color; or rather, retained a single color, the yellow of gold. Stories of caches of gold were teased out of the tales of Arab travelers, and the city became in the minds of the geographers and the merchants they served a fabulous place whose skyline was pierced with spires of gold, dreaming under the desert sun, rich beyond measure.

The legends were not entirely without merit. Of the gold that reached North

Africa in the fourteenth and fifteenth centuries, two-thirds came from, or at least through, Timbuktu, and thence across the Sahara. The coins of the doges were Ghanaian gold from Timbuktu; the guineas that fueled the English commercial expansion were from Ghana (on the Guinea coast) and came to England via the markets of Timbuktu. It was natural, therefore, to think that Timbuktu was itself the origin of the gold and not just a way station on its route. In this way the city took on an almost luminous eminence in the European imagination, a fantastic land groaning under the ineffable weight of its affluence. Unlike the mutated Arab view, it was the pretty legends that seized the European imagination, not the reality. It was loot, not lore, that they coveted.

This image of great riches and a wondrous desert civilization lasted until colonial times; grafted onto it was the newer notion of its very remoteness—never mind that Arab travelers had been going there for seven hundred years and more; Christians were forbidden, and often killed when they were caught. As late as Victoria's reign a popular saying in England was still "from here to Timbuktu," which meant "from here to as far away as you can get," adding a layer of inaccessibility and mystery to the legends of great opulence. Few men who went there, or tried to go there, or even went into the deep Sahara, ever returned to Europe, "and those who did so told almost incoherent stories of madness through thirst, unspeakable cruelties of mirages, a fierce and terrible sun, and a vast limitless ocean of sand."[1] Nothing much about money, though they knew it was there somewhere. Why go, otherwise?

◌

FROM THE VERY earliest times, they always knew *something* was there. *They* being outsiders generally, the people of the north and northeast, and *there* being the south, the other side of the Great Emptiness of the Sahara Desert. What that *something* was thought to be shifted and changed as empires' fortunes waxed and waned. Was it rods of gold sticking up from the earth, ripe for the plucking, a great city of brass shining like a beacon in the southern sun, a mountain of rubies? Or was it the existence of wealthy and wise kings, sitting on stools of gold, a benevolent presence there in the endless unknown? The stories tantalized everyone who heard them. One El Welid, "the son of Romah the Amalekite," went into the deep desert, looking, as he supposed, for the source of the Nile. "He occupied three years in preparing for his expedition, and then started with a large army, destroying every tribe he came upon. He passed through the tribes of the Soudan, and through the gold country, and there he saw golden sticks sprouting out of the ground. He continued journeying until he reached the great Lake, unto which the Nile flows." Dozens of tales like this are told, some of them seemingly transferred to North Africa from the circle of sagas that surrounded Alexander the Great. One traveler, for example, was said to have "gone to the land of the blacks, [and was] rewarded with gold and the capture of two maidens . . . from a people whose women had only one breast"—one-breasted women being two-a-penny in the Alexandrian myths.[2]

No reports survive of emissaries from the pharaohs of Egypt reaching the Sahel or the goldfields of West Africa, of Old Ghana (or Ghana-Wangara as it was sometimes called, Wangara being the Muslim geographers' name for the Middle Niger), though such penetration would have been plausible enough. That there were caravan routes across the desert by the second millennium BC is common knowledge; that Meroë and Kush traded with the rulers of Bornu on Lake Chad is known; that, indeed, there was a well-traveled route from Alexandria to the Upper Nile is known; that an easy route went west from the great lake to the Middle Niger is also known.

The earliest written reports date back to the Greco-Roman period, and a few hints are found in the classical literature. The great historian Herodotus, who was born in 484 BC, wrote extensively on Africa—his history of the Persians' invasion of Egypt and their defeat of the Ammonites in the Western Desert is a classic of historical writing—and he made several references to the penetration of the Sahara itself. One account, admitted by Herodotus himself to have been thirdhand, was the story of "some wild young men" of Cyrenaica, "who drew lots to decide which of their number should explore the desert part of Libya, seeking to penetrate further than any had done before." These young men, no doubt pumped by testosterone-fueled bravado, traveled for many days over desert sand, until they came to a plain dotted about with trees, and then to a great marsh, where they were met by "dwarfish men, black of skin," who took them to their town by a river flowing west to east. These marshes or swamps could plausibly be the Niger floodplains, the great river the Niger itself, and the city they found some precursor of Gao.[3]

It was Herodotus, too, who first described incursions into the desert by the Garamantes civilization of Libya, probably a Berber kingdom that inhabited what is now the Fezzan, in southwest Libya, and whose empire, such as it was, lasted a thousand years or more, even after it was overrun and annexed by the Romans in 19 BC.

Nothing is left in modern Libya of the Garamantes except the ruins of their ancient capitals Garama and Zinchecra, and a few rock paintings depicting the characteristic Garamantes four-horse chariots hunting the cave dwellers or "troglodytes" of the High Mountains of Ethiopia (though *Aethiopia* in ancient writings simply meant "Black lands," and there are even suggestions that the troglodytes could have been the cave dwellers of modern Mauritania, hard by the Atlantic—Tin Labbé in Mauritania is a dramatic troglodyte village that still survives, the original rock shelters and crevices finished with stone walls and mud plaster). A few enigmatic references can also be found in Herodotus and later in Pliny the Elder, who both described not only the chariots, much admired by the technologically savvy Pliny, but also their peculiar "backward gazing cattle," as Pliny put it (the animals were often shown gazing over their shoulders).

Garamantes emissaries and traders routinely crossed the desert, traveling vast distances to do so. They had traffic with Egypt to the east and with Gao (or Gao's precursor city, Kukiya, now vanished) on the distant Niger River. Ptolemy, in his history of the Persian Wars, asserts that the Garamantes governed the whole of the eastern Sahara as far as Sudan, but his meaning (and the boundaries) are uncertain. The poet Virgil used Garamantes as a metaphor for remoteness ("a land beyond the paths of sun and year, beyond the constellations"), and in that way its reputation was eerily similar to Timbuktu's in later centuries. In practice, their governance followed the ancient caravan routes from Fezzan to Bornu on Lake Chad, already well known to traders. By 500 BC Garamantian chariots were thought to be traveling from the Fezzan district of Libya to Gao-Kukiya, skirting the central Saharan massifs of Tassili, the Ahaggar and the Adrar des Iforhas, thereby pioneering some of the Sahara's most venerable caravan routes. Whether they did actual business in these chariots is less certain; in the eccentric traditions of modern historiography, French academics have actually tested such vehicles in the Saharan sands and found them wanting: they couldn't carry much more than the operator. The debate remains open: possibly caravans of draft animals accompanied the charioteers. Or possibly the Sahara was more verdant then and easier to traverse.

It was a Roman army, under the African proconsul Lucius Cornelius Balbus, who finally annexed the Garamantes and their country, which the Romans came to call Phazania (Fezzan). It was an annexation, though, and not a conquest, for the Garamantes remained influential throughout the Sahara until AD 500.

After the annexation the restless legions ranged farther afield, followed and sometimes preceded by merchant adventurers. One such was Julius Maternus, who, according to a later Greek writer called Marinus of Tyre, traveled with a Garamantes expedition to a land called Agisymba. The location of this mysterious place is widely disputed—and was even widely disputed at the time, some reports putting it as far south as the southern tropic (which would mean somewhere around the latitude of Zimbabwe), and Ptolemy suggesting it was much closer to the equator. It could even be in the northern hemisphere, as northerly as modern Lake Chad, though this is less likely. Wherever it was, Maternus saw plentiful rhinoceros there; indeed, there are suggestions he traveled to Agisymba specifically to collect the animals for the Roman games. The Romans' defensive wall around their Fezzan province was a line hundreds of miles long along the northern edge of the desert, with forts at intervals, but there were advance forts beyond that, in the remoter oases, almost halfway to where Timbuktu was to be founded, a millennium or so later.

None of these intrepid travelers discovered riches or wealthy kings, but little wisps of rumor drifted like wind-borne sand into the northern cities—somewhere to the south, and to the west, in the land of the people called Wangara or beyond it, in a space no man knew, such kings and such gold existed, and were waiting, needing only to be fetched.

౭ఄ

IN THE SEVENTH and eighth centuries Arab invaders swept across the North African littoral carrying all before them, until the final Islamic conqueror dipped his toe into the Atlantic and declared that nothing more was to be won.

Except . . . that there *was*. Wangara, or the Wangarans, still waited with their cones of gold, somewhere across the emptiness.

Even though the Garamantes had already penetrated the great desert, the new arrivals on the North African shore looked over the Atlas Mountains at the great sand seas beyond and quailed. They came to think of the wayward flowing sands of the Sahara as an immense river, across which no bridges led, a treacherous thing whose turbid currents could sweep away the unwary to lands unknown, perhaps to the primeval mud from which the sun is born. In this, they were already following the legends. After all, one Dhu'l-Adhar, a king of Yemen said to have lived at about the time of Solomon (a sure sign that mythmaking is at work), raided the Maghreb, defined as "the land beyond the borders," west of Egypt (that is, beyond civilization) and forced it into submission. His son and successor, Yasir, is said to have reached the Saharan Sand River south of the Moroccan Rif and to have halted, dismayed, unable to find passage through the "seething currents of sand." Adhar and Yasir fled back to the coast, and their lineage vanished from the stories.[4]

One of the earliest Arab invaders of the Maghreb reached a wadi at the edge of the desert with his army and stopped, as dismayed as Yasir had been. He found it to be flowing with sand like towering mountains. "He ordered [one of his commanders] to cross the *wadi* with 20,000 men. He advanced until he vanished from sight and not one of his men ever returned. Next he [sent another commander on the same mission]. He crossed over with 10,000 men but he and his companions did not return either, and they vanished from his sight."[5] (It's also fair to say that the eminent fourteenth-century Tunisian historian Ibn Khaldun, who was a notorious debunker of tall tales, thought these stories of the great rivers of sand to be a colorful fiction—others had been crossing the supposedly uncrossable for centuries, he pointed out.)

The Arab governor of North Africa, Musa ibn Nusayr, the same Nusayr who sent his legions northward to create the Muslim province of al-Andalus (now more generally known as Spain), also looked south, searching for the Valley of the Ruby, the City of Brass and the Tower of Lead, though he found nothing but pastoral families and their flocks.

No matter. Nusayr's quest gave him an honored place in the *Thousand and One Arabian Nights* and firmly planted the idea of dreaming spires of precious metal in the receptive minds of the Maghreb and then Europe.

The story starts when the fifth caliph of the Umayyad dynasty, Abd al-Malik bin Marwan (685–705), is told a tale of a ship being blown off course and fetching up in a country where the inhabitants were black of color and naked of body, and where you could catch in the waves bottles sealed with the sign of Solomon, son of David, each of which contained *djinn*, spirits and conjurers.

"By Allah," says the caliph, "I long to look upon some of these Solomonic vessels," to which the storyteller replies: "It is in thy power to do so without stirring abroad. Send to thy brother the governor of Egypt so that he may write to Musa ibn Nusayr, governor of the Maghreb, bidding him take horse thence to the mountains whereof I spoke and fetch thee therefrom as many such cucurbits [gourdlike containers] as thou hast a mind to; for those mountains adjoin the frontiers of his province."

Nusayr duly sets out, "traversing frightful wolds and thirsty wastes and then mountains which spired high in the air; nor did they leave journeying a whole year's space till, one morning, when the day broke after they had traveled all night, behold, the [guide] found himself in a land he knew not . . . and on the horizon some great thing, high and black . . . a high castle, great and gruesome, as it were a towering mountain . . . [which the guide recognized and said:] '. . . my grandfather . . . said: We were once journeying in this land and straying from the road, we came to this palace and thence to the City of Brass; between which and the place thou seekest is two full months' travel.' "

Eventually a djinn sends him to "Al-Karkar" [Kawkaw, an older name for Gao] "on the shores whereof dwell a people of the lineage of Noah . . . And which is the way to the City of Brass . . . It is near at hand [to that place]."

And so it was. And Nusayr, after a series of adventures which saw him patrolling through palaces whose "owners [were] lying dead upon mats of scented goats' leather . . . bladders of musk and ambergris . . . vessels of ivory and ebony . . . bows and bucklers hanging by chains of gold and silver and helmets gilded with red gold . . . benches of ivory, plated with glittering gold and covered with silken stuffs" duly acquired a dozen bottled djinn from the "children of Ham," gave "the King of the blacks many and great gifts" and returned to the caliph.[6]

Fanciful, of course—Nusayr himself never crossed the Sahara, and the geography is, to put it politely, confusing. But the kernel is there. The "great thing, high and black," could have been the Ahaggar Mountains; Kawkaw (Gao-Kukiya) had been in touch with the goldfields of the Black Volta for centuries by this time, and we know that the extraordinary culture of Benin, which plated its public buildings with brass and whose towns glittered in the sun from many leagues' distance, acquired a good deal of its copper from Takedda, much to the north and east of Gao, so there was traffic back and forth.

Benin's capital was one of the glories of Old Africa. It still survived in the seventeenth century, when a Dutch visitor described it thus: "[It] is certainly as large as the town of Haarlem, and entirely surrounded by a special wall. It is divided into many magnificent palaces, houses and apartments of the courtiers, and comprises beautiful and long square galleries, about as large as the exchange in Amsterdam, but one larger than another, resting on wooden pillars, from top to bottom covered with cast copper, on which are engraved the pictures of their war exploits and battles . . . Most palaces and the houses of the king are covered with palm leaves, and every roof is decorated with a turret ending in a point, on which birds are standing, birds cast in copper with outspread wings, cleverly made after living models."[7] The royal court took up almost a fifth of the city; artists belonged to the king, did their work on commission, and their work became royal property. Much of it was magnificent. The obas (kings) wore extravagant amounts of ivory and coral; vassal chiefs were decked out in pounds of bronze.

And of course there is (or was until the British colonialists demolished it) an African society for whom gold was commonplace: the Ashanti, "the people of the golden stool," near the Volta basin. I once spent some time in the museum in Kumasi, in Ashanti country, looking at their artifacts of royalty. The museum has room after room filled to the brim with gold. The sheer amount of gold worn by the Ashanti kings was reported incredulously by early travelers—gold sandals, gold anklets, gold tunics, gold amulets, gold headdresses, gold swords, gold staffs—everything in gold, including the emblem of royal power itself, the Golden Stool. (Also on display is a large brass container that had been looted from the Ashanti by Lord Baden-Powell, founder of the scouting movement. It had been full of gold dust when he took it. His widow eventually returned it, though empty of the gold.)

And so the legends and rumors of the towers of gold and cities of brass to be found "in the Wangara country" (as it later came to be called, in the days of Ghana-Wangara) were mutated reports of real refulgent buildings many hundreds of miles farther on, reports growing in the telling as travelers (and slaves from those distant parts) passed from the Niger delta to the Volta to the Middle Niger to the Maghreb, and to Egypt and beyond.

ح

GEOGRAPHERS REMAINED VAGUE about the interior of Africa for centuries. All through the medieval period and later, in Europe and even in parts of the more worldly Arab universe, it was believed that the two great rivers, the Nile and the Niger, were central to understanding the interior (though they were often conflated into only one giant river). The Niger ran parallel to the equator, and somewhere to the east of center of the continent it joined the Nile, which flowed due north. Their courses were directed by high mountains, though no one in Europe knew where these massifs began or ended, or just how they affected the great rivers, but they gave them resonant names anyway, the Mountains of the Moon, or the Mountains of Kong. In the valleys between these mountains cartographers placed a clutch of king-doms, sometimes savage and barbarous, at other times with noble cities and mighty kings. Mapmakers were forced to choose between flights of fancy or empty white spaces.[8]

The first credible geography of the Saharan hinterlands was produced by the Moroccan Abu Abd' Allah Muhammad al-Idrisi, who traveled in North Africa during his youth (he was born in 1100) and then took up residence with his patron, Roger II, of Sicily, where he began a lifetime's work of map-making and geographic writing. It is unclear how far into the desert Idrisi penetrated, and his main work, *The Pleasure Excursions of One Who is Eager to Traverse the Regions of the World*, still found much of the land south of the Atlas Mountains a zone of mystery. In any case, even had he made it all the way across the desert, Timbuktu would have been at this time not much more than a well and a nomad camp.

Abu l'Hasan Ali ibn Said al-Gharnati, who was born in 1211, may well have been the first European (he was born in Granada, in Spain) to pene-trate the Sahara, and possibly the first outsider to write about it ("may have been" and "possibly" because while he wrote a geographic treatise that in-cluded Africa south of the Sahara, much of it was based on the work of ear-lier writers, notably Idrisi, and it's uncertain whether he actually went anywhere). By Gharnati's time, Timbuktu would have begun its steady climb to affluence. We know this because by the time the next series of re-ports drifted back out of the desert, the city had already taken on an impor-tance far beyond its size.

For several hundred more years, it was mostly Arabs who visited Timbuktu and returned to write about it, among them Ibn Battuta (in the early 1300s), Ibn Khaldun (1380) and al-Makrizi (about 1400). The greatest of these, and the first to penetrate the Sahara and leave a detailed account of his journeys, was Ibn Battuta, or more formally Muhammad ben Abdullah ben Muham-mad ben Ibrahim ben Muhammad ben Ibrahim ben Yusuf, of the tribe of Luwata and the city of Tanja, Abu Abdallah Ibn Battuta. He was born, we know, in Tangier in 1304 of a family of scholars and lawyers, and went to

Mecca for his pilgrimage at the age of twenty-one. There he determined "to travel throughout the earth," and for the rest of his life he wandered about within the limits of his world, making it a basic rule "never, so far as is possible, to cover a second time any road" that he had once traveled, and marrying, on the way, numerous wives.[9] He twice crossed the Sahara to the Niger and beyond, and spent some time in the kingdom of Mali, then at the height of its power and affluence.

More than a hundred years after Battuta came and went, the ignorance about Timbuktu remained profound in Europe, and remained so until modern times. Europeans couldn't even agree on its name. In a letter written by Antoine Malfante and addressed to Giovanni Mariono at Genoa in 1447, Timbuktu is called Tambet or Thambet. Thambet is the name used by Ca' da Mosto in his *Voyages*; he also adopts the name Tambucutu and Tanbutu. A Catalan atlas made for Charles V by Abraham Cresques in 1375 referred to Timbuktu as Tenbuch. A few years later, Diogo Gomes called it Tambucutu. Other variants (sometimes many were used in the same book or document) were Timbuctoo, Timbúktu, Timbu'ktu, Tomboktu, Timbuktuh and Tombutto.

One of the earliest true geographies of the Sahara, and possibly the first to attempt a delineation of the natural boundaries within it, was that of the former slave and papal scribe called Leo Africanus, in the early 1500s. Leo, or "Giovanni Leone," born al-Hasan ibn Muhammed al-Wazzan az-Zayyati in the Moorish city of Granada in 1485, was schooled in Fez and as a teenager accompanied his uncle on diplomatic missions throughout North Africa and across the Sahara to the Sahelian kingdoms of Mali and Songhai. Leo was subsequently captured by European pirates and sold as "a very learned slave" to the pope, in Rome, who promptly freed him and for whom he dutifully recounted what he had learned in an engaging work titled *History and Description of Africa and the Curious Things Therein Contained.* Leo's African travels, rendered into colorful English prose in 1600 by one John Pory (who called him, in that careless English way, John Leo), were the only eyewitness accounts Europe had of the Sahara regions and of Timbuktu itself for several hundred years to come, and European mapmakers, in a frenzy of creative energy, imagined a place into being based on Leo's often useful but sometimes erratic memories.

The reality was to prove more complicated than Leo's tales. It was a longer, deeper, darker reality, much richer than the memories of any scribe, no matter how diligent, though filled as any storybook must be with heroes, villains, fantastic objects, saints and miracles, betrayals and redemptions, endurance of great trials, military genius, tyrants, sophisticated scholars, venal buffoons, and ordinary people making their lives and enduring their deaths in an extraordinary place.

CHAPTER TWO

ↄↄ

The Founder, the Founding
and the Legends

THE WELL OF Buktu, so-called, is a paltry little thing, about three feet across and for the moment not much deeper, and contains no water at all. A goatskin bag suspended from three slender wooden poles poked into the ground hangs-over the opening, a show-and-tell of how the water was drawn to the surface in those days when there was water, if there ever was any. The "well" is kept from falling in by a skinny scaffold of wooden sticks, the whole thing set up in a sandy courtyard that serves as a kind of anteroom to the municipal museum of history of the city of Timbuktu.

This well was probably never a well, and Buktu may never have existed; or if there was a well and Buktu, the founding mother of the mother city, really did exist, it and she were almost certainly never in this spot, and nobody really pretends otherwise. But never mind.

An old man, wizened and sly, was sitting on a bench in the shade, smoking up a storm. He'd sell you a postcard or a "Tuareg" purse or even a goatskin bag if you wanted one, but he didn't try very hard. The hard sell wasn't in him. He was too amused by life and by the improbable appearance and unlikely desires of those few outsiders who passed him by.

"Is this really the well of Buktu?"

He hesitated, assessing the visitor's credulity. But then he grinned. "It is a well of the same type," he said at last.

He offered a drag on his smoke, but I declined. Then he offered an amplification: "No one knows where the real well was. But there must have been one. Who is to say it wasn't here?"

Who indeed? We'd walked up that morning from the massive depression in the sand that would be, some day and some time, the city's first sewage

plant, passed a few boys throwing chunks of broken concrete at a wild date
tree to see if they could get any of its fruit to land in the muck below, and
then encountered a grinning child with a small bird clamped between his
teeth, its wings thrashing in its death throes. We'd skirted a butcher shop ob-
scured by a thick green curtain of flies, and been jostled by two Tuareg men
in indigo robes, striding by with that inborn arrogant swagger that seems native to all the desert nomads, on their way to a mosque that was five hundred
years old in a city a good deal older than that, and then we'd almost been
sideswiped by a motor scooter ridden hard by a young woman in baggy pants
and a T-shirt embossed with the logo of an obscure rock band. Hadn't we
seen that morning a Tuareg man in long indigo robes with an ABC News cap
on his head, lounging on a sofa reading the sports pages? So who was to say
what belonged where? The museum is one of the stops on what is always the
first morning of a first visitor's standard walking tour of the old city: the museum, the market, and the houses of the first European explorers to reach
Timbuktu and live to tell about it, the Frenchman René Caillié and the German Heinrich Barth. This wasn't our first visit and we were not for the moment interested in either Caillié or Barth, but our garrulous guide took us
there anyway, almost absentmindedly.

We peered into the well. Whatever else it was, it was an authentic type. I
had seen dozens of shallow wells just like it, scratched into wadis in many
parts of the Sahara, used by the nomads for their goats or camels or for their
own use on their wanderings across the emptiness. I had drawn water from a
number myself, though I preferred not to drink it, since it was almost always
a muddy brown and often stained with the droppings of the goats that always
seemed to surround the wells.

Still, a well of Buktu, or *Tin'buktu*, is part of the founding myth of the
ancient city, and myth can often be a revealing guide to fact, when fact is lost
in the mists of unrecorded time.

The most common version of the story is this:

Timbuktu was founded by nomadic Tuareg herdsmen around the start of the
eleventh century. These were of a group called Imashagen (or Imagcharen—the
words simply mean "nobles") Tuareg, whose range was between the Niger and
the oasis town of Arawan, about a week's journey into the desert. In the wet season, such as it is in the Sahara, they'd range to the north. In the dry season, the
summer, they'd bring their herds closer to the Niger River to graze. They set up
a camp in the dunes at a convenient place a few miles north of the river, where

they dug a well. They needn't have camped at that exact spot; any place would have done. It was merely convenient, close to the inland delta that is the Niger floodplain to the west, at a place just about as far north as the Niger's course takes it. After a few years this convenient camp became more permanent, and they'd leave their goods there in charge of an old woman called Buktu. *Tin* meaning either "well" or merely "place" in Tamashek, the language of the Tuareg, they'd refer to returning to the "Place of Buktu," or Tin'Buktu. Although there were already venerable towns on the Niger, this Tin'Buktu gradually became more important as a gateway to the desert, and traders began showing up there from the river and points south, accumulating trade goods for a venture across the desert itself, following the Tuareg paths, such as they were. The position was serendipitously strategic for commerce, situated as it was at the junction of the dry Sahara and the lush central valley of the river Niger, a waterway that constituted an easy pathway for transporting goods to and from the more tropical regions of West Africa, including their goldfields, and thence across the desert to the Mediterranean. The camp, thus used, soon turned into a permanent dwelling place.

Well, as a story it's tidy enough. The syllable *Tin* has a long connection in Tamashek to the feminine, and Buktu (occasionally written as Abutut instead) is referred to in some versions as "an old slave woman." Some traditions say the word isn't a person's name at all but means "woman with a large navel" in Songhai, the language spoken downriver from Timbuktu. In a further refinement, the word is also translated as "woman with a large lump," which is then taken to mean navel—no doubt one of the earliest references to an "outie" in literature. "Thus," say the chronicles, hopefully, "did they choose the location of this virtuous, pure, undefiled and proud city . . . a city unsullied by the worship of idols, where none has prostrated save to God . . . a refuge of scholarly and righteous folk, a haunt of saints and ascetics, and a meeting place of caravans and boats."

This romantic notion is scorned by philologists like Heinrich Barth, who pointed out with some asperity that the Songhai word for navel also means a shallow depression between sand dunes, and that Tin'buktu most probably only means "the place between dunes." On the other hand, according to many Tuareg in the region, the name comes from the word *imbakewen*, which is to say, objects. In effect, *Timbakewen* means those who guard objects. The Arab traveler who visited Timbuktu in the early 1500s, Leo Africanus, believed that the name of the city and the city itself were of Songhai origins as he argued that "the name Tombuto (was) imposed on the kingdom from the name of a town so called which (they say) king Mansa Sulaiman founded in the yeere [sic] of the Hegira 610." Abd al-Rahman al-Sa'adi, the author of the earliest surviving history of Timbuktu (the *Tarikh al-Sudan*, written in the middle 1600s),[1] wrote that "in the beginning, it was there that travelers arriving by land and water met. They made it a depot for their belongings and provisions, and it grew into a crossroads for travelers coming and going. Looking after their belongings was a slave woman of theirs called Tinbuktu, which in their language means 'the one having a lump.' The blessed spot where she was encamped was named after her."[2]

৩

THE ORAL TRADITIONS that survive in Timbuktu tell a different, more elaborate story of the city's origins, one that reveals a social history much more complicated than the simple tale of a nomadic encampment, however historically "accurate" that may be. This was related to us by Salem Ould Elhadj, who had been introduced by Halis as a scholar who would see to our instruction in the matter of Timbuktu's history. He was in fact more eminent than that, being a former city councillor, a former trustee of the Ahmed Baba Center, a member of Mali's Legion d'Honneur. We were sprawled one evening on the dunes north of the city, a vantage point much enjoyed by the Tuareg, who generally hate cities with their noise and stink, and try to get away as often as possible. Sidi Salem was sitting on a small rug, a twig in his hand that he used to draw pictograms on the sand for our benefit. He was in full didactic cry and wanted us to understand something deeper about the history of his city. He had also taken the trouble to write out the longer legend and its meaning.

"According to the patriarch of the Bellafarandi quarter, the quarter around the well of Buktu and the home of the Bella people, the first inhabitants of Timbuktu were black people," his paper says. The Tuareg, he pointed out, were a range of browns themselves but referred to themselves as "white," as they did the Arabs and the Berbers; the Bella, traditionally, were a caste or a tribe that had been enslaved by the Tuareg, and remain the servant class to this day. The patriarch was thus staking a claim to the Bella, or at least the native Songhai and not interlopers from the north, being the true founders of the city.

In any case, the legend says that "the first person to live in the city before the Imagcharen was Buktu, who was really called Gaïchatou Tin-Atouboutoute, that is to say, 'the woman with the great navel' in Tamashek. She was Songhai, originally from Khairache, a place just east of the town of Rharous, downriver toward Gao from Timbuktu.

"One day she was out at pasture with the family's goats when a large Taboragh pine (wild date) fell and pierced her through. She managed to get up, and follow her grazing goats to the shores of a nearby pond. According to the patriarch, this pond was none other than Tacaboundou, which we know was only about fifty yards from the celebrated mosque of Sankoré, the second greatest in Timbuktu, and the oldest.

"This pond was then in a forest, and surrounded by verdant grasses. All the water from the season's rainfall had collected there. Still wounded, and somewhat disoriented, Buktu decided to stay where she was. Her animals found fresh things to eat in abundance, and she herself could live on wild fruits and goat milk."

Buktu was the only girl among seven children; since the family had no news of her whatever for several months, they sent her eldest brother, Boutaghla, to look for her. On the way, he came across a large fruit he'd never seen before. He broke it open and tasted it. It was delicious. He took part of it with him. It was a watermelon.

"After a thousand and one difficulties, Boutaghla found the shores of the lake Tacaboundou. There he came across his sister, Buktu. He offered the rest of the watermelon to her; she ate it and threw the seeds to the ground. In short time the seeds germinated, grew, and yielded up wonderful watermelons. Boutaghla wanted to take his sister back to the family, to the east to Rharous, but she had taken a fancy to the countryside, and refused to go. She found the place perfect for herding animals because of the plentiful water and the abundant grasses, and watermelons seemed to grow of themselves. Eventually Boutaghla returned to Khairache by himself, but since both his parents were by then dead, he persuaded his five brothers and his own wife to return to the lake with him, to join Buktu. They settled down and began to cultivate watermelons." They were Timbuktu's founding citizens.

Among the first inhabitants to follow were Imagcharen, the Tuareg who wandered in the region. "These Tuareg were so numerous that Buktu and her family soon lost their language of origin, Songhai, in favor of Tamashek. The city slowly grew and became more important and more and more people came from all over.

"Rich merchants began to erect houses of *banco* (pounded mud), but

Buktu, her brothers and their descendants continued to live in their grass shelters. As time went on they were joined by certain slaves, especially those captured by Songhai emperor Sonni Ali Ber, and for a while the shelter settlement grew. But as the houses in *banco* increased in number, the grass shelters diminished and were then destroyed . . . and [eventually] the descendants of Buktu were placed, as Bella, in a quarter to the east of the city. This same quarter, today called Bellafarandi or the place of the Bella, also bears the significant name of Amazah, 'the place where the brothers live.'"

The "well of Buktu," by no coincidence at all, is supposedly situated at the very heart of the city, where the Bella lived before their grass huts were burned down and they were moved to Bellafarandi.

Sidi Salem pointed out that many people still living in Bellafarandi follow the old traditions and call themselves after Buktu's brothers, naming themselves thus: Ag Boutaghla after the eldest brother Boutaghla, Ag Taridar after Taridar, Ag Bikiya after Bikiya and so on. "They still to our day cultivate watermelons where the old canals used to run, or on the dunes that encircle the city." The watermelon is still a potent symbol of fecundity, a means of extracting water from sand, a metaphor for life in the desert.

A slightly more macabre version of this tale has Buktu being captured and enslaved by the Tuareg, and finally killed by her master, identified only as Sidi Mohammed, her body becoming, quite literally, the salt of the earth, and herself the navel of the city, a somewhat grisly allegory preserved by the Bella to illustrate their dependence on, and helplessness at the hands of, their overlords.

ço

FURTHER MEANING MAY also be found buried deep in the legends of the Tuareg themselves. The ancient division into classes of nobles and vassals, a distinction that persists today and forms what remains of the Tuareg political system, probably began sometime in the first few centuries of the Christian era, when a group of pastoral camel-breeding Berbers coming into the Sahara from some unknown place conquered a second, Berber-speaking population who lived mainly by goat-breeding. To give themselves legitimacy, the nobles claimed direct descent from a heroine called Tin-Hinan, who, mounted on a magnificent white camel (or white horse, the stories vary), mysteriously arrived in the region of the Ahaggar from the oasis of Tafilelt in southern Morocco. Indeed, in the heart of the central Sahara, near the oasis of

Abalessa in the Ahaggar, are tombs in which were found the bodies of two
women (said to be Tin-Hinan and her servant, Takama); on the skeletal arms
of one were bracelets of silver and gold, and with her a gold pendant and
beads, some of chalcedony from Guinea, some of aggrey, a fertility charm, a
bunch of herbs, baskets of dates and grain, milk bowls, a coin of Constantine
and much else besides, all now exhibited in the Musée National du Bardo at
Algiers. Besides the coin, the glass is Roman, and together they indicate a
fourth-century date,[3] pre-Islamic by several centuries.

Buried queens and mysterious female ancestors are common in the desert;
the Tuareg, like the Berbers before them, are a matrilineal culture, and estab-
lishing a secure female line is an important political act. Maybe Tin-Buktu
wasn't a slave. It is said in Tuareg lore, after all, that the noble families of the
Tuareg tribes are all related through the daughters of the same mother; the six
sisters are the ancestresses of them all.[4]

Whatever the truth—whether Buktu is a surrogate in legend for the enslaved Bella or for their overlords, the Tuareg—the Tuareg nomads founded
the city itself. But they didn't keep it for long. Over its history Timbuktu has
been owned by a succession of foreign emperors, kings and sultans. From time
to time the Tuareg, who lurked in the desert, ferocious and warlike, descended on the city to take it for a decade or two, or merely to loot and pillage
before retreating again. Theirs has not been an altogether happy history in
this part of the world, as will become clear. They're a proud and even arrogant culture, but their present status is uncertain and their future bleak.
Rather like Timbuktu's.

CHAPTER THREE

❧

The City, Its Site and Its Neighborhood

THE FOUR-WHEEL-DRIVE TOYOTA clawed its way to the top of a small dune—Kassis, our Bambara driver, wanted to give us a fine view of the city slumbering in the afternoon heat, a distant and smoky vista to the south—but on the summit the front wheels bit into soft sand and we just . . . stopped. We scrambled out and watched as Kassis dug himself further in by spinning his wheels first forward and then aft, to no avail. He got out too, looking sheepish. Halis looked merely resigned. Like so many Tuareg, he thought camels were much superior for desert travel—no bogging down in soft sand for them. No doubt true. But they were also slower and less comfortable and the "Toyota" (it was actually a Jeep, but Toyota is universal Saharan shorthand for any four-wheel-drive vehicle) would have to do.

By a happy coincidence, as we leaned against the car we heard a faint bleating, and a small flock of goats appeared over the next dune, followed by twenty or so camels, a couple of veiled Tuareg and a small family. They plodded easily through the sand. No bogging down for them.

"Where are they going?" I asked Halis.

"Oh, there," he said, gesturing vaguely to the north, not really paying attention. He was preoccupied with this matter of the wheels buried in the sand. Then he reached into the vehicle and extracted his sword, which all Tuareg seem to carry, either in their vehicles or secreted about their persons, though his was not really a sword, more like a large dagger, a kind of sawed-off sword. He wandered over to some scrawny thorn bushes and hacked a few of them off to use as traction.

When that didn't do the trick, he and Kassis unbolted a set of *tôles* from the roof rack. All vehicles in the desert carry these *tôles*, long plates of studded

Small caravan setting off from Timbuktu for Arawan. (Sheila Hirtle)

metal shaped like skis, used to extract vehicles from the frequent patches of soft sand, the Saharan traveler's bane.

❧

WHILE THE TWO of them were doing what they had to, we stared to the northeast, where the small caravan was still visible against the gentle slope of a distant small dune. We were pondering this business of *there,* in Halis's usage, and what it encompassed. We were due north of the city, on the main road to Arawan and the salt mines of Taoudenni, and thence through the terrible Tanezrouft to Morocco, but *road* is a laughable word under the circumstances. For a few miles from the city this "road" can just be made out, just a depression in the sand with faint ridges where tires had passed, but an hour or so further even those faint signs disappeared and the unmarked path became something only in the minds of travelers—clear enough to the desert Tuareg, perhaps, with their seemingly inbuilt navigational systems, but a mystery to everyone else.

Arawan is six days' weary slogging almost due north of Timbuktu, the last real town before the salt mines of Taoudenni and Taghaza. Modern salt gatherers still use Arawan as a way station, much as René Caillié, the French explorer, did in 1824. Caillié was in a caravan that paused for a week at Arawan on its way north. Just outside the town, it came to the last wells to be found for nearly two hundred miles. All stopped to fill their waterskins and, an ominous sign, to pray for God's mercy. Then they set forth into the void, a landscape, as Caillié described it, as nothing but an immense plain of shining sand, and over it a burning sky.[1]

The town was founded, according to local tradition, before Timbuktu, which makes it more than a thousand years old. Local legend says the name means "water hauled up on a rope" in Tamashek, the language of the Tuareg; it was in the middle of the Majabat al-Khoubr, one of many places called the Empty Quarter, but the Arawan oasis had sweet water in wells that were deep enough but not too deep, and vegetation for the camels. The caravans almost always paused there for a few days, or a week, gathering their strength, girding themselves for the forty or so grim days they were still to face on their trek north. They wouldn't see another oasis like this one until they got to the Dra'a Valley in Morocco, some eight hundred miles to the north.

Three thousand people lived in Arawan, in its heyday, in the days when caravans meant something—convoys of ten thousand camels were far from unknown. Once the town had 170 productive wells; today there are just two. With the dunes rolling relentlessly over the town, only a handful of residents are left. (Halis, when he's at home, is one of them. He was born in Arawan, and his family lives there to this day.) Was this little caravan really heading for Arawan? If so, it would travel for at least a week, then another two weeks after that if it was heading for Taoudenni. Beyond that . . . the desert north of Mali flattens into stony plains, monotonous and featureless, not even a dune or a ridge or a boulder as relief. In the Elder Days the caravans would stop at either Taoudenni or Taghaza, or both, to water their camels and rest, for the trading cities of the Arab north were a full month's travel further yet— Taghaza is more or less at the halfway point.

Not the longest or grimmest crossing in the desert, but not easy either. Leo Africanus has left a vivid description of the desert between modern Mali and Morocco or Algeria to the north. He called it Zuenziga, "a most barren and comfortlesse place," in which "many merchants are found lying dead upon the same way in regard of extreme thirst . . . For the space of nine daies journey not one drop of water is to be found, unless perhaps some raine falleth: Wherefore the merchants use to carrie their water on camels backes."[2] In modern days the only relief from the flatness is the Adrar des Iforhas Mountains, somewhat to the east, which in ancient days might have been an extension of the Ahaggar Plateau, a deeply eroded sandstone massif, barren and scrubbed by the wind, pressed in by the Tanezrouft and the Chech, great *ergs*, shifting seas of dunes.

Still, caravans streamed across those *ergs* for centuries, carrying gold from Ghana and slaves from all over the Sudan to the towns of the Maghreb, bringing back salt from the desert itself and manufactured goods from the Mediterranean.

It was forbidding country, but also beautiful. The immense sand seas (those massive stretches of caramel and beige) blend into the grays and duns of the gravel *hamadas* and the dusty silvers of the salt pans; here and there are sharp spikes of black basalt and patches of iron where some ancient tumult has punctured the planet's skin, leaving monstrous scars. To the northwest the golden dunes are streaked with reds and browns of a startling intensity. The Moroccan desert south of the Dra'a Valley contains classic crescent dunes the color of caramel; and to the east, around Gao, the dunes that border the river are over three hundred feet high and sixty miles long, the color of delicate rose. North of Gao is the valley of Tilemsi, threading its way through hauntingly beautiful mountains. To the west is the stark red Djebel Timétrine, to the east the golden rocks of the Adrars—Adrar Hebjane, Adrar Timajjalelene, Adrar Tirarar—a landscape clean and potent.

To the west of Timbuktu is desert all the way to the far Atlantic, but along the way the traveler will pass Walata, once a rival to Timbuktu but now much decayed, and the ruins of many cities and districts older by far, many of them still being discovered. Mema was there in the desert, not a city but a powerful industrial region now vanished, not even ruins to mark its passing, and Koumbi Saleh, the capital of the first of the Empires of the Sun, Old Ghana, now just crumbling rubble. Along the way you may see massive tumuli or mounds, detritus of cities long gone, or any one of many thousands of sites where iron and copper smelters once kept the smiths toiling at their forges. In their heyday these cities and towns, and those industrial sites, weren't in the middle of the desert but remained surrounded by forests, and all the great fauna of Africa still hunted there. Many venerable caravan routes led from those cities to the north too, including one that was called the Royal Road; why they fell into disuse and the cities crumbled is one of the fascinating puzzles of African archaeology—a combination, possibly, of ecological collapse, climate change, desertification partly human-caused (patches of those great forests lasted to modern times), and the turmoil of warfare and religious strife, some of it imported from Arabia, some of it purely native.

Southwest, upriver, were Mopti and Djenné, the latter much older than Timbuktu itself. Farther on was the heartland of the second of the great West African empires, Old Mali, its capital at Niani sometimes just called Melli; Niani has so thoroughly vanished that its actual location is a matter of genteel academic dispute, but it's thought to be on the Sankarani River, a Senegal River tributary. Southwest, in modern Guinea and Senegal, is where the much-coveted gold came from. The kingdom of Tekrur was on the Senegal River near the Atlantic.

To the south, the Sahel shaded into savanna, and then into woodlands before the true tropical rain forests. Gold was found to the southeast too, in what is now Ashanti country in modern Ghana, along the Volta River; to get there you had to cross the Bandiagara cliffs, where the amiable Dogon lived, and the country of the Mossi tribe, fierce and self-contained.

To the east is the "road" to Gao, the Niger city that was once the capital of the powerful Songhai kings, who ruled Timbuktu for a hundred profitable and mostly peaceful years. This road is as derisory as the road from Timbuktu to Marrakech, on which we were now bogged down, and beyond that . . . nothing very much until you get to the Aïr Massif north of the Niger city of Agadez, another famous desert capital, a month's travel by camel from Timbuktu, if not more. Still, many a caravan traversed those deserts in times past. From the northeast, from Libya, came the Garamantes adventurers. From and to the east travelers connected Timbuktu to the Hausa towns of Sokoto, Katsina and Kano and thence to Lake Chad and the empire called Bornu. From there, of course, it was a time-honored trail to the Nile, to Egypt, to Mesopotamia and thence to the caliphs of Baghdad or the Holy Places of Mecca and Medina.

❧

AFTER A FEW minutes of scuffling in the sand, Kassis got the *tôles* planted, spun onto them and hauled himself free. We returned to the city in a long, looping detour, skirting the dome-shaped reed huts of the Bella and cutting through what had once been the place where the sultans had lived but was now abandoned, used as a slaughterhouse, the sand underneath the gantries black with old blood. The sun was going down just to our right, a lurid red-orange ball looming in the smoky dusk; the city was dark—the power out again—lit only by a few flickering fires, and a red warning light on the water tower in the distance, presumably battery powered. In the past the caravans coming in from the deep desert would have been met by a commercial

agent and escorted into town along this very route under the same bloodred
sun and in the same darkness, only the tallest structure in town would not
have been the water tower but the minaret of the Sankoré mosque, already a
hundred years old when the great sultan, the emperor Mansa Musa, came to
town in the middle 1300s.

His arrival heralded the start of Timbuktu's first golden age, and its first
great expansion as the main entrepôt for the southern Sahara and a haven for
scholars of Islam. The second and most significant golden age was several
centuries later, under the rule of the askias of Gao, when the city was at its
greatest and most affluent.

Even so, then as now, Timbuktu is made largely of mud. The streets are
sand, the little highway to the Niger River port of Kabara the only paving.
The mosque called Djingareiber is of brick and some stone, and one of the
others, the Sidi Yahiya, has been corrupted by cement, and there are a few
houses made of the stone called *alhor* here and there, but the mosques are still
mainly mud. The tombs and shrines are of mud. In the newer parts of town
the streets are laid out in a grid, and the houses there are mud brick, though
often well made. In the old town, the medina, almost all the houses are made

View of the city across a sandy depression used as a soccer field. (Marq de Villiers)

of mud. The central town is a maze of narrow alleyways occasionally punctuated by secretive doorways fronting courtyards, and glassless windows, with intricately carved screens of wood, and a few Moroccan-style doors. At intervals there are ruined buildings and vacant lots that look like bomb sites, but the only bomb that has dropped is time and its inevitable consequence, decrepitude. A shrinking population has no money to repair a city made of mud, in which the buildings melt in the wet-season rains unless protected by fresh plaster. Too many of the inhabitants are living like the Romans after the barbarian invasions that led to the Dark Ages, reduced to watching their history slowly fading into the memory of the griots. Trees are few and look weary. Shallow depressions that once held water now hold a pathetic mix of garbage and small market gardens, meticulously watered by hand. Whatever canals connected the city to the river, if there ever were any, are gone.

From the air, the city is all beiges and dun, shading into the desert and scarcely distinguishable from it; only the military parade grounds and the market buildings stand out, and the stadium where the earth has packed to a dusty red. But it looks beautiful from the air, much more beautiful and romantic than it does on the ground, like an artist's loving sketch in burnt sienna and ochre.

CHAPTER FOUR

✌

The Niger's Course
and Meaning

IN THE MORNING we went down to the Niger River, the city's life-line and one of the prime reasons for its very existence in this spot, passing the statue of Timbuktu's guardian demon, Alfarouk, on his white horse, using the only paved road in town, the one that passes the airport on the way to the river. It leads to Kabara, Timbuktu's port, which was once important enough to employ a customs inspector who was a major source of revenue for the city, taxing imports from the merchant cities up- and downriver. In a faint echo of this venerable practice, a police post has been set up just outside town that flags down cars as they pass. They waved us through, however, and Halis said, darkly, "They don't stop us when they see foreigners in the car."

"What do they want?"

"Something for their tea fund," he said.

He wasn't really bitter, however. Mali is very poor, and the police probably hadn't been paid for a month or so. They were just doing their duty by their families. And not too long ago, foreigners would have been heavily taxed—they were often unbelievers, after all. Sometimes they were killed out of hand.

The Niger is a good six miles from the city itself, although it might have been closer in earlier days. Why so far away? Why not locate it on the banks of the river itself, where the animals could both graze and get water, without need of a well? Over the centuries efforts had been made to bring the two closer by constructing canals, but they never really amounted to anything. I put the question to Salem Ould Elhadj, but it seemed to him overly obvious, and for a while he said nothing, waiting for the pupil to come up with his own answer, giving me that long look that professors use for the exasperatingly

Heinrich Barth's portrayal of Timbuktu's port of Kabara. (Heinrich Barth)

slow. Eventually he shrugged and drew a crude map in the dune's sand, showing the main course of the river and the location of the city. But the Niger is
not a watercourse that stays in its place; in the wet season it can rise signifi-
cantly, overflowing into the alluvial plains that surround it, causing a bewil-
deringly twisty set of pathways and channels, some of them so shallow that it
seems the boats that traverse them are sailing across the grass; in the dry season it retreats to sullen, muddy puddles around a much narrower river. Where,
then, to locate a camp in which goods will be safe?

"But that wasn't really the reason they located it here," he said, using his
twig to erase the map. "Unfortunately, those verdant riverbanks were infested
with mosquitoes and insects of all kinds, and were the privileged home to
millions and millions of noisy, raucous frogs." The implication was clear: the
uproar of those frogs would drive a desert nomad mad. And in the low-water
season, the water and the mudflats gave off a fetid, unbreathable atmosphere,
damp and miasmic, useful perhaps for growing things but grossly unhealthy
for men of the desert, habituated to grand open spaces, quiet, and pure air. In
the end they sought a location that was better for their health and, in their
view, the purity of their thoughts.

There's another reason to stay away from the river. Desert people fear flowing water. Wells are good, but streams dangerously tricky, even wily. Partly
this fear is realistic; desert thunderstorms can cause flash floods that have

drowned unwary nomads in their camps. But it is to be feared for better reasons than that. Djinn and evil spirits live in water, it is well known. You use water to imprison demons. Djinn can trap even the wary. In Bambara legend, these spirits, called Faaro, can be protectors or destroyers of the village; Faaro itself is an androgynous being associated with the creation of the world and lives, of course, in water.[1] The Niger Valley wasn't unique in this: when the Almoravids founded Marrakech, they refused to site the city on the nearby Wadi Tensift because their people feared being so close to a river, even an occasional one, it being haunted by djinn.

For the first three or four miles from town the road passed through scrub desert, with a few scrawny trees in the gullies. Off to the left, on a small knoll, were the buildings of the venerable Baptist Mission, referred to derisively in Timbuktu as Little Washington; the missionaries there were supposed to eat hamburgers and have a swimming pool. A few miles farther, threads of river water started to appear by the side of the road, inlets from the main channel, and soon the first pirogues, pulled up on the banks. A dyke had been constructed to the right of the road, and beyond it were rice paddies, flooded at this time of high water. Dutch and Swedish aid money has been at work here, and the earthworks and their pumping apparatus were impressive, but then Timbuktu had always been self-sufficient in food; with enough water, the soil is fairly fertile, and the local practices were eminently sustainable. Beside the rice paddies were market gardens and here and there patches of watermelons. Piles of watermelons were stacked up on the roadside, presumably for sale though no vendors were present. I thought of Buktu and her brothers, and wondered if these were grown by their lineal descendants.

At midmorning, the notorious frogs were quiet, and there were few mosquitoes. Still, we were wary, for the mosquitoes carry not only malaria, which is bad enough, but also dengue fever, for which there is neither prophylactic nor cure.

Nothing very much had changed, it seemed, from the days when Heinrich Barth passed by 150 years ago. Or at least the landscape was much the same: "Ascending the sand-hills which rise close behind the village of Kabara . . . The contrast of this desolate scenery with the character of the fertile banks of the river which I had just left behind was remarkable. The whole tract bore the character of the desert, although the path was thickly lined on both sides with thorny bushes and stunted trees."[2]

However, Barth arrived at a time of political turmoil, after the disintegration of central authority and at a time when Fulani jihadists were once again sweeping through the Sahel. There was constant squabbling with the Tuareg, who were both notoriously quarrelsome and notorious backsliders, embracing a version of Islam that infuriated the purists. While he was there, it was a toss-up which of the two sides was in charge, or which one wanted his head more than the other. Writing about his path to Timbuktu, he added, "[Those stunted trees] were being cleared away in some places, in order to render the path less obstructed and more safe, as the Tuareg never fail to infest it . . . It was from the unsafe character of this short road between the harbor and the city, that the spot, about half way between Kabara and Timbuktu, bears the remarkable name of Ur-im-mándes, or, He does not hear, meaning, the place where the cry of the unfortunate victim is not heard from either side." The sky, he recorded, was thickly overcast, and the atmosphere filled with sand, and "[when I got to town] its dark masses of clay were scarcely to be distinguished from the sand rubbish heaped all round; having then traversed the rubbish which had accumulated round the ruined clay walls of the town, and left on one side a row of dirty reed huts which encompassed the whole of the place, we entered the narrow streets and lanes which scarcely allowed two horses to proceed abreast. But I was not a little surprised at the populous and wealthy character of this quarter of the town . . . many of the houses rising to a height of two stories, and in their facade evincing even an attempt at architectural adornment."[3]

Kabara was really only usable at high water—the boatmen having to get out into the water and push at other times—and has recently been abandoned for a new port, Douentza, a few miles upstream. Kabara is still there, but no longer has any purpose, and its people, too poor to move and in any case with nowhere to move to, have subsided into an abject poverty. Douentza is now where the pirogues tie up, and the transport boats from Bamako, the capital, as well as the "ferry" to the south bank. (The word *ferry* is in quotes because it seems to run on a schedule known only to the ferrymen; it can leave at once, even though empty of customers, it can leave in six hours or a dozen, or sometimes not for days, lineups of customers notwithstanding.)

We hired a pirogue at Douentza and pushed off into the river, heading for the main channel. The Niger was a little more than a half mile wide at this point, moving only sluggishly through the placid landscape. It was flowing east, a curious fact that puzzled geographers for centuries. Surely, on the western side of the continent, it should be flowing westward to the sea?

Pirogues on the Niger near Kabara. (Sheila Hirtle)

In fact the Niger (which derives its name not from the Latin for *black*, which has resulted in the many unfortunate epithets derived therefrom, but from the Tamashek phrase *gher n-gheren*, meaning "river among rivers") rises in the rain-sodden Fouta Djallon Plateau of Guinea, only 150 miles inland from the Atlantic, the same plateau that yields up the west-flowing Senegal River. It heads eastward, skirts the Sahel and keeps the cities of Ségou, Timbuktu, Gao and Niamey alive. For a thousand miles (about a third of its length) it flows through Mali. Just before Timbuktu it spreads out in a wide valley, almost an inland delta—the same delta our pirogue was now traversing, dodging the fishermen and keeping a wary eye on a petroleum barge coming downriver from Bamako. The countryside is flat, the river's flow almost invisible, and it spreads into a complex network of branches and lakes, byways and alleys. Then, somewhere past Gao, the river is pinched through a gorge called Tosaye that is barely one hundred yards wide. Timbuktu—or its port, Kabara—is on the Niger almost at its most northerly point; just after Timbuktu the river stops its northeastward flow and turns eastward, then, just before Gao, it turns abruptly south, as though disheartened by the heat and the menacing dunes confronting it. In this way Timbuktu is strategically placed between the great desert (pathway to the Mediterranean and its riches) and the river (lifeblood of the Sahel, an easy route for traffic from the south and southwest, where the land was lusher and, more important, the goldfields were).

This curious and unexpected course—it first flows northeast, then east, then takes a bend to the southeast to the Niger border, after which it heads southward and enters the Atlantic in a festering, malarial delta in the Gulf of Guinea near Port Harcourt, a further 1,550 miles or so, giving its name to two countries along the way—baffled early explorers. Herodotus, for example, confused it with the Nile, as did so many later writers.

Pliny, the great Roman naturalist, also bent his mind to speculating about the source of the Nile-Niger. Not to much effect, however; he was too busy gleefully recounting stories of the "crawling and squeaking and snake-eating men" who inhabited its course, and he was too fascinated, as so many of the early writers were, with what they took to be the undue nakedness of the Africans.[4]

Idrisi, the twelfth-century Arab geographer, believed the Niger flowed westward, and thought it had a common source with the Nile. Ibn Battuta passed through Timbuktu early in the fourteenth century, when it was already a trading depot of note, and a university town with extensive libraries. But on the Niger he was unhelpful: he left no word of its course, except to refer to it as the Nile. Three hundred years later Leo Africanus, alas, spoke of traveling "downstream" from Timbuktu to Djenné to the southwest, thereby indicating that his memory was not always reliable. The later Arab traveler now mostly known as Shabeni (his full name was Asid al-hajj Abd-Salam Shabeni) ignored its direction of flow but called it the Nile and reported its water was sweet to drink. Mungo Park, the Scottish explorer who reached (and later perished on) the Niger in 1796, on an expedition financed by London's African Association, saw for himself that the river flowed eastward, but of course he didn't know where it debouched into the sea, or if it did. A Moor in Timbuktu, he wrote, had told a friend that "below Ghinea, is the sea, into which the river of Tombuctoo disembogues itself." He was correct, but Park was unable to believe it; it seemed impossible for an eastward-flowing river to end in the Atlantic. Ghinea, or Guinea, he therefore incorrectly placed somewhere east of Timbuktu, along with Ghana, then a name of ancient renown but uncertain location. He excused the Moor by suggesting he had confused the word for *sea* with the word for *lake*; Park then repeated rumors he had heard of a great lake to the east, which he called Wangara, and which must, he thought, surely be the terminus of the river.[5] Whether this imagined lake was really Lake Chad is not known, but Wangara country is to the west and southwest of Timbuktu, not the east. It may simply have been the Niger floodplain west of Timbuktu; at high water the Niger can rise more than thirty feet above its low point, a rise rivaled only by the Amazon in world rivers, and the shallow lake it causes, Lake Debos, can be almost one hundred miles broad.

In the not too distant past—a few centuries at most—the Niger probably had a northeasterly tributary flowing from the escarpment called the Djebel Timétrine, at one time more verdant than the present, toward Timbuktu. Many stories exist of canals, really fingers of wet-season flow, approaching close to the city from the north and northeast, and then, presumably, flowing into the Niger's main channel somewhere just west of the city, perhaps even through the pond called Tacaboundou, on which Buktu had camped.

∾

WE CRUISED STEADILY upriver, in the direction of Mopti, Djenné and Bamako, passing a caramel dune stretching down to the water's edge, used by townsmen as a beach; whole families came down to the shore to picnic and swim. Here and there men were fishing from pirogues, casting their nets upon the waters, their catch mostly tilapia and catfish. The riverside villages were neat and tidy, much neater than Timbuktu, perhaps because their garbage went into the river instead of accumulating in the streets.

Halis pointed at a complex of houses on a small island. "Rich Tuareg, back from Saudi Arabia," he said.

"I thought the Tuareg didn't like the mosquitoes and frogs?"

He shrugged. I guess if you were rich enough it didn't matter. Still, the house was hardly a mansion, and women were washing laundry in the river there, as elsewhere, surrounded by children splashing and shrieking.

Halis was lounging on a bench near the middle of the thirty-foot pirogue. He had just finished what he called "a Tuareg breakfast," a fresh sheep's liver, bought from a roadside butcher in Kabara, which he grilled over a small spirit stove. We had declined a portion, to his amusement.

∾

ONCE, IN PAST centuries, the hinterlands of the Niger floodplain were covered with villages and towns, and occasionally cities, now mostly vanished. Mopti, Djenné (on the Niger tributary called the Bani), and Ségou are really the only towns left, and Djenné is old, very old, no one quite knows how old but it was a going concern at the start of the Christian era.

The riverside market at Mopti is still one of the grand sights of the Middle Niger; except that the larger pirogues and the still-larger pinasses are now driven by converted car engines, it looks much as it would have in the days of Timbuktu's founding. The market is arranged around a deep basin set into the banks of the Bani River at the southern end of the city, a few miles before it joins the Niger. The market is remarkable for many reasons, not the least of which is that its methods and commerce have changed hardly at all in the last five hundred years, or eight hundred, or a thousand. The pirogues are still made just out of town, by Bozo craftsman segregated in their own boat-building village; they are still made in the same way, pieced together from hand-hewn boards, nailed up by Bozo-made spikes cobbled together from scrap metal, even tin cans, finished with an adze and calked with baobab leaves and pitch. Their design is identical to that noted by Arab travelers in the thirteenth century: long, up to sixty-five feet, needle-nosed, with a shallow draft and very stable, roofed with arching boughs covered with thatch (occasionally tarpaulins, now). Similar but smaller "canoes" act as ferries, carrying families to and from the pottery-making villages on the far side. These boats ply the river as they always have, traveling from Ségou and Segoukoro to Mopti, Mopti to Timbuktu, and Timbuktu to Gao.

One of the curiosities of the Bozo boat-building craft is that the pirogues and pinasses, including those moored at Kabara, are made in two fore and aft halves and then, quite literally, sewn together with sturdy thread made from baobab bark. One of the many advantages of this interesting technique is that it allows the owner, if he becomes successful in his trade, to separate the two halves and insert a third section, thereby lengthening the boat and increasing its capacity.

In the dry season the market spills down the cobbled sloping sides of the basin itself. Everywhere there are pirogues, hundreds of them. Merchandise is stacked higgledy-piggledy on the cobbles. (We saw two men wrestling an ancient refrigerator onto the roof of a sturdy cargo pirogue.) On the banks are huge piles of calabashes, bundles of firewood, stacks of lumber (some of it being made into furniture on the riverbanks) plus the usual accoutrements of an African market: mounds of dried fish, bloodily butchered lambs, pyramids of mangoes, baskets of peanuts, heaps of manioc and other roots, battered aluminum cookware, great shiny balls of creamy shea butter and cheeses, mostly covered with a thick wrapping of buzzing flies.

And off to one side, spread over an area sixty-five feet long by as many wide, are great slabs of Saharan rock salt, brought by camel caravans out of the deep desert from Taoudenni and Taghaza, traded in the markets of Timbuktu and brought down here to Mopti from Kabara, whence they will make their way to the refineries and factories of the capital. The salt slabs weigh 220 pounds each and are stacked in bundles of four or five, tied with cord and piled on sticks laid on the cobbles. They are the color of dirty cream, flecked with gray.

All day the boats come and go from Mopti. The men pole the heavily laden pirogues off the cobbles and heave their way out to the open river. In shallow waters they would pole all the way to Timbuktu; when the water was deeper, they'd paddle. It could take five days or longer, and they'd sleep along the way on the banks, near remote villages, as they had always done. In remote times the Tichitt people had done the same, and then the Ghanaian traders, and when their time had gone, their successors from Mali the Great and the Songhai of Gao had carried on the tradition. And here it still is. Bambara now mostly, but also Bozo and Dogon and a polyglot mix of Arab and Berber and Tuareg, with an admixture of Fulani and Hausa and Wolof and the rest, communicating in the lingua franca, French.

✑

ON THE WAY back to Kabara we traveled close to the left bank. Along the shores, villagers were out threshing, mostly millet but occasionally also wheat. Fishermen were still casting small throwing nets into the water. Sometimes, beyond the shore, boats glided through what looked like fields of grass but must have been shallow channels. Half an hour into our return voyage we swung wide to skirt the opening of a deep basin. Our piroguier, Hassan, wanted to avoid the hippos that lived there. They were calving, he said. "Very dangerous at this time of year."

There have been hippos in the Niger for longer than humans have recorded. Ibn Battuta, in the 1350s, reported their presence in large numbers as he traveled in a small boat "made from a single tree" from Timbuktu to Gao. His companions were wary of them, he wrote, since their small boat had no motor to take them out of trouble, as ours did. He'd never seen such beasts and at first took them for deformed horses. "They have manes and tails like horses and feet like elephants . . . They swim in the river and lift their heads and blow."[6] The manes he seems to have invented, or misremembered, but the description is otherwise apt.

Their future is uncertain. The climate of the Sahel and the Niger basin is changing, though exactly how or to what degree remains unknown. Even in the good years, more than half the Niger's flow evaporates in this inland delta; in the dry years the loss can be almost two thirds. Down past Gao, near Niamey, the Niger can stop running altogether in low water, and it is being choked by water hyacinths, a water-hogging scourge throughout West Africa, imported from Europe by well-meaning missionaries. The fish catch on the Middle Niger dropped from one hundred thousand tons twenty years ago to not much more than half that in 2006.

There was clearly more water in earlier times. As suggested, some flow came in from the northeast, from Djebel Timétrine. The story of the founding of Timbuktu mentions the pond, Tacaboundou, near where the Sankoré mosque stands today, where now there is only dust, even in the gullies and depressions. At high water the river itself used to accumulate in channels and reach close to the city, near enough to take a small boat and make just a short hike to the city itself. The Arab traveler Shabeni reported seeing "close to the town of Timbuctoo, on the south, a small rivulet in which the inhabitants wash their clothes, and which is about two feet deep. It runs in the great forest on the east, and does not communicate with the Nile, but is lost in the sands west of the town. Its water is brackish; that of the Nile is good and pleasant."[7] As recently as the rainy years in the 1970s there were stories of hippos wallowing in ponds within the city itself, and many reports of stagnant ponds long after the river had receded. Betty Ford, the widow of former U.S. president Gerald Ford, once contributed money to restoring one of the city's pools, but it is dry again and is already crumbling and full of garbage (with a tiny row of vegetables growing on one bank), a monument to a well-meaning but essentially useless charity. In the histories there are confusing accounts of "canals" from Kabara to Timbuktu, though these seem to have been natural channels, not man-made (or if they were made-made, they were never completed). In 2006 a Canadian company was doing a feasibility study to see if it would be worth dredging such a canal now, but the consequences are unknown, and the water levels in the river so variable that for much of the year it would in any case be empty or at best stagnant, a repository for garbage.

As with water, so with vegetation. All the early stories about Timbuktu, folktales and histories alike, recount memories of forests, some of them substantial. Shabeni's rivulet ran through a great forest, he reported, and he later filled in his account: "On the east side of the city there is a large forest, in which are a great many elephants. The timber here is very large. The trees on the outside of the forest are remarkable for having two different colours; that side which is exposed to the morning sun is black, and the opposite side is yellow. The body of the tree has neither branches nor leaves, but the leaves, which are remarkably large, grow upon the top only: so that one of these trees appears, at a distance, like the mast and round top of a ship."[8] Shabeni's English interlocutor added that "Shabeeny has seen trees in England much taller than these: within the forest the trees are smaller than on its skirts. There are no trees resembling these in the Emperor of Morocco's dominions. They are of such a size that the largest cannot be girded by two men. They bear a kind of berry about the size of a walnut, in clusters consisting of from ten to twenty berries. Shabeeny cannot say what is the extent of this forest, but it is very large."

These forests were reported by Ibn Battuta too, and by Leo Africanus, who also saw elephants.

The elephants are gone now. Elephants still exist in the Sahel; a recent GPS-assisted satellite survey found 322 animals migrating between Burkina Faso and southern Mali, watering at Lakes Gossi and Banzena. But around Timbuktu . . . nothing. Only scrawny desert thorn trees are left. To some degree this was human-caused: Sonni Ali, the tyrant of Gao, hewed down whole forests to build an armada to torment his upriver enemies; and Gao's rulers cut down more to build boats in a vain attempt to repel the Moroccan invaders in later centuries, using them instead to evacuate the population. But the forests would probably have vanished anyway, through gradual human attrition and from increasing desiccation.

Some of the changes are very recent. Miranda Dodd, a former Peace Corps volunteer who married a Tuareg and is now living in Timbuktu, spent some years in Mauritania in water and resource management. "Areas that are dry now, arid and waterless, were forested only three decades ago. The woods contained many animals, even large ones like lions, all gone now." Halis, who was born in Arawan in the 1970s, remembers seeing a giraffe not far from Timbuktu. The same thing is happening on the northern fringes of the Sahara. A French military man, Lieutenant Gralt, writing in 1945, pointed out that "not long ago it was possible to travel from the Aïr to Termit [to the southeast, in Niger], finding water every day where now there are no wells for 250 kilometers [155 miles]."[9] In Roman times in certain eastern oases the wells were no more than thirteen feet deep; now, some of them go down nearly four thousand feet, and the water tables are still dropping.

Timbuktu itself is not short of water. Its municipal wells have maintained their steady flow; the bulk of the aquifers deep below the surface consists of fossil water left over from earlier, more verdant times, but they are still being recharged by the Niger and show no signs of dropping. Still, the city's immediate neighborhood is changing. When the three medieval mosques of the city were last renovated, huge banks of desert sand had first to be removed, and the streets are once again six inches deep in sand. The dunes are closer to the city than they were—indeed, the newer sections to the north are built on top of dunes—and with the trees gone there is little to stop their continuing encroachment. The computer models set up to forecast the effects of global warming are sometimes ambiguous and hard to interpret, but it seems clear that the desert regions of the world—the American Southwest, the Sahara, the Bedouin lands and the Gobi—will all get even drier than they are now. Timbuktu is unlikely to escape.

CHAPTER FIVE

Ↄ

The People of the Region

WANDERING THROUGH THE produce and artisanal markets of Timbuktu yields a cheerful cacophony in a Babel of languages. Narrow aisles lead through towering stacks of watermelons and bitter melons, piles of white and black rice, basketball-sized roundels of shea butter from the karité tree, used as a skin-care and moisturizing lotion, baskets of twisted tubers, gourds of improbable shapes, plastic sacks of pomegranate juice, bottles of Evian water that may have come from France (or maybe were just refilled from the Niger), bundles of wilted greens, manioc and cassis flour in baskets. In tubs, large mounds of peanut butter, dark brown. Packets of spices. Dried medicinal herbs. Fresh herbs for cookery. Cucumbers, okra and other greens. Mangoes, yellow and green peppers. An array of more-or-less dried fish, rank in the hot sun. Peeping out from under the lid of a covered basket, a row of viper skulls, a powerful fetish. Produce vendors are mostly women, in a rainbow of hues and an assortment of sizes, elegant Fulani; skinny Tuareg; Bambara of what the novelist Alexander McCall Smith calls "a traditional build," plumply pretty; Arabs in black aba robes with their veils pushed back; Dogon with their curiously squarish faces; Hausa women, tall and imperious; brassy young women of all hues in Western gear with T-shirts that say things like AL'S PLUMBING, PITTSBURGH; or women in the brilliant plumage that is their signature all over Africa from Cameroon to Chad, long robes in bright pinks, emerald greens, fuschias and reds and golds, headgear yards of brilliant cloth wrapped and swirled and tucked and fluffed, each one subtly different. Nothing very much speaks "Islam" about any of this; only rarely is a woman veiled, and they display their beauty proudly, even ostentatiously, especially the sleek Fulani in their light cotton gowns. Here and there are tiny charcoal fires kept alive with bellows the size of a teacup and even tinier anvils on which the (mostly male) artisans fashion jewelry for sale. The men are more drably dressed in long robes in dusty white, some in Tuareg blue and a few in orange, but many in Western attire. The languages are Hausa and Songhai, Tamashek and Arabic, Bambara and Fulani, or "Peul" as its usually called in Timbuktu, with a French overlay where all other communication fails. Almost everyone speaks two or three languages other than French.

A young lad with curly hair and startlingly pale eyes tried to pick my pocket, but Velcro defeated even his slender hand, and when I wagged my finger at him he grinned cheerfully, unrepentant, gave me a finger back and slid into the crowd.

At the rear of the market, in a dusty and relatively deserted alleyway, a row of donkeys was waiting, patiently, with heads bowed. "Taxi stand," said Halis, only half joking. Walking a little farther, we passed a straw shelter where three Bella women were pounding millet. (It's their only source of income. They live in huts on the outskirts of town and pound grain into flour for bakers or households in town, for a few pennies a day.) They were tall, upright and lean, the two older women craggy and dignified, the younger woman oval-faced and very black, like a Nubian princess, her face in a scowl, clearly angry at the unwanted and unwonted scrutiny from outsiders.

The polyglot ethnicity of Timbuktu makes it a different sort of desert city. In Algeria and Libya and Morocco the towns are much less mixed; there would be a few Hausa, perhaps, but generally the population would be Berber or Arab or Tuareg. Agadez, the other southern desert capital in Niger, is a mix of Tuareg and Hausa, with an Arab blend; Gao is still largely Songhai. Timbuktu has always been different, with admixtures from all the many ethnic groups of the region. A cheerful cacophony it might be, but no one in Timbuktu has any trouble identifying the neighborhoods where the various ethnic groups congregate. The Bella of course live in Bellafarandi to the northeast; to the southeast are "people from Ghadamès," which usually means Arabs, Ghadamès being in western Libya; the quarter around the largest mosque, the stately Djingareiber, is where "the masons" live, which generally means either Arabs or the Mande-speaking people like the Bambara, these days Mali's dominant ethnic group. The Sankoré neighborhood was traditionally the home of the uléma, the scholarly community, whose origins varied as the city's governance did, Malinke under the mansas of Mali, Songhai under the askias of Gao, also Berber or Arab.

Halis in the marketplace with a vendor of leather buckets. (Sheila Hirtle)

In this way the city is a reflection of its neighborhood—its hinterlands, its region—and its history.

ಌ

TO THE NORTH, in the earliest days, were the Berbers, the indigenous people of the North African Mediterranean littoral; they lived on the shores and in the fringes of the northwestern Sahara, along the Atlas, the Anti-Atlas and the Moroccan Rif. Still, this word *indigenous* begs a substantial question; little is known of their real origins.

Their own legends tell of a crossing from Egypt, Arabia, Yemen, Uzbekistan, Afghanistan—there are many versions. The Berbers are often classed as *Mediterraneans,* a term difficult to define. Some Berber groups in the Moroccan Rif, middle Atlas Mountains and the Djebel Nafusa of northwestern Libya include many individuals with fair skin, blue eyes and light hair, particularly in their beards.

Ibn Khaldun, the medieval Berber historian, wrote that the Berbers had been divided into two tribal blocs from the earliest times, and that their "mutual hostility and incessant quarreling had been the dominant factor of their history" long before the arrival of the Arabs, but persisting afterward.[1] There were a bewildering array of factions under a sliding and slippery array of names, but the two confederations to remember are the Zanata, who generally inhabited the regions east of Tunisia and west of Egypt, and the Sanhaja, who lived in the central Maghreb. A further group of Sanhaja lived in the west, along the Atlantic coast as far south as the Senegal River; their subdivisions included the Lamtuna in the south and west, the Massufa in the north and east, the Guddala to the west, and the Tarka. These were (probably, collectively) the ancestors of the Tuareg, though the old writers often used the terms *Tuareg, Massufa, Berber* and *Sanhaja* interchangeably; Massufa were commonly found in Old Mali and Timbuktu when Ibn Battuta reached the Niger in the fourteenth century. The Sanhaja controlled the important salt mines at Awlil and governed the salt trade to Ghana from the town of Audaghost.

It was the Sanhaja who in their fury later boiled out of the desert, swept over Morocco and, as the Almoravids, founded Marrakech.

෨

IN A WAY, the Tuareg were the most recalcitrant and farthest-traveled of the Berbers (for they almost certainly were Berbers in origin). The conventional history recounts how, for century after century North Africa—the modern countries of Libya, Tunisia, Algeria and Morocco—was invaded by a succession of armed colonizers: the Phoenicians, the Carthaginians, the Romans, and then the Vandals, who arrived in the fourth century, followed by the Byzantines. Then the Arabs, from their new base in Egypt, swept across the coast in the seventh and again in the eleventh centuries. Each of these conquests and invasions caused havoc among the settled Berber population and drove many of them from the desert fringes, where they lived pastoral lives, into the deep desert. Some of them drifted south and west, encountered the settled kingdoms around the Senegal River and evolved into what are known as the Moors, the people who run modern Mauritania. Some of them drifted south and east, across the dunes and gravel deserts of Algeria, picking through the dry riverbeds and mountains of sandstone and volcanic rock, from oasis to oasis, fetching up in the secretive fastnesses of the Ahaggar and the Aïr, which gave them an extraordinary combination of remoteness and survivability, places from which to raid and plunder between Ouargla and the Sudan. The desert came to be home, and they the masters of it. Secure in their refuges and elusive on their swift camels, these new Tuareg roamed the desert freely, submitting to no man's control, not even the Mali kings, greatest emperors of antiquity. They became what in their own eyes they remain: adepts of the uttermost desert, the Kel Tamasheq, sand riders and camel masters.

But the Tuareg themselves have a rather different, and much older, explanation of their history, believing that they were expelled from Arabia in pre-Islamic times, when they took the veil to preserve their identity from their enemies, and made their way westward across the Great Emptiness. Many tantalizing snippets can be found in Greek and Roman sources, such as Herodotus, Strabo, Pliny and especially Ptolemy, to suggest that the proto-Tuareg had reached the Niger Bend more than eighteen hundred years ago.

Whatever the truth, the Arab invaders, in AD 666–67, found an indigenous population that included what they called the "veiled Sanhaja," a people that Ibn Khaldun acknowledged had traveled between the Mediterranean coast and the Bilad-al-Sudan (the Land of the Blacks) for many centuries before Islam.

❧

THE DOMINANT BLACK African people along the Niger were the Mande people. The Mande governed two of the most eminent empires of ancient Africa, and in Mali today the Bambara, a Mande clan, still govern the country and are its majority ethnic group.

The Mande are divided and subdivided into a variety of ethnic and tribal affiliations, some of them substantial but most tiny. The most important are the Soninke, the Malinke (sometimes called Mandingo), the Bambara (sometimes called the Bamana) and the Dyula (sometimes called the Wangara by Arab chroniclers, and who may simply be a class, not a clan).

The Soninke sprawled over a huge swath of territory from the banks of the Senegal River to the Niger itself and ruled the early empire of Ghana.

They were among the earliest West African people to convert to Islam, following their contacts with traders from Sidjilmasa and the Dra'a Valley. Their towns and cities were described by the Cordoban geographer Abu Abdullah al-Bakri in the eleventh century and by Idrisi in the twelfth, but there is clear evidence their existence went back a long way before that.

For centuries, either in fact or in Soninke legend, their state was centered on a place called Wagadu; whether this was some Soninke equivalent of Eden or a real place remains unclear, but the legends say the people fled south from it after a terrible drought that lasted seven years, seven months and seven days, and may (depending on its date) have had some something to do either with the founding or with the demise of the Ghanaian Empire (hereafter called Ghana-Wagadu to distinguish it from the modern state called Ghana).

The Dyula, for their part, were the merchants of their day and carried on most of the long-distance trade in gold. In fact, the word *Dyula* may simply refer to Soninke families who made their living as traders, the merchant princes of their day. As the popular historian Basil Davidson put it, "the story of Dyula enterprise runs like a vivid thread through the records of West Africa from the early times of Mali to the republics of today."[2]

They were interesting as much because of their internal organization as for their enterprise. They were not really tribally based, but organized around what sounds remarkably like a modern corporate structure—even to appointing company chiefs, or *Dyulamansas*, to run their affairs. They founded many market towns and cities, and made their money as middlemen in interstate trade.

Several of the great families of Timbuktu's history were of Soninke origin, among them the Haïdaras and the Baghayoghos.

☙

THE FULANI, OR Fulbe, or Peul, are an interesting people who have spread throughout the African savanna, and late in Timbuktu's life had a more or less disastrous effect on its politics. Their origins are in Senegal-Gambia, the product of admixture between native Wolof and incoming Berbers, yielding a modern people who are dark of skin with Arab or European features; indeed, newborn Fulani are often white, though they quickly turn dark. Throughout history the prickly Fulani were notorious for their fanatical views on their own racial purity and their insistence on their own beauty, even to the extent that an ordinary-looking Fulani man would encourage his wife to give birth to the sons of better-looking men so as to improve the race. This fanaticism was later transferred to religion, and when the Fulani adopted Islam in later centuries their zeal gave rise to waves of jihadist warfare that roiled Timbuktu and its region for generations. About seven million Fulani are now spread out across a dozen countries.

On the Niger, they settled somewhere around 1400 in Masina, west of Timbuktu; the *Tarikh* of al-Sa'adi often referred to the *Masinakoï*, or sultans of Masina. For reasons unknown they drew the unyielding hatred of the Songhai tyrant Sonni Ali and later, in 1498, became the unwilling subjects of the Songhai, when Askia Mohamed defeated them in battle, but they resisted to the last and maintained their own unrelenting hostility to their conquerors until after the Moroccan invasions of 1590.[3]

The pre-Islamic Fulani had a complicated cosmology. Most African societies, though animist, believed in some sort of supreme being, but the Fulani were more explicit than most; making them fairly easy converts when Muslim proselytizers came through in the centuries after Muhammad. They also had a creation myth that speaks eloquently, if rather cynically, of resurrection and redemption.

> At the beginning there was a huge drop of milk,
> Then Doondari came and created stone.
> Then stone created iron;
> And iron created fire;
> And fire created water;
> And water created air.
> Then Doondari descended a second time.
> And he took the five elements
> And he shaped them into man.
> But man was proud.
> Then Doondari created blindness and blindness defeated man.
> But when blindness became too proud,
> Doondari created sleep and sleep defeated blindness;
> But when sleep became too proud,
> Doondari created worry and worry defeated sleep;
> But when worry became too proud,
> Doondari created death, and death defeated worry;
> But when death became too proud,

Doondari descended for the third time
And he came as Gueno the eternal one,
And Gueno defeated death.[4]

ᘒ

SOUTH OF THE river, between the goldfields of Akan and the Niger, were the Mossi kingdoms. The Mossi seem to have immigrated from somewhere around Lake Chad to the east and may be relatives of Nigeria's Hausa. They were a quarrelsome people who mostly seem to have been spoilers; in later years they sacked Timbuktu, raided the Lake Debos region and besieged the trading town of Walata. The Songhai emperors kept a constant eye out for Mossi incursions, and Sonni Ali led three military missions against them, to no real avail. Their power, such as it was, was based on cavalry—armored cavalry for defensive purposes but swift light cavalry for long-range raiding; the Mossi seldom stayed long enough to fight pitched battles, but plundered and were gone. Their own towns were frequently walled, and even villages were constructed to easily withstand sieges. Mossi rulers helped protect weaker and smaller cultures to the south from the empires to the north and thus deprived those empires of the booty (and slaves) they considered rightfully theirs. The Mossi resisted Islam to the last and retained their religion, which, as with the cultures of indigenous North America, deified the earth itself. The major center of Mossi life was at Ouagadougou, the present capital of Burkina Faso.

ᘒ

BETWEEN THE MOSSI and the Niger River are the Bandiagara cliffs, home to the Dogon, a small, intense culture that has long stayed out of great affairs.

When Islam swept through the Sahel like a gale, there were pockets of resistance. Not through warfare but through a belief system so attuned to the lives of the people who practiced it that it remained impermeable not only to the proselytizers of Islam but to the Christian missionaries who followed them.

The Dogon are not the only people between the desert and the forest who have chosen to withdraw from modernity. The Kirdi people of Cameroon, who like the Dogon withdrew from Islamization, are similarly looked down on by Muslims as being "uncivilized." But the Dogon people might be unique, both in the seamlessness and thoroughness of their complex belief system, and because those who do make the crossing into a modern urban culture still seem immune to that culture's blandishments.

The cliffs of the Bandiagara escarpment are a natural wonder. They drop precipitously from plateau to plain, sheer for hundreds of feet, and are pierced by numerous caves. In these, the early people took refuge, and there they still bury their dead.

The Dogon and the boat-building Bozo are ethnic cousins, and in legend the cliff dwellers owe a perpetual debt to the river people, for in one of the great droughts that afflicted the region, a Bozo father fed a hungry Dogon family on his own flesh, cutting off slices at need, and thus kept them alive.

☙

FINALLY, TO THE east are the Songhai, for many years rulers of Timbuktu. The Songhai origins are obscure. As with the Tuareg, there are theories that they had arrived centuries before from Libya, or even Yemen, but no one knows for sure. The capital, Gao, or at least its precursor, Kukiya, has been a going concern at least since the year 300 and possibly much earlier. They may be contemporaries of the Garamantes, and even of the pharaohs. It was under the Songhai rulers of Gao that Timbuktu achieved the second and greatest of its golden ages.

CHAPTER SIX

༄

Precursors: The Empires of the Sun

THE GREATEST EMPIRES of Old Africa sprawled along the Senegal and Niger rivers, and their stories even now are not thoroughly understood. From the west to east, these were: Tekrur, Ghana, the short-lived Susu, Mali, and Songhai. Mali succeeded Ghana and Songhai succeeded Mali, but there was also considerable overlap.

Until recently it was thought that Ghana was the oldest organized polity in West Africa. This was Old Ghana, or Ghana-Wagadu, "Golden Ghana" as it was called, partly for its storehouses of real gold but partly because the kingdom glittered, in the estimation of its neighbors, as bright as gold itself. This was not the modern state called Ghana farther to the south, which was cobbled together by Kwame Nkrumah in the 1950s after independence from the English colonialists; Nkrumah took the name deliberately, to give his new country the gloss of ancient respectability. Ghana-Wagadu was flourishing by the third century and was already old when the first Arab traders arrived, sometime around the eighth century. The lesser-known kingdom of Tekrur, which was west and south of Old Ghana and reached the Atlantic, may be almost as old, or even older; at any rate, it was the first organized southern Saharan state to adopt Islam. At its height, sometime after the eighth century, Tekrur traded extensively with the Zanata Berbers of Morocco, mostly in gold and slaves.

But within the last decade or so great gobs of new information have been streaming out of the Niger basin and bubbling into the archaeological literature, the product of new techniques such as satellite imagery and a more regional approach to site exploration (as opposed to the meticulous toothbrush-and-dust-pan excavations of traditional archaeology). Some of the language used by field archaeologists to describe what they are learning can hardly be contained within the emotionless limits of academic jargon, and unscience-like words such as *amazing* and *massive* keep cropping up in their reports. "The flood plain of the Middle Niger . . . is lined with hundreds of ancient tells rivaling those of Asia both in area and in clues to the emergence of city life . . . the Middle Niger is dominated by numerous monumental tumuli."[1] (Tells are artificial hills, usually of debris from large settlements; tumuli can be the same thing, although in some cases they also mean burial mounds.) All over the Niger basin archaeologists have discovered truncated pyramidal burial mounds for the military and political elites, sometimes sixty feet high, containing an astonishing (another unacademic word) array of grave goods, including three-foot-tall terra-cotta effigies of heavily armed cavalrymen, of the kind so famously found near Xi'an, in China. In the region of Mema, on the north bank, thousands of smelter sites have been found, in an area where there are (now) neither forests for fuel nor any ore to smelt. Dozens of large cities, hundreds of towns and literally thousands of villages are scattered in the area, most of them abandoned about seven or eight hundred years ago.

Some of this seems to coordinate neatly with known climate changes in the southern Sahara: the ending of the Atlantic wet phase starting about 2500 BC until about 300 BC; the transitional arid phase, from about 300 BC to AD 300; a renewed wet phase from AD 300 to 1100; and another dry phase that lasted four centuries, from about AD 1100 to 1500. Thus, after about 300 BC the climate went into serious decline, severely reducing the extent of the annual Niger flood, but allowing the colonization of the former wetlands. The wet phase starting in AD 300 was the signal for a fairly continuous expansion and intensification of settlement, since it yielded more arable land and conditions suitable for farming. It was in the subsequent dry phase, with its downturn in rainfall, that most of the settlements, including Mema and its hinterlands, were abandoned. The founding of Timbuktu also corresponds with the start of the last dry phase and may explain why the nomads showed up where they did at the Niger River.[2]

ꟾꟷꟷꟾ

IT IS BECOMING increasingly clear that the ancient south-of-the-Sahara commercial and trading system was far more independent of the Mediterranean, far older, far bigger and far more widespread than previously thought, and not just in the Upper Niger—in the Middle and Lower Niger basins too. To take one example of many, a long-established trade route reached from Gao-Kukiya to the Ife people in modern Nigeria. Ife has always been anomalous in equatorial Africa; it was unique in its region, for example, in developing a highly figurative and representational art.

Recent excavations have shown just how much the outside world has underestimated Ife; it was a commonplace of even recent historical writing to assume that equatorial Africa never developed cities or major monuments of any kind. This has now proved to be spectacularly wrong. For example, one site is Igbo Ukwu, a royal burial place in which massive quantities of manufactured goods have been found, including many that came from the Mediterranean and even from India, via Gao-Kukiya. Ife-Ife itself, the capital city, was surrounded by a ring wall forty feet high and twenty-five miles in circuit, and that wasn't the only one, or even the largest: Africa's largest single monument is a sixty-five-foot high wall with a moat sixteen to twenty-three feet wide that surrounded the city of Ijebu, the wall measuring an astounding one hundred miles in circumference.

The earthworks around the capital city of Benin—already mentioned as a city plated in brass—are larger yet; the UNESCO world heritage site register describes it as "a six thousand five hundred square kilometer [2,500 square mile] cluster of community earthworks, which run for about sixteen thousand kilometers [10,000 miles] in the Benin rainforest zone." In its central core, its walls reached sixty-five feet in height with densities of a little over four and one-third linear miles of earthworks per every third or so of a square mile. It is, very likely, the largest ancient earthworks anywhere.

This robust culture, which flourished from around the fourth century and vanished around the fifteenth, traded extensively with Gao and the polities of Ghana-Wagadu; there's no doubt that some of the products of the smelters of Mema found their way thousands of miles downriver to the Bight of Benin. We already knew that copper was brought into Mema from near Agadez, in modern Niger, gold from the Volta basin to the south, iron and ore for smelting from the southwest. The Garamantes people of the Fezzan, all the way across the great Sahara, twenty-five hundred miles away, visited in their chariots, centuries before Islam, centuries before the Arab people began their explosive expansion across the ancient world. Trade goods from Egypt, from India and even from southeast Asia have been found in these new digs.

The region is, says the historian John Hunwick, what the Nile Valley is to Egypt: "An ecological treasure and a civilizational magnet."[3]

❦

WHEN OLD GHANA was founded, Timbuktu was still a thousand years in the future. But there is a linear progression from the early industrial capacity of the Middle Niger and the accumulation of population there, through the kingdoms of Ghana-Wagadu and then Mali, which were both disturbed by the coming of the Arabs and by Berber predations, which led in turn to a shift in international trading routes, all of which, in the end, favored the growth of Timbuktu. Without the growth of the earlier kingdoms, and the trade (in gold and copper and salt) that they fostered, the commercial rationale for the growth of Timbuktu would not have existed. And without the unrest set in motion by the Berber movements and the Arab invasions, the western trans-Saharan caravan routes would have continued to prosper, and there would have been no need for a Timbuktu.

It may have been founded as a nomad camp, but that it grew so rapidly was really a consequence of much deeper, and much older, commercial and political forces.

❦

THE EARLIEST REAL evidence of political systems at all analogous to modern states—that is, Ghana-Wagadu—dates from about the ninth century. But in some cases their origins were much older, maybe a millennium and a half older. Such, for example, was the so-called Tichitt culture, or Tichitt Tradition. A town called Tichitt still exists in Mauritania, a 250-mile hard slog across stony desert from Walata, but it's a sorry thing, seldom visited now. Local legends say that seven earlier towns have been superimposed on this site, but the one that survives is irretrievably sinking beneath the dunes; only the upper stories of a few houses are visible; the rest have been swallowed by the sand. Ironically, most of the surviving town was destroyed a few years ago, not by wind-blown sand but by unexpected rains, leaving by some miracle only the mosque with its distinctive square-topped minaret, now seven hundred years old.[4]

When it was founded, the countryside was clearly much more verdant, for the town survived on its agriculture. At its height, the Tichitt settlements numbered more than four hundred villages strung out along the Tichitt escarpment for more than 120 miles. It was strategically situated, close to where Ghana-Wagadu would later emerge, and close also to where the great

Saharan trading center of Audaghost (Tegdaoust) would be built in the third and fourth centuries.

The same people were responsible for both the Tichitt Tradition and the Ghana Empire—the Soninke.

The Tichitt culture fell into crisis in the centuries before the present era. Many of the now-abandoned settlements had watchtowers and massive fortifications, a defensiveness that seems to have been a response to an invasion, perhaps from the Garamantes, whose soldiers showed up with horses and ox-drawn chariots; since many of the local villagers were cave dwellers, this might explain the otherwise enigmatic reference in Pliny to the Garamantes "hunting troglodytes." The incursions weren't enough to explain the culture's rapid decay, however. An ecological collapse seems to have followed; agriculture failed, and famine resulted.

Out of this chaos, and in the aftermath of the Garamantes' withdrawal (they were being attacked by the Romans to the north), came the gradual consolidation of the culture we now call Ghana-Wagadu.

☙

AT ITS HEIGHT, Ghana-Wagadu covered a formidable stretch of territory. Judging from the geographer al-Bakri's lengthy description of the towns and cities of the kingdom, it seemed to stretch from the Senegal River in the west, the border with the still independent state of Tekrur (though now much reduced), to the Niger River in the east. To the south, it dominated the rich gold-bearing region of Bambuk before petering out in the mountains of Mandingo; to the north it reached into the desert and thus dominated the Berber trading center of Audaghost. By doing that, it also dominated an important Saharan resource, the famous salt mines of Idjil, several hundred miles to the northwest. Al-Bakri reported in his *Book of Highways and Kingdoms* that the salt from these mines was "transported to Sidjilmasa, Ghana-Wagadu and other countries of the Sudan; work there continues uninterruptedly and merchants arrive in a constant stream for it has an enormous production."[5]

The Arab astronomer al-Fazari, writing in the eighth century, described the country as a place 1,250 miles long by 100 miles wide; it was a place of great riches he called "the land of gold." A hundred years later another Arab writer, the encyclopedist al-Hamdani, asserted that the richest gold mine on earth is that of Ghana in the land of the Maghreb (*Maghreb* in his definition meaning "beyond borders"). The geographer and traveler ibn-Hawqal, writing somewhere around the 960s, expanded on his predecessor's assertion by saying that "Ghana is the wealthiest king on the face of the earth because of his treasures and stocks of gold extracted in olden times for his predecessors and for himself."[6]

Toward the country's eastern edge, between modern-day Timbuktu and Gao, was a city called Tiraqqa, which has now completely vanished but was for a while one of the great commercial centers of the Middle Niger. Idrisi in the twelfth century described it as "one of the towns of Wanqara [sic], large, well populated, and unwalled, subject to the ruler of Ghana, to whom the people go in litigation." Tiraqqa seems to have remained an important market until the thirteenth century, at which time Timbuktu replaced it.[7]

Wangara, or Wanqara, is in the Middle Niger Valley area. Idrisi described the land, or "island," of Wanqara thus: "This country of Wanqara . . . is an island 480 kilometers long and 240 wide [300 by 150 miles], surrounded by the Nile on all sides during the whole year . . . In the land of the Wanqara there are flourishing towns and famous strongholds. Its inhabitants are rich, for they possess gold in abundance, and many good things are imported to them from the outermost parts of the earth."[8] This probably puts Wanqara along the junction of the Bani and Niger rivers, which is even now an island at high water.

The capital of the country was called Koumbi Saleh. To get to Koumbi Saleh now, you have to travel either from Nouakchott, Mauritania's capital, or go north from Bamako, the capital of Mali, through the old Soninke heartland in what is now the national park called the Boucle de Baoulé, and then farther north into the desert scrub. The land flattens out in the Wagadu, once a verdant forest but now stone and scrub, devolves into folds and wrinkles in the Valleé du Serpent and at Nara, the last town south of the Mauritanian border, turns into arid stonelands and dunes. Koumbi Saleh is about thirty miles or so into Mauritania, but nothing is left except a few tumbled ruins and the bustling camps of resident archaeologists.

But contemporary descriptions exist. In the middle of the eleventh century, al-Bakri, in his *Book of Highways and Kingdoms*, was effusive, suggesting that the capital had an army of 200,000 men, some 40,000 of whom were archers, and a strong cavalry. For years this was assumed to be an exaggeration; after all, al-Bakri never went there himself but based his account on the reports of merchants and travelers, among them Abraham ben Jacob and Yusuf al-Warraq. The city itself was thought to have had, at its height, a population of no more than 40,000 or 50,000. More recent archaeological fieldwork suggests, however, that the population of the "metropolis" that surrounded it might have been much greater. "Within 30 to 100 kilometers [18 to 62 miles] of the Koumbi Saleh ruins are the mounds and tumuli of other urban sites . . . Many . . . of considerable size . . . their material culture resembling that of Koumbi Saleh. In their day they would have formed important nodes in the dense interacting networks of the Ghana-Wagadu system. If the ruined sites were simultaneously inhabited between the 9th and 14th centuries, the heartland would have had an enormous population. In light of this possibility, al-Bakri's reference to an army of 200,000 may not have been far off the mark."[9] Indeed, al-Bakri had hinted as much: "The best gold in his land comes from the town of Ghiyaru, which is eighteen days travel from the king's town over a country inhabited by tribes of the Sudan whose dwellings are continuous."[10]

Al-Bakri went on to describe the capital in some detail.

The city of Ghana [identified as Koumbi Saleh] consists of two towns situated on a plain. One of these towns, which is inhabited by Muslims, is large and possesses twelve mosques, in one of which they assemble for the Friday prayer. There are salaried imams and muezzins, as well as jurists and scholars. In the environs are wells with sweet water, from which they drink and with which they grow vegetables. The king's town is nine kilometers distant from this one and bears the name al-Ghaba. Between these two towns there are continuous habitations. The houses of the inhabitants are of stone and acacia wood. The king has a palace and a number of domed buildings all surrounded with an enclosure like a city wall. In the king's town, and not far from his court of justice, is a mosque where the Muslims who arrive at his court pray. Around the king's town are domed buildings and groves and thickets where the sorcerers of these people, men in charge of the religious cult, live . . . These woods are guarded and none may enter them and know what is there . . . The king's interpreters, the official in charge of his treasury and the majority of his ministers are Muslims . . . The king adorns himself like a woman, wearing necklaces and bracelets, and he puts on a high cap decorated with gold and wrapped in a turban of fine cotton. He sits in audience or to hear grievances against officials in a domed pavilion around which stand ten horses covered with gold

embroidered materials . . . Behind the king stand ten pages holding
shields and swords decorated with gold, and on his right are the sons of
the vassal kings of his country wearing splendid garment and their hair
plaited with gold.[11]

This twin city sounds oddly like a medieval version of modern hub development, complete with strip malls—the considerable population was supported by the produce of surrounding farms, which were irrigated from wells.
Al-Bakri described the court as displaying "many signs of power, and the king
had under him a considerable number of satellite rulers." Much of his revenue
came from taxes on trade, and the basis of trade was gold. Ghana's own merchants brought the gold from the south and traded it for salt, which the north-
erners brought in from deposits in the Sahara.

The ruins that archaeologists are now investigating are believed to be the
"foreign," or Muslim, half of the city—they have yet to locate the ruler's
half. Some suggest that the Muslim town was surrounded by a double or
triple wall and was densely built with three principal streets and many smaller
ones, and a large public square, which could have served as a market or as a
parade ground for troops. Around this square were sixty blocks of single and
multistory stone houses. The surrounding wall or walls have vanished, but
vestiges of a monumental gate can still be seen.

When was the kingdom of Ghana founded? The archaeologists can only
guess. It could have been built in the fourth century, but it seems to have
been much older than that. Leo Frobenius, a sometimes erratic German
ethnographer, reported the existence of a "vellum manuscript," which he said
recorded the names of seventy-four rulers before the Soninke dynasty in
Ghana, "which there occupied the throne in 300 AD, running through
twenty-one generations."[12] (Still, no one else has been able to trace this manuscript.) The oral traditions of Timbuktu maintain that there were twenty-
two kings in Ghana-Wagadu before the start of the Islamic era. In any case,
by the time the Islamic proselytizers got there in the eighth century, it had
long been ruled by the Soninke group called the Cissé. The earliest extant
Arabic reference to a kingdom of Ghana dates from the close of the eighth
century. It remained an animist society until near the end of its existence,
though one of its eminent kings, Tunka, allowed Muslim merchants to build
mosques there in the tenth century. The first mosque, called the Great Mosque,
dates from the late tenth century.

Archaeologists at the Koumbi site have picked up considerable numbers of decorative objects, including ceramics, copper artifacts, gold weights and glass, much of it imported from the Maghreb and from Spain.

The town itself covered about 110 acres, but a 620-acre area beyond the walls is also covered with ruins and includes two massive cemeteries of about three-quarters of a mile each, with numberless tombs, including one massive commemorative tomb surrounded by columns and six walls, a style imported from the north. Beyond the cemeteries are the watchtowers, a row of them stretching about five miles, and beyond that numerous large square structures that might have been warehouses, or *fondacs (funduqs)* as they were later called in Timbuktu.

The leftover Tichitt towns and the district called Mema were two important provinces in the Ghana-Wagadu kingdom, essential for their manpower and their industrial production in the lengthy fight with the Sanhaja Berbers on the one hand and the emerging kingdom of Kawkaw (Gao) on the other.

Its hard to see any sign of civilization in Mema today. The whole Mema basin, covering almost 9,300 square miles, is arid, with sparse grasses that support a sparse population of goats and an even sparser population of human herders. But the available evidence suggests that in the first millennium the basin was covered with streams and forests and supported a dense population in urban clusters. Ruins of these towns can be seen, if you have the eye of an archaeologist to help: large habitation mounds, ancient fields, huge slag heaps. It's possible to pick out from aerial photographs over 250 habitation complexes in the Mema basin alone. A survey of a small area, some 15 by 20 miles, in the 1990s found 137 sites, 15 of them specialized iron-producing factories. Many thousands of smelters have been found. Clearly this was the industrial engine that powered the empire's expansion. The Memans were obviously involved in manufacturing on a large scale; certainly iron production was much too great for local consumption only, so exports were certain. Excavations in the Péhé district of Mema have yielded terra-cotta statuettes of armed horsemen, cowry shells, iron lance heads, copper and bronze objects, spindle whorls, imported luxury ceramics, glass beads and semiprecious stone beads. The basin has no iron ore of its own; it was brought in, either from the south, or perhaps from the northwest, since the mountain at Khedia d'Idji, in the Adrar region of Mauritania on the Royal Road, has a vast reservoir still estimated at around eight billion tons.

Farther upstream was the commercial center of Djenné, which is still a trading city of some twenty thousand people on the Bani River, in the Niger floodplain. Modern Djenné is a picturesque little town justly famous for its magnificent mud mosque and its fabric weavers, who make the extraordinary Malian "mud cloth," but Djenné itself is relatively "new": two miles away are the ruins of Djenné-Djenno, Old Djenné, a major city that was mysteriously abandoned almost seven hundred years ago; archaeologists rummaging through the debris left from the old town have found jewelry and other artifacts of exquisite beauty, much of it locally produced but some of it of exotic provenance. Old Djenné has been dated to somewhere around 200 BC and was a thriving city by AD 300, when jewelry, copper objects and decorative ceramics were being mass-produced. That it was trade-oriented was clear; glass beads in the tillage were chemically analyzed and found to range in date from 200 BC to nearly AD 1400, the earliest of all likely to have been made either in India or somewhere in East or Southeast Asia.

Djenné, or Djenné-Djenno, wasn't the only such city in the Middle Niger; nor was it the largest. "There were contemporary urban clusters that were five times as large in area, had three times the resident population, and had organized hinterlands of satellite settlements many times the size of Djenné-Djenno's."[13] Ghana-Wagadu had a network of markets, a developed agriculture, a sophisticated art, an evolved politics and, early Arab recollections suggest, a tax-collecting bureaucracy, before the Europeans emerged from the Dark Ages.

Djenné-Djenno, the towns and smelters of Mema, and Koumbi Saleh itself decayed before the upstart Muslim empire of Mali began to associate Ghana with corrupt pagan practices. Djenné-Djenno disappeared, by what may be a coincidence, with the arrival of Islam; perhaps the newly pious just wanted to start again and moved the city two miles downstream. Or maybe the ravages of the Sanhaja Berbers were sapping the agricultural lifeblood of the kingdom. Or maybe there was some ecological catastrophe; it is known the region undergoes periodic dry spells, and perhaps the Niger dried up or moved, and its tributaries failed, especially the major tributary in the region, the now-vanished Fala de Molodo. Or maybe the smelters and pottery and glass factories had ruined all the forests and they ran out of fuel.

Or maybe all of these. By the late twelfth century or the early thirteenth, none of the large cities were left and all the smelters had closed. The legends give a clue to what really happened: Dinga, the mythical ancestor of the Soninke, is said to have founded the capital of Wagadu, Koumbi Saleh, after wandering for many years from (in some versions) the Middle East. Central to the kingdom was the sacred forest of Wagadu, where the guardian serpent-god, Bida, used to live. Every year, this djinn demanded the sacrifice of a young woman, the most beautiful virgin in the kingdom. "Once the choice fell on a young woman named Sia. Her betrothed, Mamadou Lamin, decapitated the snake, and rescued his beloved, bringing a dreadful curse on the place. Ever afterward calamities fell on the city [Koumbi Saleh], whose inhabitants fled following a drought which afflicted the whole Ghana region."[14]

This may be. But the area is swarming now with archaeological field teams. In the language of police procedurals, investigations are ongoing.

❧

TEKRUR AND SUSU (or Soso) were two small states that survived the collapse of the Ghanaian kingdom.

Tekrur had been Ghana's main rival in the west and kept the Ghanaians from the Atlantic. It was governed by a tribal alliance of Wolof and Tukolor, the latter a corruption of the word *Tekrur*. As reported, it was the first organized state in West Africa to adopt Islam, which allowed it to cooperate with the Sanhaja and challenge Ghana for control of the Bambuk goldfields. But the Tukolor rulers seemed to lack the gene for imperial expansion; the kingdom remained small and ethnically uniform, which may help to explain why it outlasted Ghana for several hundred more years before being scooped up in the imperial maw of the mansas of Mali.

Susu, which seems to have been stitched together by Soninke clans north of Bamako, had a brief, and not very glorious, existence. No written documents about it survive; it is known only from the oral traditions, but these claim that it was founded by a clan of Malinke blacksmiths with magical powers. Whoever they were, they were fervently, even rabidly, anti-Islamic and soon developed a reputation for ferocity in battle. The rulers of Koumbi Saleh, weakened by the loss of their industrial heartland and by constant raiding (and a twenty-year occupation) by predatory Berbers, themselves harassed by invading Arabs, were no match for these terrible warriors when they appeared in sight of the watchtowers in the first half of the thirteenth century, and Koumbi was taken and sacked. Not long after it fell, Ghana-Wagadu drifted out of the history books.[15]

CHAPTER SEVEN

&

The Coming of the Arabs

THEN CAME THE Arabs, who stirred up everything.

The Islamic conquest of North Africa was awesomely swift, in historical terms. After overrunning Syria, Mesopotamia and Iran in just a few years, the victorious Arab armies surged into Egypt in 641, ousting the Byzantines from Alexandria and forcing the patriarch Cyrus to ratify the conquest of his province. This wasn't enough. The conquering general marched into Cyrenaica, which had been a province of Egypt, and took it without resistance in 643. Just a year later he marched into Tripoli. The exarch Gregory, who had governed the city, was defeated in a brief and savage battle; he and his daughter were killed, and his people fled in all directions.

A subsequent Arab general took so many prisoners and demanded so much tribute that the population petitioned him to accept a massive ransom, if only he'd go away. He took the terms and the gold and duly departed in 649.

The bribery was convenient but not really necessary, for while the Islamist armies had every intention of completing their conquest of North Africa, they were diverted for nearly twelve years by a civil war raging at home, the struggle to install Ali, husband of the prophet's daughter Fatima, as caliph, or God's deputy on earth. While they were absent from Africa, the Byzantines did themselves no good at all by trying to impose on the recalcitrant population the same kind of ruinous ransom ("taxation") paid to the departed Arab generals; as a result, they were facing a revolt when new Arab armies returned in 665, and easily rolled up what remained of the Byzantine forces.

The invaders pushed westward into Algeria and worked out a modus vivendi with Kusayla, the ruler of an extensive confederation of Christian

Berbers. Kusayla became a Muslim, and Arab and Berber forces controlled the region in turn until 697. It was the Arab general of the time, Abu al-Muhajir Dinar, who dipped a toe into the Atlantic and declared that there was nothing left for the victorious forces of Islam to conquer. The next—and last needed—commander in chief of the Islamic armies was Musa ibn Nusayr, the governor of the Maghreb who made his way, as reported earlier, into the legends of the *Thousand and One Arabian Nights* and whose armies, under Tarik ibn Ziyad (Tarik's Mountain = Djebel Tarik = Gibraltar), made their way into Spain. The whole thing was over by 711.

The conquest, in retrospect, might seem to have an air of inevitability about it, but in reality it was a conquest more fractious than most. No more than one hundred thousand Arab soldiers actually invaded, and their tyrannical ways soon led to revolt. In the chaotic political conditions that followed, three major kingdoms emerged, roughly corresponding to the three modern countries of Morocco, Algeria and Tunisia.

ↄ

THIS FIRST WAVE of Arab invaders was part of the astonishing flowering of Islamic culture, immigrants full of zeal for spreading Muhammad's newly revealed Word. But although many of the new arrivals intermarried with the Berbers, and with the leftovers of half a dozen old kingdoms—Romans, Carthaginian and Phoenician remnants, Jews and Judaized Berbers—theirs was nevertheless primarily a military invasion which hardly penetrated beyond the coastal mountains, and thus had no great effect upon the composition of the interior population or their way of life.

The second Arab wave, the invasion of the Bedouin tribal confederation called Beni Hilal in 1050 and the subsequent rampages of another such group, the Beni Soleim, both of them coming from Egypt, not Arabia, was a different animal altogether, and it was to have a profound and lasting effect on the entire Sahara, including Timbuktu.

Most contemporary writers seemed to believe this invasion was a calamity. The judgment of the modern historian Edward Bovill ("[that it] was an evil day for North Africa when, in the 11th century, the Beni Hilal poured out of Egypt westwards, along the coast; knowing no home but a tent and abhorring any more lasting structure [they] systematically pillaged every town and destroyed every solid building they encountered") was widely shared at the time. As early as 1360 the historian Ibn Khaldun described the Beni Hilal as "a plague of locusts," though he admitted their epic poetry was pretty enough.[1] It is said to be possible to trace the increasing desertification of the north, its loss of forest cover and Roman-built water conduit system, to the destructive effects of the Beni Hilal.

No part of the desert, not even the remotest, was unscathed by these Arab invasions, and the effects were felt far beyond the desert itself. Those Berbers who resisted the invasion and the consequent forced conversions to Islam were driven into the desert itself, there to join their deep-desert cousins; some of these mutated into the Moors and the Tuareg, others formed loose tribal confederations of their own, or, where such confederations already existed, clung to them more fiercely than ever. As they did so, the leftover native Nilosaharans, who had been there since the verdant times, retreated to the Sahel, the Niger and to Lake Chad. Even the gold- and silversmiths of the desert, who considered themselves to be Jews, blended almost completely into the Arabized tribes. South of the Sahara proper, tribes like the Dogon, who now live high in the cliffs of Bandiagara, took up their refuge in that inaccessible place because of the invasions, the Mossi to the south making it impossible to retreat that way.

The Arabs, many of them Bedouin, followed the retreating Berbers into and across the desert, until every part of the Sahara had its population of Arabs. Few inhabitants of the deep desert escaped conversion to Islam. The Tuareg, who were pinched into the deep desert by war and invasion, resisted for many centuries (and succeeded in remaking Islam in their own idiosyncratic way), and the Tubu in Tibesti did not give up the fight until the twentieth century, after more than a thousand years of often fierce resistance, but in the end, they all succumbed.

The founding of Timbuktu was part of the turmoil that followed the invasions, as the western trade routes across the desert were closed off, one by one, and new ones eagerly sought.

౨

FOR THE COMMERCIAL empire of Ghana-Wagadu, inheritors of the Tichitt industrial economy, political and military trouble had started on the northwest frontier as early as the ninth century. It had come from the Berbers, among whom the Arabs descended like a stick thrust into a hornet's nest.

All across the desert, from Libya in the east to the Atlantic coast, two broad and, for the most part, mutually hostile groupings of Saharan Berbers, the Sanhaja and Zanata, emerged and competed for dominance. Their quarrels spilled over to the southwest, and there was constant raiding against Ghanaian outposts. During the mid-eleventh century the Lamtuna Sanhaja, located between the Dra'a and the Senegal River, came under the rule of the puritanical Sunni Malikites,[2] who proceeded to diligently enforce the strictest of Qur'anic injunctions in favor of community prayer and against alcohol and unclean foods. And also against unbelievers, which meant the rulers of Ghana-Wagadu, among others. "Now and then," says Ibn Khaldun in his *History*, "they inflicted defeats on the more settled agriculturists of the Ghanaian empire."[3] This is a pretty dispassionate way of putting it; these terrible nomads boiled out of the desert with their scimitars, killing the farmers, then the farmers' protectors, then whole caravans of traders who had headed north across the sands with saddlebags of gold. But the initial confederacy was short-lived; the nomads had nothing to unify them except a sense of historic grievance against the Zanata, their own narrow faith and an ethos that glorified robbery as conquest, and they soon fell to fighting among themselves.

For a while the Ghanaian kings reasserted themselves and once again took control of the oases and the caravan routes, pushing the nomads back and subduing those who could be subdued. The rest remained in the deep desert, out of sight, nursing their anger; and after a while the tribes began to cohere once more, into a loose confederation whose center was around Audaghost, just north of the northern frontiers of the Ghanaian kingdom, but under its occasional control.

It wasn't until early in the eleventh century that this new confederation took on a more menacing form. A chief of the time, Yahya ibn Ibrahim, made a pilgrimage to Mecca and brought back with him an Islamic scholar from Morocco, Abd Allah ibn Yasin. Yasin, who was born in the Sahara and had lived in Muslim Spain for seven years, was a zealous preacher, and at first his teachings went well; his ideas, encompassing a more militant, puritan faith with little room for backsliders and apostates, spread rapidly. His underlying political purpose seems to have been to unite the Sanhaja and then launch them against the Zanata to, as he put it, "defend the right, abolish illegal taxes and impose the Qur'anic prescriptions." A secondary purpose was to put down what he considered Islamic heretics in southern Morocco, and at the same time to reassert control over Sidjilmasa and Aghmat, two northern termini of the Sudanic trade. Zanata Berbers also infested (his word) Audaghost, though that southern town was still under the influence of Ghana.

In the end, though, his teachings rankled the prickly Guddala Sahaja, among whom he had settled. They didn't take kindly to an outsider telling them to reform their morals (Yasin's notion that they should restrict themselves to four wives when they had been used to ten was particularly resented), and after Yasin launched them against a neighboring Lamtuna tribe in an attempt to unite them by force, they rebelled. What made it worse was that Yasin didn't necessarily practice what he preached: he had, as the chronicles put it delicately, "a marked fondness for the goods of this world . . . and a fondness for women."[4] The Guddala seized all his possessions and drove him from the country.

Destitute and humiliated, Yasin fled to Sidjilmasa. But he soon regrouped, this time taking refuge among the Lamtuna Sanhaja, whose ruler, Yaya ibn Turjut, or Tilutan, a man with great ambitions and political talent, gave him free reign.

Yasin was a man of limited intellectual talents, but in a way this is just what was needed, for he soon cobbled together a simplified form of Malikite Islam easily understood by the tribes, and as soon as he felt strong enough launched a sortie against the Guddala who had rebuffed him earlier. He prevailed, too, "massacring all those who had declared themselves against him and killing a large number of individuals who merited it on account of their crimes or their impudence," and within a few years he had united all the Sanhaja of the central and western Saharan regions. The expansion of his influence was made easier by a convenient doctrine he enforced when he was able, extracting fully a third of a tribe's property for his own use, "in order to make it lawful for them to use the other two thirds."[5]

Eventually these partisans, or rather those of his patron Turjut, became known as the *al-murabitin*, the Almoravids, a name elusive of definition but which could be derived from the Qur'anic meaning of the root word, *ribat*, which is very close to that of *jihad*. (Another version of the origin of the name is that Yasin called them *murabitin* after witnessing their great courage in a campaign against a tribe of polytheists in the Dra'a.)

In 1054, angry at what he saw was the great disparity in wealth between his own partisans and the Zanata rulers across the Atlas, Yasin launched his people against the north, taking Sidjilmasa, crossing the Atlas and sacking Fez. Yasin himself died in an obscure battle against a heretic tribe in 1057, but the Almoravids continued his work; it was the Almoravids, under their generals Abu Bakr ben Umar and his cousin Yusuf ibn Tachfin, who founded Marrakech in 1062. A year later Yusuf entered Fez without resistance, and in 1085 he "came to the assistance of the Spanish Muslims," and by 1102 the Almoravids ruled from the Senegal to the Ebro.

In an interesting sidelight, the Almoravids followed the Tuareg Berber custom of veiling their faces and often called themselves "the veiled ones." In Muslim Spain the veil was considered a privilege of the true Almoravids, forbidden to all but the Sanhaja; it became something in the nature of the uniform or distinctive dress of the ruling class.[6]

By the middle of the century the southern Almoravid armies under Abu Bakr were united enough, and free enough, to turn their attention to the still-pagan rulers of Ghana, and they began to conquer the productive lands of that kingdom. In 1076 they occupied the Ghanaian heartland, suppressing pagan practices, building mosques and schools, burning statuary and smashing clay idols.

It was the end of the old empire. The Sanhaja occupation lasted only twenty years, after which the Berber armies, responding to an urgent appeal from their Moroccan brethren for help against their enemies, the Zanata, departed whence they came. But by that time the authority of the Ghanaian kings had been fatally compromised. Perhaps that wouldn't have mattered had not the Almoravids' raids and constant fighting also undermined the country's agriculture and thus its prosperity; and had not the massive industrial capacity in the Mema heartland begun to fall apart under political and ecological pressures. Whatever the ultimate reasons, the empire began to break apart. Satellite kingdoms such as those of the Mande gradually began to assert their independence. Finally, as recounted, the capital was overrun by the Susu. That really was the end.

⁊

THE DECADENCE OF Ghana had a direct impact on Timbuktu. The commercial equilibrium had been upset. The Royal Road, the most westerly and most common caravan route from Ghana to the Moroccan towns, was cut off by Sanhaja predations and general banditry. Walata replaced Audaghost as the new southern axis, the gateway to the desert and thus to the north. But as the Massufa Berbers (or the Tuareg—the names are by now used interchangeably in the old histories) took control of the salt mines at

Taghaza, they began to bypass Walata, too, and headed straight down to the Niger—using Timbuktu to get to Djenné, which had maintained its commercial importance. The relatively new little town of Timbuktu had the double advantage of being a convenient gateway to the desert and only a few days away from the rich central delta and the metropolises of both Djenné and Gao, and this was decisive in its rapid growth.

After a while Walata itself began to send its commerce through Timbuktu; it had grown fat in provisioning the Ghanaian Empire, and as the empire faded, so too did Walata's trade.

And to the east, after the establishment of a dynasty called the Sonnis, Gao once again increased in importance and became the largest city in the eastern Niger basin.

Timbuktu was thus strategically located between the leftover commercial enterprises of Ghana-Wagadu (Djenné and Walata), and Gao. The *Tarikh al-Sudan*, the history of Timbuktu written in the sixteenth century, put it this way: "At the beginning, it was there that travelers coming by land and by water would meet. They constructed depots for their grains and their trade goods. Soon it became a main route and stopping place, for travelers stopped there both coming and going to the Sahel from the north. Later, as it began to become established, it grew by the goodness of God, and the population expanded. People came there from everywhere and from all sides . . . and it became a place of commerce. At first the people of Wagadu, Ghana, were those who came to trade in the greatest numbers, and they became merchants for all surrounding regions."[7]

Salem Ould Elhadj put the same point this way: "For Timbuktu, the great wealth was from salt, which came down from Taghaza and was transported on pirogue to the Middle Niger, and on the Bani to Djenné. Timbuktu would never have grown as important as it did if it hadn't been the main entrepôt for the merchants of Djenné, which sent here a large number of businessmen and men of letters. Djenné contributed greatly to the growth of this new city, and the approaches from Djenné were available by water for most of the year. This led to the establishment in Timbuktu of a great number of merchants' houses. They imported ivory, cola nuts, cereals, spices, baobab flour, shea butter, slaves and powdered gold. From the north came salt, fabrics, dates, eggs and feathers of ostriches." Timbuktu fast became the crucial node; to and through it came merchants from Tuat, Sidjilmasa, the Dra'a, Tlemcen and the port of Honein, from which there was in turn traffic with Europe.

Scholars came to Timbuktu at this time too, abandoning the fading Walata and the beleaguered west. That was also critical to the city's growth— and to the diminution of what remained of Old Ghana.

❧

EVENTUALLY, IN 1235, the Mande clan called the Keita, kings of Mali in the uppermost Niger Valley, took control from the Susu, who had seized Ghana, and incorporated what was left of the kingdom into their own, considerably more extensive, and militantly Islamic, empire.

Sundiata, the Magician King, "of the country of Mema," of the Tungara tribe, emir of the Malinke, kin to the Songhai of Gao, became the first Malé (Ruler) of what was to be the successor, and greater, empire.

CHAPTER EIGHT

ↄ

Mansa Musa and the First Golden Age of Timbuktu

A CRUMBLING MUD-AND-STONE staircase, "guarded" by a crumbling wooden door, leads to the roof of the Djingareiber mosque, one floor up. The roof itself is crumbling too, but if you gingerly skirt the softer spots, it's the best place for an overview of the city of Timbuktu. To the west are flat scrub plains that in the old days were flooded at high water from the Niger; to the northeast is the line of what could have been a city wall and beyond that straggling rows of new houses; to the east is an intricate maze of alleys that is the main city itself, to the south beyond the market buildings the new quarter, flat and featureless and without any discernible character. I peered over the parapet into a street below, where the guide who had opened the door, a Tuareg called Mohamed Ali, waited patiently.

The Royal Mosque, as it is called, is a massive structure, maybe a thousand feet on a side. Imposing walls are pierced with deep doorways and capped with what look like watchtowers and of course the minaret from which the muezzin call the faithful to prayer. This they have been doing in an unbroken line from 1325, when Mansa Musa, the most powerful king of the most powerful kingdom to arise in Africa, took control of the city and imported architects from Andalusia to build him an appropriate home (now vanished) and an appropriate place to make his obeisance to Allah.

We revisited the mosque again in 2005, but it had been abruptly closed to visitors on the advice of engineers hired by the Aga Khan, who reported the roof was on the point of collapse, its *banco* substructure crazed with fissures and its roof beams rotten through. The faithful still prayed, though tucked away into a corner, and the imams were forced to appeal to their captive audiences for donations to help save the building.

When it was first built, it was a potent, though pious, symbol of the royal power of the mansas of Mali.

⁊

EXCEPT THAT THEY occupied the Upper Niger Valley south of Bamako, the origin of the House of Keita is unknown. It is possible their origins go back to the founding of Djenné-Djenno itself. The oral traditions—no doubt influenced by their later need to appear as Islamic as possible—suggest the dynasty goes back to Bilal, the black companion of the prophet himself. Ibn Khaldun records a Keita king called Barmandana as the first Islamic king of Mali, though he provides no dates.

But Sundiata is regarded as the ruler who brought the Keitas into the wider world and imposed them on the Middle Niger. He was, it seems, from Mema, or at least lived in Mema for a time, and was the son of the king of the Keita and his second wife. He was named Sogolon Djata (or sometimes Mari-Djata) but was given the name Sundiata, the Hungering Lion, in his youth.

So much for the facts, as far as they are known. This is what the bards say of Sundiata.

He was a powerful child, though weak on his feet, and the people asked, "Why doth thy Sundiata always slip about the ground?" In those days there was but one great Sira tree in all of Mande. Whoever swallowed a pip of the fruit of this tree became King of Mandingoland. As a boy Sundiata went to this tree with his family. Many had tried to get one of its fruits by hurling up cudgels at it, but none could throw sufficiently far. Now instead of a cudgel, Sundiata picked up a man, and the man so thrown up struck against a fruit, broke it off and hurled it down. Sundiata gulped down the whole fruit, thus hindering the birth of any rival to his might. And then he seized the whole gigantic tree, plucked it out of the ground as another would have torn up a little plant, carried it into town and planted it in his mother's compound.

His father was reported to have said (as well he might): "Haha! Sundiata has arrived at man's estate and now one may set about his circumcision."

Of course, it wasn't as simple as that. It never is, in this matter of hero stories. Sundiata had a jealous brother, son of the king's first wife, Sasuma, who appealed to the Nine Witches of Mali to have the upstart killed. They failed, but Sundiata was forced to flee his country for his own protection. He took refuge with the king of Mema (believed to be the ruler of what was left of Ghana-Wagadu). While he was there, he asked the sand oracle to divine his fate. The oracle replied, "Before thou arrivest where thou wouldst thou wilt thrice be stirred to wrath. Yet, if thou let not thine anger overcome thee, thou shalt be king of Mandeland."[1]

Presumably, though the bards are silent on this point, Sundiata successfully overcame his wrath, because ruler of Mandeland he indeed became, suppressing along the way the Susu, who had tried to emulate Ghana-Wagadu, without much success, but who did succeed in dominating the trade routes to the detriment of all; the Susu king, Sumanguru, had seized Koumbi Saleh and was trying to put together a successor empire. (Another legend says of Sumanguru that while he was briefly in control of Mali he had poked fun at Sundiata, whose constant falling down he maintained was typical of the frailties of the Keita people, a rather large mistake on his part, for he was later painfully put to death. This may not in any sense be "true," of course. I have a photo of a small signpost near Nianan Kulu, by the highway near Ségou, on the road from Mopti to Bamako, which says, IN THIS PLACE SUMANGURU KANTE DISAPPEARED, IN 1235. Apparently like Sundiata, he was a magician and disappeared using a magician's tricks, fleeing into a cave in the escarpment and vanishing from human sight.)

Sundiata's victory over Sumanguru gave him control over the trans-Saharan caravan routes as well as all the internal trade routes over which gold was transported. He ruled from 1230 to 1255, making the city of Niani his capital. This little town, sometimes called Niani-Niani, was probably (though not certainly) on the Sankarani River, a small and unimportant tributary of the Niger, but close to the primary goldfields—this is where the golden rods of Ghana were supposed to be found, according to the legends then still circulating in the Maghreb. Niani was older than the empire, for it had once pledged allegiance to Ghana, and it remained the capital of Mali for some three hundred years. It is gone now, obliterated by time, even its location disputed.

At Sundiata's death he was succeeded by his son, Mansa Wali (sometimes referred to as Mansa Uli). Wali made the pilgrimage to Mecca sometime after 1260 and worked at the consolidation of the empire. Wali was followed by another brother, Khalifa, a sociopath who apparently liked killing people for sport. He was murdered by his courtiers, and the throne passed to a collateral line, that of Abu Bakr, who seems to have been a grandson of Sundiata, and was named for the Sanhaja general who had dominated Koumbi Saleh in earlier times.

After Mansa Abu Bakr there was an interruption in the line as power was seized by one Sakura, "a man of servile origins," in about 1298. By all accounts, he was a bastard (literally as well as morally) but proved a superior ruler, able enough to impress Ibn Khaldun, who reported about seventy years later that "under his powerful government the possessions of the people of Mali were expanded, and they overpowered the neighboring nations . . . Their authority became mighty. All the nations of the Sudan stood in awe of them, and the merchants of North Africa traveled to their country."[2]

Sakura died on his way back from his hajj, and he was followed in rapid succession by Mansa Qu, son of Mansa Wali, then by Mansa Muhammad, and then by Abu Bakr II, the immediate predecessor of the greatest Malian emperor of them all, Mansa Musa.

Everything we know about this Abu Bakr II, or Abu Bakari, comes from Mansa Musa himself, from a conversation he had with the son of the sultan of Cairo, the gist of which was published by the Cairo encyclopedist al-Omari as a chapter in his most famous work, the *Masalik al-Absad*, in 1340.

"If I have become the master of Mali," Musa confided to his host, "it is only because my predecessor refused to believe that the ocean was infinite."

Apparently this restless and energetic monarch had traveled the length of his growing empire and had spent—or so the griots say—too many hours staring out over the Atlantic, which he came to see as a barricade to his expansionist ambitions. Somewhere out there must be other lands for a king to conquer. "Therefore," Mansa Musa said, "my predecessor sent a preliminary reconnaissance fleet of four hundred ships towards the unknown and shadowy horizon. Only one returned, but that one told stories of a mysterious river in the middle of the ocean."

Those stories were enough. For Abu Bakari, his fate was decided.

"Not in the least discouraged," Mansa Musa said, "the emperor ordered the building of two thousand more vessels, a thousand for the men, a thousand for supplies." When the fleet was ready, he led his entourage once more down to the coast. There, he placed himself in the lead boat. "He assigned to me his authority and power until such day as he should return, but to this day no one has ever seen him again."[3]

Abu Bakr II set sail for America somewhere between 1310 and 1312. Did he ever get there? On this subject the griots are, of course, silent. Historians of the Americas are similarly silent, and except for a few African-looking stat-ues in fifteenth-century Mexico, and a few Spanish texts describing "black men from Ethiopia" near the Darien isthmus in 1513, which may or may not have anything to do with any of this, Abu Bakr's hubristic journeying has vanished from memory.

☙

MANSA MUSA, SOMETIMES called Kanka Musa or Gongo Musa after his mother, came to the throne in 1312 and died in 1332.

Under his rule the empire reached from the shores of the Atlantic, west of Tekrur, to the borders of modern Nigeria, and from the margin of the trop-ical forest northward into the Sahara. Al-Omari was told by a fellow Egypt-ian, who had lived for thirty-five years at Niani, that "the kingdom is square in shape, being four months [of travel] in length and at least as much in breadth." Leo Africanus was slightly less expansive: "the kingdom of Melli (Mali) extends three hundred miles along a river that falls into the Niger, bordering on Guinea, northward on deserts, westward to the ocean shore, and eastward to the territories of Gago [Gao]."[4] The mansas systematically expanded their domains. They reinvigorated the trade routes from Djenné toward new goldfields that were being opened along the Black Volta and far-ther south still, into the Akan region of modern Ghana, and to Benin and the Ife and Yoruba in Nigeria. They swept through Tekrur and reached the At-lantic. They extended their power beyond what had been the eastern frontiers of Old Ghana, to the cities of Timbuktu and Gao, termini of the shortest trans-Saharan routes. They began sending caravans laden with gold across the desert to the Maghreb states and to Egypt, using more easterly routes across the desert. (For a century or so, the western routes closed altogether as the countryside deteriorated south of Morocco into brigandry.) The Niger River became Mali's east-west conduit, and Timbuktu its hub. Soon, Malian mer-chants were trading south to the Gulf of Guinea, east to the Hausa city-states in modern Nigeria, especially the newly thriving market town of Katsina, and to the Islamic centers around the eastern Mediterranean and the Gulf of Arabia. Universities were founded at Timbuktu, Djenné and Ségou. Islam spread with the traders, and the Malians, and then the Hausa, converted en masse. The arts flourished. The country became wealthy, so wealthy that the kings were profligate with money, as though it were in inexhaustible supply.

❦

THE MOST EXTRAVAGANT expression of this extravagant wealth—an expression that finally brought the mansas and Timbuktu itself to the hardheaded attention of the Venetian traders—was the pilgrimage Mansa Musa made to Mecca in 1326. It was on this same voyage that he had stopped in Alexandria, where he had caught the attention of the encyclopedist al-Omari.

The reports of this journey vary in the details, but all agree on the astonishing wealth he showed. He is said to have taken with him 60,000 fellow pilgrims, plus 500 or so slaves. However, what seems to have astonished the scribes of Alexandria and Cairo more than the size of his retinue was the amount of gold he carried with him. Again, the reports vary. Some say 100 camels laden with gold, others 1,000 camels each with 100 pounds of gold, or no camels but 150 kilograms of gold, or 500 slaves carrying 6 pounds of gold each, plus 300 camels with 300 pounds of gold, or 500 slaves each carrying a rod of 2 kilograms of gold. Volume 4 of the authoritative UNESCO *General History of Africa* makes an even more extravagant claim, surely a mistake: "The great ruler took 60,000 porters with him. Each porter carried 3 kilograms of pure gold, that is, 180,000 kilograms or at least 180 tons of gold."[5]

Which of these, if any, is "true" is of course unknown. The one with 1,000 camels laden with 100 pounds of gold each is a Tuareg story, told mostly to make the point that the king "had to take a Tuareg [with him] as his prime minister to get him through the sands the Tuareg ruled, otherwise he would have been robbed."[6] He was also said, in a more pious version, to have built a mosque along the way at every place he stopped for Friday prayers. The commonly expressed notion that his money was so lavishly spent that the economy of the Middle East crashed and the value of currency debased for a decade seems to be a modern gloss on the old story.

The best account, and one that contains a few piquant details not recorded elsewhere, is that of al-Sa'adi in his chronicle, the *Tarikh al-Sudan*.

> He made the pilgrimage to the Sacred House of God departing—God knows best—in the early years of the eighth century [of the hegira]. He set off in great pomp with a large party, including 60,000 soldiers and 500 slaves, who ran in front of him as he rode. Each of his slaves bore

in his hand a wand fashioned from 500 mithqals of gold [that is, over 4 pounds of gold each, for a total of 2,200 pounds].

He took a route through Walata in the upper lands and through Tuat. Many of his party stayed behind in Tuat because of a foot ailment that befell them on the journey and settled there. The foot ailment was called *tuwat* in their language and so the place was named after it.

The Easterners who chronicled his visit were astonished at how mighty a ruler he was. However they did not characterize him as open handed or generous since despite the great size of his kingdom he gave out no more than 20,000 mithqals of gold as his charity.[7]

(Al-Sa'adi compared this niggling amount with the more than 100,000 mithqals that Askia Mohamed donated along his way a century of two later; but this is no doubt because al-Sa'adi was himself under the protection of the askias, and such a beneficial comparison would have been prudent.)

Wealthy he may have been, but Mansa Musa was obviously a bit of a spendthrift and clearly lacked a controller to keep track of his expenses. Al-Sa'adi, who is himself quoting the traveler Ibn Battuta (who actually visited Niani a few years after Mansa Musa's death), recounts how the mansa had run out of money and had to borrow some from a Cairo merchant.

Mansa Musa . . . stopped at a garden belonging to . . . Siraj al-Din at the pool of the Abyssinians outside Cairo. He was in need of money and borrowed it from Siraj al-Din; the amirs also borrowed from him. [Afterward] Siraj al-Din sent his agent with them to recover the money but he stayed in Malli. Then Siraj al-Din himself went with his son to recover the money. When he reached Timbuktu he was given hospitality by Ishaq al-Sahili. It was fated that he should die that night. People talked about it and suspected that he had been poisoned. His son said to them, "I was with him and ate exactly the same food that he ate. If it had been poisoned we should both have been killed, but his appointed time had come." His son went to Malli, recovered the money and went back to Egypt.[8]

Whatever the truth, later historians, such as ibn al-Iyas (who died in 1525), mentioned Musa's visit as the outstanding event of the year.

And for the first time, Europe took real notice: in an atlas of the world made for Charles V (*El mapamundi de Abraham y Jafuda Cresques*) in 1375, three of the cities of Mali were mentioned: "Ciudad de Melli," the capital, Tenbuch (Timbuktu) and KaoKao (Gao). It shows Mansa Musa himself, drawn seated holding a large ball of gold and wearing an oddly European-style crown. He was described in the text: "This Negro lord is called Musa Mali, Lord of the Negroes of Guinea. So abundant is the gold which is found in his country that he is the richest and most noble king in all the land." The map clearly shows the Atlas Mountains, with a gap where the Dra'a Valley is, and the caption "Through this place pass the merchants who travel to the land of the negroes of Guinea, which place they call the valley of the Dra'a." Musa is shown facing a nomad on a camel. The accompanying text reads: "All this region is occupied by people who veil their mouths; one only sees their eyes. They live in tents and have caravans of camels. There are also beasts called Lemp from the skins of which they make fine shields." These veiled ones, presumably the Massufa Berbers or the Tuareg (who may be one and the same), controlled the trans-desert traffic.

∾

ON THE STREET outside the Djingareiber mosque, roadwork was going on, or rather "roadwork" because it was a desultory thing, two men in a hole with shovels, a pile of dirt in the middle of the road and one other worker, a bucket on his head, strolling casually toward them. The street was otherwise deserted; it was noon, and hot, and it was time to rest. The hole was where a UNESCO-funded sewer would go, in due time; Timbuktu had done without sewers for nine hundred years or so, and another few wouldn't do it any permanent damage. Around the corner, along the south façade of the mosque, the city, or UNESCO again, had laid cobblestones, and they looked curiously inappropriate, being too neat and finished. While we watched, a woman emerged from a nearby house and dumped a bucket of household garbage on the cobbles. Perhaps she too felt the neatness was inappropriate. Or maybe that was just where she and her neighbors habitually dumped garbage. The city has no sanitation workers, after all.

Timbuktu would have been a substantial presence even before Mansa Musa caused his massive mosque to be erected here. A few hundred yards to the north, its minaret clearly visible from the Djingareiber's roof, was the oldest mosque in the city, Sankoré. It had been built sometime in the late 1100s, in what was to be called the Sudanese style, made of packed mud from the Niger

Street work outside Djingareiber mosque. (Sheila Hirtle)

baked to clay, its façade pierced with stone beams like porcupine quills, a ready-made scaffold from which to repair the building when it rained, as it occasionally did. No one knows who built Sankoré, except that it was the gift of a wealthy woman, but a few years after its erection a Qur'anic school was founded there, a school that in time, under the askias, became the University of Sankoré and is now once again just a school, where young children sit in the sand and learn the sutras of the Qur'an by heart.

Sankoré's development was a sign that Timbuktu had matured by the end of the thirteenth century. Its trade had attracted wealth, wealth had created leisure and leisure had brought in scholars and holy men, collectively called the uléma, from many parts of the desert and the Maghreb. It was already becoming a commercial and intellectual center. But its government was still uncertain. Old Ghana had not paid it much attention. Indeed, for much of Ghana's existence Timbuktu was not yet even a nomad camp, and in the last century of Ghana's rule the state was hard-pressed to deal with incursions from the north and in the immediate vicinity of the capital and had few resources to spare for acquiring outlying provinces.

Both Timbuktu and Gao soon caught the eye of Mansa Musa. Gao's trade with the north was still substantial, and the city retained a route to the goldfields of the Black Volta. Timbuktu, for its part, was already beginning to supplant Walata as a commercial center, and the canny traders of Old Djenné were shifting their enterprises there. Along with that shift went many of Djenné's eminent scholars, which created, in turn, a resentment against Timbuktu that was a curious mix of snobbery and envy, and that was expressed in legend, as we shall see. Djenné regarded itself as cultured and cultivated and Timbuktu as a brash upstart; analogous attitudes can be found in our day between St. Petersburg (sophisticated) and Moscow (brash), or between Montreal (cultivated) and Toronto (commercial) or between Rio (worldly) and São Paulo (industrial).

At the same time, the city's newfound wealth had attracted the unwelcome attention of the nomadic bands of deep-desert Tuareg, whose predations on caravans and occasional short but savage raids on the city itself kept the merchant class in a constant state of nervous excitement.

In 1326, the same year the mansa made his pilgrimage to Mecca, his forces formally annexed Timbuktu and Gao. One of his lieutenants, Sagamendian, took an expeditionary force to the two cities and scooped them up into the empire. He met, it seems, no resistance at all; indeed, he was apparently eagerly awaited and had the keys to both cities, if such keys existed, pressed into his hands. It's possible he was even invited in.

On his way back from Mecca, therefore, Mansa Musa took a different route from the northerly one he had traveled earlier. He and his retinue went first to Gao and then to Timbuktu. On his way, he very likely came down through the Ahaggar and Aïr regions. Another of his main sources of wealth were the copper mines of Takedda, to the west of Agadez, which is now in Niger. We know this because Mansa Musa himself mentioned it to an Arab trader, ibn amir Adjib, in Cairo, reported by Ibn Battuta, "There is nothing in all my empire which is such a large source of taxes . . . as the import of this unworked copper. It comes from this mine and from no other. We send it to the lands of the black pagans where we sell a mithqal of it for two-thirds of gold."[9] These black pagans were presumably the brass workers of Benin, far away on the Atlantic to the south.

As Heinrich Barth put it, Musa now had control of "the four large territories of the western part of Negroland: First, Baghena, formed out of the remnants of the kingdom of Ghanata [Ghana-Wagadu]; secondly Zagha, or the western Tekrur, together with Silla; then Timbuktu, at that time still, as it seems, independent of Gogo [Gao]. Jinni [Djenné] however, probably owing to its nearly insular character, seems not to have been subjected to Melle

[Mali] at this period, although it was engaged in continual warfare." Timbuktu, as a consequence, lost its independence but gained much more. "And being thus well protected against violence offered on the part of the neighboring Berber [actually, Tuareg] population, and in consequence of the town increasing rapidly, it soon became a market place of the first rank, so that the most respectable merchants from Misr, Tawat, Tafilalt, Darah, Fez and other places migrated to Timbuktu."[10]

In his own capital, Niani, the new *hajji* Mansa Musa built a palace and an audience hall, already having a mosque. In Gao he built a palace and a new mosque, and in Timbuktu, another, altogether greater, mosque.

On his way back from Mecca he had stopped again in Cairo, partly to borrow money but also to hire those he thought he needed, artisans and workers skilled in stonework and ironmongery. There, he added to his retinue one of the most eminent people of his time, the celebrated poet and architect from Andalusian Granada, Abu Ishaq es-Sahéli al-Tuadjin al-Granata. The architect's fee for building a house of worship in Timbuktu was substantial: some fifty thousand mithqals of pure gold, about 440 pounds of the stuff, dozens of slaves of both sexes, clothing, foodstuffs, land along the river and other perks.

Es-Sahéli chose a site then called Bissaouthiré, now called Djingareiber (or Friday Prayers), to build the great mosque. Work started late in the year, and by 1330 the building was finished, constructed to es-Sahéli's plan, essentially the same building that stands now, modeled after the Great Mosque in Damascus, which es-Sahéli had himself replicated in Almoravid Spain, in Cordoba and elsewhere. A massive thing, the new mosque had an imposing façade forty feet tall with great wooden doors and a single minaret; inside, there were nine vaulted spaces where thousands of the faithful could worship, apartments for the imam, rooms for students, storage for holy objects and for books. For the first time in the city a building was erected of brick, with a façade of imported limestone that glittered in the desert sun; previous building in Timbuktu had been *pisé*, or pounded clay, which the locals call *banco*. The mosque easily eclipsed the Sankoré, across town to the north.

The architect built a second grand edifice. Mansa Musa was never to live in Timbuktu—it was never the capital city of Mali—but he wanted a decent place to stay when he was in town, and es-Sahéli built him a *madugu*, a House of a Master, a building that has now vanished and whose plans no longer exist, but from all accounts a place of complementary massiveness and ostentation.

To protect the city from the Tuareg who prowled the desert to the north, he built a rampart and a stone fort.

❧

THE INDEFATIGABLE IBN Battuta, one of the greatest travelers of his or any other time, left us what is by far the most engaging portrait of life in the Mali of the mansas, with some sharply observed if condescending anecdotes about life on the road and at court. He reached Niani just a few years after Mansa Musa's death, when his brother Sulaiman was in charge; but presumably nothing much had changed in the few years that had passed.

Battuta left Marrakech via Sidjilmasa, departing from that city in February 1352, in company with a number of merchants. Their caravan stopped briefly in Taghaza and then headed for Walata.

At an oasis he called Tasarahla (Bir al-Kusaib now) the caravan stopped for three days and dispatched a *takshif* to Walata, which was then still an important commercial center, though not any longer as important as Timbuktu. He described this *takshif* as a Massufa agent hired to alert the city that a caravan was coming; he would carry letters to people in town asking for houses to rent. "Sometimes this *takshif* perishes in the desert and the people of Walata know nothing of the caravan or its people, or most of them perish too. There are many demons in that desert. If the *takshif* is alone they play tricks on him and delude him till he loses his way and perishes. There is no road to be seen in the desert and no track, only sand blown about by the wind. You see mountains of sand in one place, then you see they have moved to another."[11]

Caravans coming into Timbuktu from the north tended to hire their *takshifs* at Arawan.

The caravan reached Walata after a two-month journey from Sidjilmasa. It was the seat of the first region governed by the mansas. Sulaiman's deputy was Farba (governor) Husayn. Battuta was not impressed.

When we arrived the merchants deposited their goods in an open space and the blacks took responsibility for them. The merchants went to the *farba* who was sitting on a rug under a shelter; his officials were in front of him with spears and bows in their hands. The Massufa notables were all behind him. The merchants stood in front of them and he spoke to them through an interpreter as a sign of his contempt for them, although they were close to him. At this I was sorry I had come to their country because of their bad manners and contempt for white people. I made for the house of Ibn Badda, a kind man to whom I had written asking him to let a house to me, which he did.[12]

Battuta's bad humor persisted, and he let his irritability show.

The [customs] inspector of Walata, Mansha Ju, invited those who had come in the caravan to a reception, but I refused to be present. My companions urged me strongly to accept, and I went with the rest. At the reception coarsely ground *anli* [a local grain] was served mixed with a little honey and curdled milk. This was put in a half gourd, which they make like a large bowl. Those present drank and left.

I said to them "Is it for this that the Blacks invited us?"

"Yes," they said. "For them it is a great hospitality." I then became convinced that no good was to be expected from these people, and I wanted to join the pilgrims traveling [north] from Walata, but I decided to go and see the capital of their king.

To his credit, Ibn Battuta later discovered, and reported, that this meager "meal" of *anli*, honey, and milk was never supposed to be a banquet; it was purely symbolic, part of the ritual of hospitality, and he later apologized, sort of. "I stayed in Walata about 50 days. Its people treated me with respect and gave me hospitality. Most of the inhabitants belong to the Massufa. The women are of outstanding beauty and are more highly regarded than the men."

He hired a Massufa guide to take him on the twenty-four-day journey from Walata to the capital, which he called Malli. He traveled with only three companions. There was no need for a caravan, he reported, for the road was safe and travelers were not molested.

The countryside soon changed from the arid deserts of Walata to thick forests. He was particularly taken with the immense baobabs along the road. "A caravan can shelter under a single one of them. Some of them have no branches or leaves but the trunk gives enough shade to shelter men. Some of these trees have rotted inside and rain water has collected there, as if it were a well. People drink this water. In some of these trees are bees and honey, which people collect. I passed by one of these trees and found a man inside

weaving; he had set up his loom and was weaving. I was amazed at him."
Baobab leaves were supposed to cure impotence, which impressed him even
more. "Also, in this jungle between Walata and Malli are trees whose fruit
resembles plums, apples, peaches and apricots, but they are not exactly the
same."

The countryside was productive. There was no need to carry food, for it
could be bought along the way with pieces of salt, glass trinkets or articles of
perfumery. Food was transported in huge calabashes, "from which they make
bowls, beautifully decorated."

After traveling for two weeks or so, they reached the Niger, or the "great
river, the Nile," as he called it. He recounted how he saw a crocodile near the
town of Zagha. "One day I went down to the Nile to satisfy a need and one
of the Blacks came and stood in the space between me and the river. I was
amazed at his appalling manners and lack of decency. I mentioned it to someone who said, he did it to protect you from the crocodile by putting himself
between you and it." The crocodile was so large, Ibn Battuta reported, that it
looked like a small boat.

ఆ

FINALLY, THE LITTLE group reached the capital, where, according
to Battuta, he received a warm reception.

> I arrived in the city of Malli, the capital of the king of the Blacks,
> alighted at the cemetery and proceeded to the quarter of the white peo-
> ple, where I sought out Mohamed Ibn Al-Faqih. I found that he had
> rented a house for me opposite his own. I went there and his son in law,
> the jurist and Qur'an reader Abd Al-Wahid, came with a candle and
> food . . . I met the *qadi* [judge] of Malli, Abd al-Rahman, who came to
> me. He is a black, a *hajj*, an excellent man with noble qualities. He sent
> me a cow as a welcoming gift. I met the dragoman Dugha, one of the
> most distinguished and important of the blacks; he sent me a bull . . .
> they provided for me completely, God recompense their kindnesses. Ibn
> al-Faqih was married to the daughter of the sultan's paternal uncle and
> she concerned herself with our food and needs.

For a few weeks he and his companions were ill; something they had eaten,
they suspected, and it was some time before he actually saw Mansa Sulaiman.

Mansa means sultan and Sulaiman is his personal name. He is a miserly
king and a big gift is not to be expected from him. It happened that
I spent all my [early] time in Malli without seeing him on account of
my illness. Then he arranged a mourning meal for our master,
Abu'l-Hasan, God be pleased with him, to which he invited the amirs,
jurists, *qadis* and the preacher, and I went with them. They brought out
the Quran cases, and the whole Quran was read. Then they prayed for
our master and for the Mansa Sulaiman. When this was over I advanced and greeted Mansa Sulaiman. The *qadi*, the preacher and Ibn
al-Faqih told him about me, and he replied in their language. They said
to me, The sultan says to you, give thanks to God. I said praise and
thanks to God in all circumstances.

His notes were in the same tone they had been in Walata, dismissive and
more than slightly contemptuous. He scribbled the following heading: *Account
of their meager hospitality and exaggerated opinion of it*. Below it he wrote:

When I had left [the palace] a gift of welcome was sent to me. It was
sent to the *qadi*'s house; he sent it with his men to Ibn al-Faqih's house.
He came hurrying barefoot and came in to me. He said, stand up! The
sultan's things and gift have come for you. I stood up, supposing them
to be robes of honor and money, but there were three rounds of bread,
a piece of beef fried in *gharti* and a calabash with curdled milk. When
I saw it I laughed and was greatly surprised at their feeble intelligence
and exaggerated opinion of something contemptible.

In reality, however, it was the sultan who had not been impressed with his
visitor and had thought him unworthy of serious attention. Ibn Battuta later
rather grudgingly changed his mind and wrote in his careful hand how he
had daringly upbraided the king for his stinginess, in a section he titled *An
account of what I said to the sultan afterwards and his kindness to me*.

After I had received this gift I spent two months during which nothing
reached me from the sultan. He held an audience in the first days of Ramadan. I stood before him and said, I have traveled through the countries of the world and have met their kings. I have been in your country
for four months but you have not treated me as a guest and you have not

given me anything. What am I to say about you before other sultans? He said, I have not seen you and I know nothing about you. The *qadi* and Ibn a-Faqih stood and answered him, saying, He greeted you and you sent food to him. Thereupon he ordered that a house be provided for my lodging and my current expenses. On the night of the 27th of Ramadan he distributed money to the *qadi*, the preacher and the jurists, which they called *zakat*, and he gave me at the same time thirty three and a third mithqals. When I left he gave me a hundred mithqals of gold.

The daily workings of the court also made it into his journals. He described the sultan sitting on a raised cupola to receive delegations from the countryside. On the side of the "audience hall" were three arches of wood covered with silver, below which were three more covered with gold or silver gilt. The whole was surrounded by curtains, whose raising was the signal that a royal session was to take place. When the sultan took his seat, a silk tassel was inserted into one of the arches; at this, drums were beaten and trumpets sounded. Then some three hundred slaves came out, some with bows, others with short spears and leather shields. "Then they brought out two horses and two rams; they say they are useful against the evil eye."

As the sultan sat, three slaves ran to call his deputy. The notables of the court—soldiers, emirs, and jurists—sat in the front. "Dugha the dragoman stands at the door of the audience hall, dressed in splendid clothes of [a brocaded fabric made in Alexandria] and other fabrics; on his head is a turban with a border arranged with exceptional artistry; he is girded with sword in a gold scabbard; on his feet are boots and spurs. No one except him wears boots that day. In his hand he has two short spears, one of gold and the other silver, tipped with iron." Everyone else sat outside the audience hall, in a wide thoroughfare lined with trees. "Each *farari* (military captain) has in front of him his men with spears, bows, drums, trumpets made from elephant tusks and musical instruments made from reeds and gourds, which are struck with sticks and make a pleasant sound . . . If anyone wishes to speak to the sultan he must first speak with Dugha."

Ibn Battuta described how the people showed their respect to their king: "[by] taking off their clean clothes, putting on dirty ones, and then on the ground in front of him sprinkling dust on their own heads. I was astonished they didn't blind themselves. To pour dust on themselves is good manners among them."

On prayer or feast days, "the sultan comes out on horseback and a tent is erected for him in a field. There are armor bearers with splendid weapons, quivers of gold and silver, swords ornamented in gold, as are the scabbards, spears of gold and silver and maces of crystal. Dugha the dragoman comes out with his four wives and his concubines, who are about a hundred, in fine clothes. On their heads are bands of gold and silver, with gold and silver apples attached to them. There are dances and acrobatics and singing, and the sultan gives gifts of gold."

ADMINISTRATIVELY, TIMBUKTU BECAME a province of Mali, ruled by a *farba*, a governor who in this case doubled as a military man, who lived in the *madugu* and ran the province like a king. He had his court and his council. He ensured order and peace, collected taxes imposed on the merchants, and mediated between the various ethnic groups. Both Mansa Musa and the *farba* had secretaries and court officers; records were kept and sent as the government, while still personal, became more systematic. Ibn Battuta, who spent a few days in the town in 1353, visited the *farba*. "I was present one day when he promoted one of the Massufa to be emir of a group," he wrote in his journals. "He gave him a robe, a turban and trousers, all colored, and seated him on a leather shield. The chiefs of the tribe lifted it up above their heads and bowed their heads to him." The emir's function was to judge conflicts and to furnish soldiers for the *farba* when called on.

While he was there, Battuta visited the grave "of the illustrious poet Abu Ishaq al-Sahili of Granada, known in his own country as *al-Tuwaijin*, 'the little cooking pot' [this provided without explanation], and also of Siraj al-Din b. al-Kuwaik, one of the great merchants of Alexandria." This "al-Sahili" was the es-Sahéli who built the great mosque—and the same man at whose house the Cairo merchant had died.

EVEN IN HIS personal absence, Mansa Musa's largesse had a galvanizing effect on Timbuktu. Richer merchants hired the skilled workers imported from Egypt to build their own houses, which they made of stone, thus contributing greatly to the embellishment and extension of the city.

The masons and ironworkers settled in and prospered. Both formed powerful guilds, the masons in the Djingareiber quarter, the blacksmiths in a quarter then called Sareïkeïna. New people flocked in from the west, mostly Soninke from Mema and Walata. More Soninke came from the south, from Wangara, and settled in the quarter around the mosque called Sidi Yahiya, which was then close to a branch of the Niger flooded at high water, where they set up a market; the sector came to be known as Wangarakunda, the quarter of the Wangara. Little by little Timbuktu took on the cosmopolitan population it was never to lose, a city in which Arabs, Tuareg, Soninke and Fulani lived side by side. The ethnic mix also included Wolof, Tukolor, Bambara, Bozo, Songhai and Berbers.

The city profited from the Mali-imposed peace in two significant ways. It grew larger than either Djenné or Gao and became, in effect, the cultural (and religious) and commercial center of the empire.

On the cultural front, the tolerant governance of Mansa Musa and his successors continued to attract scholars and savants from all parts of the Sahara, the Maghreb and from Egypt, and a population of theologians, doctors, teachers and writers accumulated around the mosques. One of the most celebrated was Khatib Musa, imam of the Djingareiber mosque for more than forty years, the author of dozens of luminous texts of Islamic exegesis. The standards of scholarship had already been high. The *Tarikh al-Sudan* gleefully reports the fate of the Egyptian savant Sidi Abd el-Rahman Tamini, who accompanied Mansa Musa to Timbuktu when he returned from Mecca, expecting to take a teaching role there. Instead, he found the standards so rigorous he was obliged to depart for Fez and Marrakech to further his studies before he was allowed to teach at any of the city's schools.[13]

The city also profited commercially. Some of the traders who settled in Timbuktu built up enormous fortunes. As Walata faded further, Timbuktu became the main terminus for the trans-Saharan traffic in gold, slaves and salt and the spices of Guinea. Caravans of ten thousand camels made the arduous trek across the desert to Sidjilmasa and Marrakech. At certain seasons the city's population could swell by more than fifteen thousand people. The standing army kept the Tuareg at bay, and visitors to Timbuktu often remarked that they had been guaranteed, and had received, a safe stay in the city.

Europeans had pretty well ignored Africa since Carthage had fallen, but there were Venetian and Genoese trading firms in Alexandria, and these alert and hardheaded gentlemen paid serious attention to Mansa Musa's extravagant spending; reports of the king of Mali and his immense wealth quickly spread through southern Europe. Traders from Grenada, Genoa, Venice and the Flemish markets to the north turned up in the Maghreb towns like Messa, Marrakech and Fez, trading manufactured goods for gold.

೧೦

TIMBUKTU'S NEW CELEBRITY status in the empire and abroad didn't always sit well with the citizens of Walata or Mopti or Gao or especially Djenné. This jealousy lives on in folklore.

Later in the day, after we'd seen what there was to be seen at Djingareiber and Sankoré, we went to pick up Salem Ould Elhadj, then tooled around the traffic circle at the head of the Kabara road, on our way to the dunes outside the city. The savant was talking about the pious nature of the early population, and how it was famously a city of 333 saints, when we rounded the statue of Alfarouk, rearing up on his white charger.

"Was Alfarouk one of the saints?"

"No no, Alfarouk was a genie, a demon. A protecting demon, our guardian demon, but still a demon."

The oral tradition, he explained, asserted that Alfarouk always appeared in a white cloak, turbaned in the manner of the Tuareg, in a human form, mounted on a white horse. He was the protector of the city in the early hours of the morning and seemed on the face of it to be an incredible busybody. He would come to the city at nightfall, patrolling every alleyway, "casting his eagle eye in every direction to see if he could spot a pedestrian or solitary voyager in these wee hours. If he spied one, he rushed up to him and sounded the tinkling bells of his horse, and urged the errant one to return home. Every citizen of the city knew he had to obey an order from Alfarouk to return home." Around three in the morning, always before dawn, he withdrew to the river at Kabara. He could not survive in the sun.

Later, Sidi Salem gave us a pamphlet he had written containing some of the legends of Alfarouk. The most interesting was one that casts light on the uneasy relations between Djenné and Timbuktu, and on Djenné's jealousy, and at the same time neatly illustrates official Islam's mastery of demons.[14]

The backdrop to the tale was a riddling game between Alfarouk and Sane Chirfi, a notable of the city and imam of Djingareiber, the subject being verses from the Qur'an. To his fury, Alfarouk was unable to prevail before dawn and had perforce to leave. Knowing he would want his revenge, the imam hurried to see the *qadi* of the city, Sheikh Alkali Aïba, imam of the

Sankoré mosque, a wise and virtuous man. This holy personage, the author of many miracles, listened attentively to the story, and the following night lay in wait for the demon at the Sankoré mosque. In due time, he heard the sound of tom-toms and saw a procession heading his way. It was Tuareg, dressed all in blue, who were beating the drums. Alfarouk, in his white cloak at the head of the procession, spotted the *qadi* at once and galloped over, yelling, "Qadi Alkali Aïba, do not interfere between Sane Chirfi and me."

The *qadi* was affronted. Demon or not, it was the first time anyone had addressed his holy person in such a discourteous manner. He continued to face the genie, then he lifted his cane, drew money from his purse and hurled it to the ground.

"Chamharouche!" he called. "Chamharouche! Come to me!"

This Chamharouche was the chief and grand priest of the race of genies. He appeared before the *qadi*, covered in sweat.

"I order you this instant," the *qadi* said, "to take Alfarouk, who here is beside you. Take him immediately to Djenné, sink him to the bottom of the waters of the Bani, and he will rest in prison there seven hundred years."

Without saying a word, Chamharouche seized Alfarouk and whisked him off to Djenné. He deposited the demon, now greatly chastened, in front of the grand mosque, where the uléma of that city were gathered.

These persons, it turns out, had been searching for Alfarouk for years. The reason concerned a young man from Timbuktu who had committed an unmentionable act in their vicinity, by refusing to take off his shoes in salute as he passed them by. This was of course intolerable, and he had of course to be killed, made to vanish forever. "We entrusted the task to two great specialists among us, who would do the deed at sunset."

"O Honorable Chamharouche, supreme chief of the genies, we waited impatiently for the sun to set. But the shadows lingered late and the day refused to end. Young people coming in from surrounding villages were astonished to find that in their villages the sun had set, but in Djenné the brilliant sun was still above the horizon. This is because one of us, a traitor, had gone in to inform the young man what had happened. Affronted, he had said to his informant: 'If the sun doesn't set they can do nothing against me.'

"Of course, we immediately judged the informant, who soon after was seized by a incurable flux of the bowels. He no longer divulges our secrets."

It was, of course, Timbuktu's fault.

"O honorable Chamharouche, the ill educated young man in question was the son of a grand marabout of the Djingareiber quarter in Timbuktu. He knew, by miracles he performed, all the dangers that would beset his son in Djenné, and had given him many scientific techniques to defend himself against danger. The very day we were to act against him, he entered his house, put on his robe and pantaloons backwards, arranged his prayer mat backwards, sat down on the mat with his prayer beads in his left hand and not his right, towards the west and not the east. In this way his father in Timbuktu was able to judge the danger that faced him. He would use whatever means he could to protect his son. One of these means was, of course, Alfarouk—wasn't his task the preservation of the people of Timbuktu, after all?

"Honorable Chamharouche, this is why the population of Djenné have long been opposed to Alfarouk and to Timbuktu whence he comes. Through my voice, the uléma of the town ask you to deliver him to us that we might inflict a suitable punishment."

And so he did, attaching manacles to Alfarouk's feet and casting him into the waters of the Bani. However, some say that Alfarouk was buried with other genies in a large plain behind the town, a plain that it was impossible in later years to cross without hearing lamentations.

This particular legend doesn't record the reaction of the people of Timbuktu. "Though at least," Salem Ould Elhadj said, "he does live on here in the popular imagination. Even if he is still in prison in Djenné, his son protects Timbuktu, and he himself has been 'officially' rehabilitated. Still named after him in the city are an FM radio station and the football club; even an association for the protection of ancient manuscripts uses the name. And as you see, the statue of Alfarouk on his white horse stands at the Timbuktu terminus of the Kabara road."

Interestingly, he added, there were "reliable sightings" of the demon until sometime in the 1950s, after which electricity came to the city, presumably abolishing shades and shadows simultaneously.

Still, the seven hundred years must be just about up.

❧

BATTUTA WAS IN Mali only a few years after Mansa Musa died, but already there were signs of dynastic troubles to come. Some of this was precipitated by a rash action of the great man himself. He had been wont to appoint his son Magha as his deputy while he was away on political or military affairs, which he was frequently, and also appointed him his heir. This was a controversial thing to do, since he was depriving his brother Sulaiman of his right to the throne as the eldest male. He seems to have mistrusted his brother, a miserly person, but he was unable to control events after his death, and Magha's rule only lasted four years, raising the suspicion that he was killed by his uncle.

It is hard to know how much of this is legend—the story is an interesting echo of Sundiata's own struggles of fratricidal strife at the dynasty's founding—but at least Ibn Battuta saw some of it firsthand and recounted a version in his journals. He tells the story of Sulaiman's principal wife plotting with an exiled prince, Djata, against her husband, though he is mostly oblivious of its meaning.

It happened that the sultan became angry with his senior wife, the daughter of his paternal uncle, who was entitled Qasa, a word which means queen among them. In accordance with the custom of the blacks she shares in the kingdom and her name is mentioned along with his in the pulpit. She was confined in the house of one of the military leaders and the sultan replaced her with his other wife, Banju, who was not a king's daughter. People talked much about this and disapproved of what he had done. His uncle's daughters came to congratulate Banju on becoming queen; they put ashes on their arms but they did not put dust on their heads [as a gesture of respect]. Later the sultan released Qasa from confinement and his uncle's daughters came to congratulate her on her release, pouring dust on themselves in the customary way. Banju complained to the sultan about this and he was angry with his cousins. They were afraid of him and sought refuge in the congregational mosque. However he pardoned them and invited them to see him. It is their custom to take off their clothes and come naked into his presence which they did. He was pleased with them and for seven days they kept on coming to the sultan's gate, morning and evening, for this is what people do who he has pardoned.[15]

જી

SULAIMAN'S QUEEN WAS forgiven and a coup d'état was avoided, but soon after Sulaiman's death civil war erupted.

The succession of Qasa, Sulaiman's son, was challenged by Mari-Djata, son of Magha, who was probably the "exiled prince" mentioned by Battuta.

Mari-Djata killed Qasa and seized power, thereby avenging the deposition of his own father by Qasa's father and restoring the house of Mansa Musa.

But all this did the kingdom no good at all. Mari-Djata reigned for fourteen years, from 1360 to 1374, and was, by all accounts, an inept and oppressive ruler, depleting the treasury and nearly ruining the kingdom.

CHAPTER NINE

~

The First Tuareg Interregnum

THE GARDEN OF Peace in Timbuktu is a forlorn thing, surrounded by crumbling concrete brick walls, more sand dune than vegetation. Nelson Mandela planted a Peace Tree in the garden on one of his visits; every dignitary who comes here does the same, but no one can tell you whose tree is whose, or indeed whether they're still alive, which is improbable, for the garden is mostly dead from drought and neglect, even the desert acacias drooping in the heat. As political symbols go, the garden lacks a certain potency, especially since just down the block, at one of Timbuktu's few cafés (and even fewer places to get a glass of beer), trees seem to be thriving. Across a dusty plaza, however, past where scrawny camels are hobbled, is a much stronger symbol, a crumbling monument in concrete and iron in which more than sixteen thousand automatic weapons are encased, weapons confiscated during the civil war of the 1990s or turned in during the armistice that followed.

The peace is holding, but memories are long and the bandits who sometimes infest the routes from the city are driven as much by the bitter taste for revenge as they are by the sour imperatives of poverty.

The previous evening at dusk we had been in the dunes outside the city once again, watching the cerulean blue of the sky shade to violet and purple and the sober beiges of the city turn dusky with shadow, and had fallen into conversation with two Tuareg. One of them was from a family based in Arawan, to the north; the other had spent three years in exile in Mauritania, returning to Mali in the armistice, in 1994. After a little guarded to-ing and fro-ing, this second person told us in the most matter-of-fact of voices how his parents had been killed by government troops. "My wife was pregnant," he said, "but she was shot in the leg as we fled. We got away."

He was silent for a moment, got up, wandered away to the crest of the dune, came back.

"They poisoned the wells," he said then, looking away. "Every one they could find, they poisoned. They tried to kill us all."

I tried to remember what I could of Mali's politics of the period. The country had become independent of the generally benevolent but neglectful colonial power, France, in 1960. At first, the French had insisted on a federation with Senegal—logically enough, since the old empires of Ghana-Wagadu and then Mali had incorporated both places, and it seemed sensible to give this new country an outlet to the sea—but the ethnic politics of the time wouldn't permit it to take hold, and the federation lasted only a few months. Mali then went through the apparently inevitable flirtation with socialism and its corollary, Soviet "advisers," which ended in an army takeover in 1968, under Moussa Traoré.

Traoré was a Bambara—a Malinke like the mansas of old—and he governed from Bamako, neglecting the north, the Tuareg and Fulani strongholds. He built a highway downriver to Djenné and Mopti, and from there on the south bank to Gao, but deliberately excluded Timbuktu. Under his rule you couldn't reach Timbuktu by any real road, and you still can't. Under his rule, too, the economy continued to deteriorate, and frequent reports emerged of Traoré's antics in Switzerland, where he had stashed a great part of the country's wealth in personal bank accounts.

Then came the terrible droughts of the mid-1980s. Mali received aid from the UN—not as much as Ethiopia and Sudan, but some aid did arrive. Traoré made sure it went to his tribespeople first, and not to the unruly nomads in the desert. Or at least, that was the nomad view.

French colonial policy had discouraged nomadism, by the simple expedient of taxing the Tuareg into submission, but all through the long Fulani wars and through the colonial period Tuareg tribal leaders had never given up their search for control over their own affairs. After the aid fiasco, riots took place in Taghaza and Taoudenni and Timbuktu and Gao, the Tuareg taking up arms as they had so often before and assaulting army posts. That's when armed convoys began interdicting the desert trails and poisoning the wells.

"It was genocide," our informant said. "They wanted us to die."

"We had heard of the troubles," I said. "But genocide?"

"They wouldn't let anyone in to see," he said. "And who would care?"

To this, there was no real answer.

He had fled with what remained of his family to a squalid camp in Mauritania, and while he was there, in 1992, Traoré was himself overthrown in another army coup, under Amadou Toumani Touré, aka ATT.

Nothing, so far, very surprising. Except that in June 1992 Touré fulfilled his promise of holding multiparty elections, and when Alpha Omar Konaré was elected president, he resigned as promised.[1]

Just before he did so, he signed a "declaration of national reconciliation" with the Tuareg. Konaré called on the Tuareg to come home.

❧

A DAY OR so later we had dinner at the home of another Tuareg who had been in Mauritania. We were sitting, desert fashion, on a carpet on the roof; a charcoal brazier was flickering, and we were eating *toucassou*, a savory stew, from a communal bowl, though in deference to visitors we'd been given separate plates. Our host was in a ruminative mood. We had been talking about his time in the camps. "It was a bad time," he said. "We had to make a difficult choice." Did Touré, and then Konaré, mean what they said? In the aftermath of an attempted genocide, the answers were far from clear. Could they trust the new government?

"In the end," he said, "I argued that we had to take the risk. We didn't know how long Mauritania would let us stay, and things might get worse for us rather than better. We needed faith. I argued that we should go home."

It wasn't an easy or popular position and didn't endear him to all the Tuareg, especially those who had lost family in the civil war, but in the end he and those who thought as he did prevailed. Konaré upheld his part of the bargain, and when firearms began to be turned in, he laid plans for the monument to peace.

The monument is a clumsy, lumpish thing, like an old-style Soviet memorial and equally neglected, but you can touch some of those weapons, or pieces of weapons, if you choose. Here a gun barrel protrudes from the crumbling concrete, there a trigger guard, here another deadly piece—bits of weapons bulging everywhere, spikes from a deadly bush, a powerful symbol, death imprisoned in stone; you can lay your hands on them, but they are useless, powerless . . . I wondered whether the peace would hold. The Tuareg themselves are not optimistic. Even in a democracy, an ethnic majority can be neglectful or spiteful, and the Tuareg are no more than 10 percent or so of Mali's population.

"A generation, maybe two, then our way of life will be gone," the Tuareg in the dunes had said, killed by neglect and by modernity in equal measure. It was a gloomy forecast, but no one would contradict it.

ↂ

HOW SIMILAR THIS sorry tale of ethnic rivalry and warfare is to the events of the distant past.

The oppressive Mari-Djata of Mali died of sleeping sickness and was succeeded by his son, Musa II. The chronicles record him as a well-intentioned but ineffective king; real authority during his fourteen-year rule was held by his chief adviser, also confusingly called Mari-Djata. Musa II died in 1387 and was succeeded by his brother Mansa Magha II, who lasted less than a year before he was assassinated. The throne was then seized by one Sandaki, probably a slave. "This usurpation was avenged a few months later by a man from the house of Mari-Djata II. In this ferment the throne once again changed hands, taken by Mahmud, a descendant of Mansa Qu, [who took] the name of Mansa Magha III in 1390."[2]

Unsurprisingly, the empire became enfeebled in all this turmoil, its authority in the hinterlands diminished. As early as 1336 a force from the Mossi state of Yatenga, south of the river in what is now Burkina Faso, took advantage of the chaos and invaded Timbuktu. They, too, had heard of the city's already legendary wealth. They drove the scholars from the city (most fled to Walata or Djenné), looted what they could, and withdrew. Al-Sa'adi put it this way in his *Tarikh:* "The sultan of the Mossi penetrated into the city, destroyed it, put it to the flame, ruined it and having killed all he could find and stolen all he could lay his hands on, returned to his own city."[3]

The mansas restored what order they could, and most of the scholars returned. Their nominal authority lasted until the first decades of the next century; they "ruled" for almost a hundred years after the Mossi incursion, although Timbuktu traditions say that the *farba,* the provincial governor, "so far from the capital at Niani, conducted himself [more and more] like an independent king."

Nevertheless, during this time Timbuktu was constantly raided and ravaged, both by the nomadic Tuareg and the newly resurgent monarchy of the Songhai people, at Gao, with the Mossi still a threat to the south.

The Tuareg by now completely dominated an immense quadrangle of land, between Tadmekka and Walata, Timbuktu and Taoudenni. Their mobile *meharis,* camel-borne warriors, would slip into town overnight, kill the garrison, steal what they could and slip away. The *Tarikh al-Sudan* again: "Unstoppable because of their high mobility, unpreventable because they surged in everywhere at once, insatiable because they demanded everything, the Tuareg warriors occupied the region and ravaged on all sides and in all ways."[4] The inhabitants of the city, especially the scholars and holy men, were notoriously poor warriors and depended on Mali's garrisons for their protection; when these garrisons were overcome, or, later, when they were drawn home by the imperatives of tumultuous palace politics, the city was helpless.

∓

IN 1433 TIMBUKTU bowed to the inevitable and was taken over by desert Tuareg under their *amenekal* (leader), Akil Ag-Amalwal, who knew a political vacuum when he saw one and declared, "the sultan who does not defend his territory has no right to rule it."[5] The legends say that he was aided by an army of miraculous child warriors, who attacked the Malian governor's palace and killed everyone they found in it. Akil ruled for forty years.

In fact, Timbuktu didn't do too badly under the Tuareg—far better for the city to have them inside keeping others out than to have them outside wanting to come in. Aside from the Malian garrison, now gone, the population of the city was made up of merchants, men of letters, and artisans, all of whom needed peace to ply their trades. The merchants needed more than that; they needed secure routes to and from the north, and the Tuareg could guarantee them those, for a price. The *amenekal* taxed them heavily, but it seemed to them a fair trade, for he also guaranteed that their caravans would arrive and depart in peace and security. "They needed time to play with their riches," as Salem Ould Elhadj put it, rather cynically. And he added, "What made it easier, of course, was that the majority of the population of the time were Massufa, just as the nomadic warriors were—they were relatives."

Life returned more or less to normal. Arrogant he might be, but the *amenekal* was also a wily ruler and went out of his way to pacify the wary uléma of the city—with positive results. The *Tarikh al-Sudan* describes him approvingly, saying that he ruled "not as a Berber but as a pious Moslem, who venerated and respected the great *uléma* of Timbuktu."[6] His governing style, it seems, was to be seen and felt as little as possible. In fact he came to town as infrequently as he could; he was a deep-desert Tuareg and much preferred the open skies of the great *ergs* to the musty confines of the twisting alleys of

Timbuktu, no matter how much wealth they were thought to conceal. The imams and uléma he left with considerable freedom, perhaps more than they were used to under the Malian kings.

As a masterstroke, he named Mohammed Naddi, one of the military commanders of the previous regime of the mansas, as his deputy and governor of the city. Naddi was widely admired in the city as "a man of parts"; he was well liked by the common people and respected by the wealthy; Ibn Battuta had noticed him as chief of the Massufa. It helped that he was a Tuareg like Akil and hailed from Chinguitti, to the west, an influential center of Berber affairs under the Sanhaja.

Naddi became the true power in Timbuktu and even carried the Malian title *Tombouctoukoï* (ruler of Timbuktu), wielding administrative, financial and judicial power. His politics were to retain good relations with the Tuareg and establish ties with the renascent Songhai dynasty to the east.

Two-thirds of the revenue he collected from the merchants Naddi sent to the *amenekal*, who in turn distributed the money to the chiefs of the principal Tuareg tribes, thus keeping those fissiparous entities more or less on his side, and kept a third for his own expenses. He also levied taxes for his own account: a sales tax on the markets, a consumption tax on other commercial transactions and an import levy on caravans entering the city. All of this made him rich. "He lived like a king, surrounded by courtesans and disposing of a considerable army," as Salem Ould Elhadj put it. None of this troubled the city. He was a favorite of the Sanhaja Berbers, who considered him one of their own, and as a pious Muslim was given the stamp of approval of the uléma, who thought his rule healthy for their own place in the world and for their religious practices.

For the pious, his masterstroke was to invite his old friend Sidi Yahiya el-Tadelsi ben Abd al-Rahim al-Tha'alibi, a Sufi sheikh who claimed sharifian descent, to come from Morocco and live in the city. As a lure, he apparently built him a mosque of his own not far from the governor's palace and proclaimed him imam in 1440. ("Apparently," because there is another version of this story, slightly less positive about Naddi's role in the affair; the oral tradition in Timbuktu asserts that the mosque was in fact built forty years earlier, in 1400, by a wandering marabout, Sheikh el-Mokhtar Hamalla, at the instructions of a now-unremembered saint. It was only forty years later that Sidi Yahiya crossed the desert from the north, presented himself at the mosque and claimed the keys. Only after that did Naddi name him imam.)

Whatever version is "true," the Sidi Yahiya mosque, the youngest and smallest of the three medieval mosques, is still Timbuktu's most popular. Sidi Yahiya himself, who continued to hold classes in "his" mosque until the end of his life, is regarded as the patron saint of the city; his mausoleum still attracts the faithful for veneration. He had a significant effect on the city during his lifetime. He had a reputation across Islam for wisdom and piety and attracted hundreds of adherents from all parts of the Islamic world, "causing for them a number of miracles," including healing the sick and conjuring up rain in drought years.

Sidi Yahiya died in 1463, just a week before his patron, Mohammed Naddi. They were buried side by side under the minaret of the mosque.

The new influx of wealthy scholars attracted to the city by Sidi Yahiya, which swelled the already significant intellectual quarter around Sankoré, had several spinoff effects: their presence caused considerable commercial growth in what we would now call the service sector; and the growth in services attracted yet more merchants and more long-distance traffic. In the early part of the fifteenth century caravans arrived from Taoudenni, Tichitt, Chinguitti and Sidjilmasa almost every week, some of them enormous ten, fifteen thousand camels at a time, swelling the temporary population of the city. This traffic in turn attracted artisans and tradespeople, who mostly settled in the Sankoré sector to the north of the city, where the original masons had settled.

The Sankoré mosque, for its part, continued to expand its influence. Its Qur'anic school system expanded, and attracted the saintly figure of Moaddid Mohammed el-Kabari as imam. He, too, was said to be a miracle worker.

It was at this time that the founders of Timbuktu's two greatest families arrived in town. The first was Mohamed Aqit, a Berber from Masina who had lived variously in Walata and then in the Raselma region. In Raselma he allied himself with Akil Ag-Amalwal, who invited him to Timbuktu. Of the founding ancestor of the second great family, Abou Abdallah Anda Ag-Mohamed, little is known, except that his daughter married into the Aqit family and became the mother of the *qadi* Sidi Mahamoud the Great and of Ahmed, the grandfather of Timbuktu's greatest scholar, Ahmed Baba al-Sudani, as he styled himself—"Ahmed Baba of the land of the blacks."

∾

AFTER A WHILE, though, all this urban piousness—especially this affluent urban piousness—began to grate on Akil and his people. The Tuareg leader was growing older but no more affluent himself, and it began to seem to him that he and his weren't sharing the wealth sufficiently. In the end, he began to countenance raids, by his own people, on the city itself.

At the death of Mohammed Naddi in 1463, his son Amar was installed as governor by the Tuareg. But the new chief failed to play his part as proper puppet and incurred the aging *amenekal*'s enmity. After a while, Amar stopped responding to instructions and, worse, stopped sending tribute. Predictably, pillaging and looting picked up. As the *Tarikh al-Sudan* puts it, "the end of the domination of the Tuareg was marked by odious actions without number, and by acts of violent tyranny."[7]

Caravans were once again interdicted and stripped; the bodies of merchants dumped at the city gates. The corpses piled up. Travelers reported violent storms and birds of ill omen. Healers failed at their tasks, and miracles stopped working. Commerce threatened to come to a standstill once more. Rumors were abroad—again—that the Mossi were massing for an invasion.

The city was therefore at the mercy of Sonni Ali Ber, the Songhai chieftain. Sonni the Merciless, he was called, and it proved to be so.

CHAPTER TEN

∾

The Coming of the Songhai

SONNI WAS A Songhai, from the city of Gao.

Gao was old, older than Timbuktu by far, older than many other of the cities along the Niger. Al-Bakri asserted that it had been founded in the late seventh century by Sorko fishermen and was originally named KawKaw or GaoGao, a name that was supposed to mimic the fishermen's drums. It, or at least its settled region, is probably far older than that; some stories suggest it goes back to biblical times. Be that as it may, by 872, three hundred years before Timbuktu was a twinkle in a Tuareg eye and generations before Buktu was born, al-Yaqubi wrote that Gao was "the greatest kingdom of the Blacks."[1] As already stated, it had been transshipping gold from the Black Volta through to the North African coast for many centuries; traders from Egypt and the Garamantes turned up in the city; there was regular traffic to the east, to Kanem-Bornu on Lake Chad, and via the Adrar des Iforhas to the north. Sometime later the historian al-Masudi, who died in 956, said the city's mosque was second in size only to the Great Mosque at Koumbi Saleh, and that the king had his own city, and "nobody inhabits [his palace] with him, or has resort to it, except a eunuch slave . . . They are all Muslims . . . The king's treasure-houses are spacious, his treasure consisting principally of salt."[2] By the twelfth century, the geographer al-Zuhri remarked that "silk and other objects of gauze and linen are imported into their country, and from al-Andalus are imported saffron and cloth from Murcia and turbans and Susa cloth from Ifriqiya. [They are] the richest and the best dressed of people."[3]

Tribally, its rulers were Songhai, but whether they were indigenous or whence they came remains unclear. Some theories suggest they had arrived many centuries before from Libya or even Yemen.

Gao's first Songhai dynasty—called the Zá, or Zuwa—claimed a legendary tie to Yemen; the founder of the line was Zuwa Alayman, and the *Tarikh al-Sudan* translates his name as *ja'a min al-yaman*, or "he [who] came from Yemen." Alayman settled first at Kukiya, near the modern Gao, which the *Tarikh* says intriguingly was already there in the time of the pharaohs, "and it was there that he [Pharaoh] found the sorcerers for the trial of strength with him to whom God spoke [Moses]."⁴ Alayman was supposed to have settled the hash of the tribesmen already living there by killing and eating their fish-god, after which they made him king. The first of the Zá rulers to come to the attention of the outside world was Zá-Kusoy, already the fourteenth of the line's thirty-two rulers; he converted to Islam in 1009. Tombstones of Moroccan marble, inscribed in what looks like Andalusian script, have been uncovered in Gao. One inscription from the year 1100 reads, HERE IS THE TOMB OF ABU ABDULLAH MUHAMMAD, THE KING WHO DEFENDED GOD'S RELIGION AND WHO RESTS IN GOD. Which of the Zá this was remains unknown.

The last of the Zá, Zuwa Bada, was succeeded after some confusion by the first of the Sonni (or Sonyi) dynasty, the national hero Ali Kulun (sometimes spelled Golom). John Hunwick, an eminent historian of the region, believes he might have been a Zuwa prince who had been left in charge of Gao by Mali's rulers, probably under the scrutiny of a Malian governor, but then revolted and asserted his line's independence. Hunwick points out that in the traditional tales of Songhai magicians, Sonni Ali Ber was sometimes known as the *za beri wandu*, "the great and dangerous Zá." Sonni Ali Ber was the eighteenth of his line.

℘

SONNI ALI BER, Sonni the Great, came to power in Gao in 1464. A man of huge appetites and ferocious cruelty, he reigned, the *Tarikh* says, "for 28 years, waged 32 wars of which he won every one, always the conqueror, never the conquered."⁵ His emotional appeal was to the traditional paganism of his people, which he set against the "false cosmopolitanism" of Mali's Islam. Early in his rule his cavalry began raiding the Malian heartland, several times entering Niani, the capital. This accelerated that city's long decline; it began shrinking in the fifteenth century until it was finally abandoned a hundred or so years later. Sonni Ali destroyed the Mali empire by his ceaseless warfare and reigned in its stead, from his capital at Gao.

This "great tyrant and famous miscreant" as Ahmed Baba called him, was cruel, but far from stupid. He ran his armies in the Roman way, using a staff of generals with specific delegated responsibilities. He developed the only navy in North Africa, building a fleet of armored pirogues, or war canoes, and in doing so decimated the forests around his capital and Timbuktu. In civil administration he oversaw large-scale irrigated agriculture; at one point he contemplated a canal between Timbuktu and distant Walata, a project that defeated even his enormous energy. He developed a sophisticated tax bureaucracy with a sliding scale of levies (the wealthier you were, the more you paid). Later in his life, despite his own heartfelt paganism, he tried to pacify the uléma of Timbuktu and even took on an Islamic name as a gesture of good faith.

His relations with Timbuktu were fraught and complicated. When he came to the throne, Mohammed Naddi, who was still running Timbuktu, sent him a letter of felicitation. He tactfully suggested that he might even be a distant relative, a member of Sonni Ali Ber's family. He was the sovereign of Timbuktu, he wrote, and wished to remain so, but nevertheless prudently pledged his allegiance to the Songhai ruler. As a result, Sonni Ali left the city alone (or perhaps this was because he was merely busy elsewhere, raiding Mali and dealing with the Mossi). Naddi's son Amar, however, was neither as tactful nor as shrewd. He wasn't content to alienate the Tuareg, who were still sowing destruction and pillaging everywhere they could; he needled the Songhai too. He sent Sonni Ali an insolent letter: "My father has quitted this earth without owning anything more than two pieces of linen. For myself, I have a large force at my disposal, and all those who would obstruct me will have to deal with this force."[6]

The aging Tuareg leader, the *amenekal* Akil, was appalled. It was all very well for the stupid boy Amar to be provocative, but Akil knew that to Sonni, Timbuktu was still nominally Tuareg, and it was the Tuareg he would come after. Come with a large army, too, and demand tribute that the *amenekal* was loath to pay.

Amar then proceeded to make things worse. Thinking better of his earlier arrogant tone (or perhaps just discovering a better way of getting rid of the Tuareg), he sent a discreet envoy to Sonni Ali. If only the great one would come to Timbuktu himself, he wrote, he would deliver up the city to him without a fight. The old *amenekal* was the problem, he wrote. He just wouldn't listen . . . In this way, as Salem Ould Elhadj puts it, "he [Amar]

showed his weakness and the feebleness of his authority, and his lack of phys-
ical vigor."

It wasn't as though Sonni Ali was an unknown quantity. The *Tarikh*
points out that Mohammed Naddi sometimes fought alongside him, as a ju-
nior partner, and knew that the Songhai ruler had at his disposal a massive
and well-trained army, with considerable experience in war. His own skills
were legendary; his soldiers named him Dali, master of sorcery, and he was
said to have inherited from his mother six spells of power; in battle his horse
was said to take to the air, swift as lightning. His tactics were the blitzkrieg—
massive raids conducted at great speed, overwhelming the enemy by velocity
and ferocity, the shock and awe of its time.[7]

He had spared Timbuktu and its fabulous wealth only because of his regard for Mohammed Naddi, or so the *Tarikh* asserts. Now he seized the opportunity offered by Amar's craven suggestion, rewarded the envoy well for
the message and said to tell Amar he would be along shortly.[8]

Typically, he wasted no time, and just a day or so after the ambassador returned, his army began to mass on the Niger's far shore.

From a dune on the left bank, Akil the Tuareg watched the cavalry "filling
the horizon" and decided he wanted no part of it. He detached a thousand
camels and fled into Sankoré to organize an exodus of the uléma and men of
letters to Walata, a prudent distance away. Al-Sa'adi, in his *Tarikh*, was scornful: "Their exit preoccupied them more [than their honor]," he wrote. These
old men, he suggested, had no sense of civic patriotism. Their reason for being in Timbuktu had been to acquire either wealth or knowledge or prefer-
ably both; they knew nothing whatever of war. To abandon the city, then,
seemed only natural. "On the day of departure for Birou (Walata) one could
see aged men, all bearded, trembling with fright as they attempted to mount
a camel, and falling to the ground as soon as the animal rose to its feet. This
is because our virtuous ancestors had kept their children close to their bos-
oms, in a way that these children grew up not knowing the least thing of life,
because when they were young, they had never learned anything."[9]

Sonni Ali was well aware of the exodus and determined to put a stop to it.
The *Tarikh al-Fettach* recorded that he dispatched a courier to the city with
this ominous message: "The Chi [Sonni Ali] announces that everyone who
remains faithful [to him] must pass this night at Boukiy [on the right bank of
the river] and that anyone who contravenes this prescription will be killed."[10]

That was all the signal the people of Timbuktu needed. They headed for

Walata or farther, the farther the better. Most of them took nothing but a little food with them, not even coverings to sleep on. They left on foot and on horseback, "and the only people left in the city were those too ill to move, who could find no one to help them."[11]

Amar, for his part, helped Sonni Ali's troops cross the Niger by sending them boats. But at the last moment, perhaps recalling his earlier insolent letter, he took fright and fled to Walata himself.

In January 1468 Sonni Ali's army entered Timbuktu without resistance, the city having been abandoned by its chiefs, and there followed, according to al-Sa'adi, "the greatest, the most immense and the most terrible ravages. His troops set fire to everything, broke everything down, and massacred a huge number of people."

Nor did the fugitives all escape. Troops under the direction of the new Sonni Ali-appointed governor of Timbuktu, the *Tombouctoukoï* el-Mokhtar, followed them into the desert and caught up with a caravan at Tadjil. There "the most eminent among the jurists and councilors were all killed."[12]

❦

THOSE WHO REACHED Walata didn't do too well either. The Mossi forces were still alert on the southern borders and looking for action. With Sonni Ali Ber in the way, they could do nothing about Gao or Timbuktu, and even Djenné seemed too close for comfort, so they sent an army against Walata itself.

For four months they ravaged the town, whose riches revived their cupidity. The prudent fled once more, some of them back to Timbuktu, where the Songhai suddenly seemed the lesser of two evils. This was a good call; the Mossi stripped Walata of its riches and took as captives most of the inhabitants who were left; many of the older savants of Timbuktu were thus sold into slavery. It was the final ruin of Walata; the town has never recovered.

Nor did the Mossi profit greatly from all this. A massive army from Sonni Ali intercepted them on the way home and inflicted a catastrophic defeat.

Sonni Ali, in the end, did arrive at an entente, of sorts, with the Muslim community of Timbuktu. He was still hostile to the idea of Islam, which he apparently likened to a plague on the black world; and he was generally contemptuous of what he called the white men, the Arabs. The West African historian Sekéné Mody Cissoko says "[he] accorded little importance to the white man, who he knew only as a marabout or shepherd. It was as much an opposition between animism and orthodox Islam, as between the culture of Negro Africa and Islamic values."[13]

His contempt was exaggerated by the spineless behavior of the Timbuktu intelligentsia in fleeing to Walata. Sonni Ali was a military man, a man of action, and their flight seemed to him childish and petulant; better to face death with honor than to preserve a miserable life at any cost. Djenné he admired. Djenné didn't invite him in but resisted to the bitter end. The *Tarikh*, no doubt embellishing a good deal, said the siege of Djenné lasted "seven years and seven months and seven days" before Sonni Ali finally prevailed.

His army was encamped at Joboro and they would attack the people of Djenné daily until the flood encircled the city. Then he would retire with his army to a place called Nibkat Sunni, the hillock of Sonni. His army would remain there and keep watch until the waters receded and then would return to Joboro to fight . . . This went on for seven years. Then famine struck and the people of Djenné grew weak. Despite that, they contrived to appear strong so that Sonni Ali had no idea what condition they were in. Weary of the siege at last, he decided to return to Songhai. Then one of the sultan of Djenné's senior army commanders . . . sent word to Sonni Ali and revealed the secret. Then the sultan [of Djenné] took counsel with his commanders. He proposed they should surrender to Sonni Ali and they agreed. The sultan then sent a spokesman to Sonni Ali to inform him of their decision, and this man was well received and handsomely treated. So the sultan of Djenné and his senior army commanders rode out to meet Sonni Ali and when he got close to him he dismounted and walked to him on foot. Sonni Ali welcomed him and received him with honor. When he saw that the sultan was only a young man, he took hold of him and seated him beside him on a rug and said, Have we been fighting with a boy all this time? Then his courtiers told him that the boy's father had died during the siege and that he had succeeded him as sultan. This is what lies behind the custom of the sultan of Songhai sitting together with the sultan of Djenné to this day. Sonni Ali married the young sultan's mother after asking him for her hand. Sultan Abd Allah told me [that is, the author of the *Tarikh*] that it was this marriage that added seven days to the aforementioned seven years and seven months.[14]

In Timbuktu, by contrast, the stories that surround his rule are much more dire. Sonni Ali never actually lived in Timbuktu—his main palace was still at Gao—but he had a residence at the port of Kabara on the Niger, from where he could easily dispatch forces to Djenné or Gao itself. The city watched his rule with sometimes horrified fascination. "In 1477," Salem Ould Elhadj told us, "while he was at his palace in Kabara, Sonni Ali issued an order to bring to him thirty virgins, all the daughters of Timbuktu's savants, to distract his soldiers. These young women, leaving their protected homes for the first time, couldn't manage the nine kilometers between Timbuktu and Kabara. Since they were incapable of continuing, and therefore fulfilling the purpose he had designed for them, Sonni Ali ordered them all to be killed. The place of execution is now called the Passage of the Fate of the Virgins."

In 1486 Sonni Ali had the *Tombouctoukoï* el-Mokhtar thrown into jail for reasons unknown, but probably merely for not running the city in the draconian way he had been instructed.

Still, there were good reasons of state why Sonni Ali decided to make up to the uléma of Timbuktu. To the heart of his kingdom—the Songhai-speaking lands from Gao southward to Dendi—he had added the inland delta region between Timbuktu and Djenné, as well as the Bandiagara highlands. His purpose was clear enough: to control the Middle Niger and more specifically the gold trade passing through Djenné and then Timbuktu. But the constant warfare he waged for the first decade of his rule—against Djenné and the Mossi as well as Timbuktu—had the opposite effect. The gold traders of Dyula began to bypass the Niger altogether and took a more direct route eastward from the Volta goldfields to the newly prosperous trading cities of the Hausa, especially Kano, whence they would be transshipped to the Mediterranean via the venerable caravan routes past Lake Chad and through Bilma, east of Agadez. To change this situation, he attempted to repair his relations with Timbuktu.

One of his first acts was to invite back to the city the most prominent of those who had fled, or at least those of them he could still find. Among the returnees who survived the Mossi at Walata were the Aqit family and Anda Ag-Mohamed. He would leave them in peace, he said, as long as they didn't agitate against him. He even paid compensation to the poorer of the uléma to lure them back, and reinstalled the family of Mohammed Naddi as the city's governing elite, appointing one of them, Habib, as *qadi*.

He struggled, too, to overcome his distaste for men of letters. Even the *Tarikh,* rather grudgingly, admitted that he was trying, that he "knew the merits of savants. Without savants, he said, there would be in this world neither agreement nor pleasures. Because of this, we must be sure to keep enough of them among us and to give them some regard."[15] He made some good appointments, for example, naming the well-respected Sidi Abdallah et Bilali, an eminent jurist of the city, imam of Djingareiber.

Clumsily, he tried to overcome the early debacle of the virgins and sent a large number of captive women as gifts to the notables of Timbuktu, "some to savants and others to saints," as the *Tarikh* puts it. They would, he said, make excellent concubines. It didn't help, though. As Salem Ould Elhadj put it, "those who remained true to Islam knew that the women were nobles taken by force and not during a holy war. They therefore liberated them or married them as free women. The author of the *Tarikh al-Sudan* affirmed that he himself was descended from one of these women, who was a Peul [Fulani]."[16]

Disapproving they might be, but the intellectual classes of the city decided to put up with Sonni Ali and his often haphazard professions of respect for Islam because he could—obviously—protect them from the Mossi and the predatory Tuareg. If they had to put up with the schools teaching pagan traditions along with Islamic practices, as Sonni Ali's governors insisted, so be it. It seemed a reasonable bargain.

☙

SONNI ALI BER died on November 6, 1492. The conventional story is that he died on campaign, but not from warfare—he drowned instead. This might not seem surprising for a man who was an adept user of the river—at its most potent, Sonni's empire boasted four hundred war barges at Gao alone—except that he died in the Gurma district, an arid expanse well south of the river. Apparently he was encamped in a wadi and was drowned in a flash flood, a surprisingly common occurrence in desert regions. His commanders and his sons were then said to have removed his entrails and packed his body with honey to preserve it, and then took it somewhere—exactly where they took it they never said, and Sonni Ali Ber vanished from history. More recently, scholars have suggested a more lurid interpretation, that Sonni Ali was actually assassinated by the man who succeeded him, and that the apparently authenticating details of the entrails and the honey were added later as part of an intricate political cover-up. No doubt this interpretation fits our modern worldview rather better than an accidental drowning, but the argument is nonetheless interesting.[17]

A month later his eldest son, Sonni Baru, ascended to the throne.

His nomination set off an uproar in Timbuktu. The notables knew Baru only too well and didn't like what they saw. He was even more scornful of Islamic ways than his father—he seemed not to understand why his father had apparently fudged his principles on the matter—and was of the same general character: a military man, blunt to the point of arrogance, who found it difficult to hide his contempt. He was regarded as bloodthirsty and crude.

The traditions say that "the professors, uléma, students and all true adherents of Islam" prayed to God that Baru be overthrown, but they seem to have done a good deal more than that, not only whipping up public opinion against him (there were near riots in Timbuktu and a population in more or less open revolt) but actually looking hard for a substitute, a Muslim warrior who would remove Sonni Ali's and Baru's "taint of semi-pagan rule" in John Hunwick's words.

Such a man wasn't hard to find. He was called Mohamed ben Abu Bakr Sylla, though he was called by many other names too. He had been Sonni Ali's governor in the Bandiagara highlands, home of the Dogon. He was to take the title of *askia*.

Askia Mohamed, later Askia al-hajj Mohamed, was to usher in the second and greatest of Timbuktu's golden ages.

CHAPTER ELEVEN

❦

The Rise of Askia al=hajj Mohamed and the Second Golden Age

ASKIA MOHAMED HAD been part of the governing Songhai elite. He seems to have been a Soninke, from either the Sylla (Silla, Sîlla) clan or the Thure clan. His mother was either the daughter of a chief of Kura, a large island in the Niger, or was called Kasay and was a sister of Sonni Ali Ber, as the oral traditions would prefer. He grew up in Gao, in the Songhai court itself, with all the privileges that would imply. Whatever the truth of his origins, all sources agree that he was a friend of Islam, a man of substantial piety himself, respectful of religion and learning, from the point of view of Timbuktu's uléma an ideal sovereign for a Muslim people. Ahmed Baba, writing more than a hundred years later, gives the approved Timbuktu version: "God made use of his service in order to save the true believers from their sufferings and calamities."[1]

Certainly, Timbuktu claimed him as their own. Still, it's probable that this approving tone was an after-the-fact adoption by the Timbuktu elite; considerable evidence suggests that the first askia paid rather smaller attention to Timbuktu than the chroniclers of that city would have posterity believe, at least at first.[2]

His accession to power was not a given. He easily mastered the western provinces of Djenné, Timbuktu, Tindirma, Masina and Hombori, all of which were much more Islamic than the eastern part of the empire, consisting of Gao itself, Kukiya, Gurma and the Dendi plains south of the river.[3] His brother was governor of Tindirma, so that part was easy. Masina quickly came on board, and of course Timbuktu could hardly wait to get rid of Sonni Baru. But Baru still had formidable forces under his control. Gao itself and the Dendi region had always been strongly animist and nativist, and still regarded Islam as Sonni Ali had, as something imposed on them by foreigners. The Islamic leaders in Gao had come to an accommodation of sorts with the Sonnis, tolerating deviations that dismayed the more orthodox.

The first battle was fought at a place called Danagha, on February 18, 1493. The rebels attacked first, and their assault lasted the whole day and into the next. Both sides suffered massive losses, but in the end Baru prevailed and pushed the rebels back.

It's at this point that the received story, as recounted in the two *Tarikh*s, departs rather sharply from what seem to be the facts.

The "official" Timbuktu story is more or less this: the first battle against Baru was not a rout; the rebel forces at least prevented the emperor from counterattacking either Tindirma or Timbuktu, and both the chronicles emphasize that the "Islamic forces" were not discouraged—the mosques were filled to overflowing, and the prayers to God must have been deafening. In this way the uléma—and the chronicles—position the conflict as an explicitly religious one, a question of Islam and civilization versus animism and barbarity, rather than the more tawdry rising of a general against his legitimate sovereign.

To give his army time to regroup, the story goes, the rebel commander recruited three of the most illustrious of Timbuktu's notables, including the eminent Mohamed Kati, to petition the emperor to embrace Islam and so end the conflict. If true, this would have had the effect of turning his subsequent assault from a mere rebellion into a jihad, a righteous response to wrongdoing. But there is considerable doubt these embassies ever happened.

Still, the story has it that the emissaries met the expected response: the emperor categorically refused to discuss anything at all. And so the second battle took place not far from Gao, on April 2, 1492. This time the rebels triumphed, overrunning the enemy and leaving great slaughter in their wake. As the *Tarikh al-Sudan* puts it, "the combat was terrible, and each side suffered enormous losses."[4] Sonni Baru fled south to the Dendi and, like his father, vanished from history.

Mohamed Abu Bakr took the throne with the titles of *emir of Mumenin* and *khalifa el Moslemin*, and adopted *askia* as his royal title. The origin of the title is obscure, but the *Tarikh* offers this explanation: "When the news [of his victory] reached the daughters of Sonni Ali, they said, *a si kia*, which means in their language, *he shall not be it*; on hearing this he ordered that he be given no other name but that."[5] He would henceforth be known only as Askia Mohamed, or later, after his pilgrimage to the Holy Places, as Askia al-hajj Mohamed.

The notables of Timbuktu were triumphant, the *Tarikh*s say. "They had participated by their prayers and their encouragement at the fall of the Sonni dynasty. Through prayer and their sacrifices God had answered them." To outsiders, these "sacrifices" must have seemed elusive, even fictional, and even their participation in the triumph illusory. Still, their triumphant tone was real. It certainly suited them to claim the new ruler as one of theirs.

At first, when Askia Mohamed neglected Timbuktu, they understood. He did, after all, have a lot on his mind. The newly crowned king began to systematically extend his holdings beyond the Central Niger kingdom of Sonni Ali and his son, soon controlling, as Heinrich Barth put it, only exaggerating slightly, "from the centre of Hausa almost to the borders of the Atlantic, and from the pagan country of Mósi, as far as Tawát to the south of Morocco."[6] To the east, his influence took in the Tuareg sultanate of Agadez and the Aïr Massif, which included the huge copper mines at Takedda. He also tried to assert his control over the Hausa city-states, especially Katsina and Kano, the principal mercantile cities, with mixed results: they seem to have paid him some tribute but never really submitted. To the west, he made colonies of the lands all the way to the Senegal River and thence to the Atlantic, conquering what had been the heartland of Old Ghana-Wagadu and Mali, from Mema to Niani, killing most of its leaders; and to the north he took control of the crucial Taghaza salt mines, leaving a local Tuareg chieftain in charge but co-opting him into the ruling class.

His overall objective was simple, if complicated in its execution: it was to control the north-south trade in gold and salt and slaves, the principal articles of wealth in the Sahel.

The southern boundary of his realm was still the Hombori district along the Bandiagara cliffs, with the fractious and quarrelsome Mossi to its south a problem that had yet to be dealt with. That was the first order of business.

To fulfill the conditions for a legitimate jihad, the askia needed first to formally solicit the Mossi's conversion to Islam, as he was supposed to have done with Sonni Baru, and sent them an emissary too, probably as fictional as the ones supposedly sent to Baru. The *Tarikh*s report that the Mossi chief, Nasiri, was hesitant. He had to consult his ancestors in the other world, he told the askia's messenger. "So he went to the idol-house with his ministers, and the emissary went with them to see how the dead were consulted. When they performed their customary rites there appeared before them an old man. Upon seeing him, they prostrated and told him what had happened. He spoke to them in their own tongue, saying, 'I am against your ever doing that. On the contrary, you should fight them to the last of your men and theirs.' Nasiri then said to the emissary, 'Go back to the Askia and tell him there can be nothing between us but war and strife.' After people had left the house, the emissary said to the one who had appeared in the form of an old man, 'I ask you in the name of God Almighty, who are you?' He said, 'I am Iblis [the devil]. I lead them astray that they may die as unbelievers.'"[7] And so the jihad was waged and their country duly devastated, though without permanent result.

℘

TO RUN HIS affairs, the askia governed through a cabinet of regional officials. The most important of these was the governor of Tindirma Province, called the *Kurmina-fari*, who was viceroy for the western provinces and governed the empire while the king was away. His brother, Omar Kumzaghu, was already installed in this post, and he was left in charge. The other important post was called the *Dendi-fari*, governor of the Dendi region, whose occupant wore special clothing and had the right to speak his mind to the askia; the first appointee was another brother, also called Omar, recalled from Walata, which he had governed for the Sonnis. (Appointing brothers to important posts was widely regarded as an eccentricity; it was the medieval custom, in Gao and all through Byzantium and the Arab world, for a new ruler to have his brothers strangled so they couldn't rise against him.) Other high officials in the cabinet included the governor of Dirma Province, who had the unique privilege of entering the askia's courtyard on horseback and who was, also uniquely, allowed to build a two-story house; the *hugokokoï*, who was a eunuch and ran the palace itself as a kind of general manager of palace affairs; and the *Kabara-farma*, who was the harbormaster and customs collector at the river port of Kabara. Other important though lesser officials were at places like Taghaza, and still others were in charge of boats and river traffic. The sultan of Djenné, with whom the Sonnis had made an accommodation, was still recalcitrant, and the askia hauled him to Gao and imprisoned him there until he died, installing his own man at Djenné as *Djennekoï*.

Timbuktu was conspicuously absent from the cabinet, which didn't go unnoticed. Like Djenné, the city was run by a *Tombouctoukoï,* a regional

governor, but the real power in that assertive city was wielded by the imams
and the uléma who congregated around the university at Sankoré. It was becoming clear to them, at least, that Askia Mohamed did not pay them the attention they felt they deserved.

కా

IN THE AFTERMATH of his military campaigns, Askia Mohamed
made his pilgrimage to Mecca. Piecing together the event from Ahmed Baba's
history and from the *Tarikh's* more fanciful version, Barth described the journey: "[The pilgrimage] brought him into contact with the princes and learned
men of the East, and made him more famous than any other of his enterprises. The most distinguished men of all the tribes under his command accompanied him on his great journey . . . and 1,500 armed men, 800 of them
cavalry. In passing by Egypt, he made the acquaintance of the great scholar
es-Sayuti, who gave him advice on running his empire on Islamic principles.
He took with him 300,000 mithqals but behaved so generously that he was
obliged to contract a loan of 150,000 more."[8]

The *Tarikh al-Fettach* obligingly lists a number of the scholars who accompanied him, but the list, which seems to have been interpolated into the
manuscript as late as the nineteenth century, is not to be trusted—at least one
of the escorts wasn't even born at the time, and at least two others had already died.[9] The really interesting thing about the list goes unmentioned by
the author of the *Tarikh*: that no one from Timbuktu made the journey. Either they boycotted it, or they weren't invited. Either way, it is more evidence
against their centrality to the askia's power.

On the way to Mecca from Cairo, the party was said to have witnessed
a miracle. "A hot wind blew on them and evaporated all their water. When
they were nearly dead with heat and thirst, the Askia sent word to the Friend
of God Most High who was among them, Salih Diawara, to intercede with
God through his Prophet Mohammed, to provide them with something to
drink. The holy one upbraided the messenger vigorously, saying that the
Prophet was too exalted to be used for intercession in such a mundane matter. Then he prayed to God Most High, and He immediately sent them rain
which came and satisfied their needs."[10]

In Mecca, the askia had an official investiture performed by Sharif al-
Abbasi (the Abbasid prince Moulay El Abbas) as "the eleventh *khalif* of
Tekrur"—Tekrur in this instance being Mecca shorthand for the whole em-

pire, thus harking back to the fact that Tekrur had been the first organized state in the western Sudan to convert to Islam. The prince placed on the askia's head a green bonnet and a white turban, and in his hand a sword, saying, "Whoever removes these orders in this country, disobeys Almighty God and his Envoy." While he was there, the askia founded a charitable institution in Mecca "for the people of Tekrur."

"It is of no small interest to a person who endeavors to take a comprehensive view of the various races of mankind," an admiring Heinrich Barth wrote in his journals, "to observe how, during the time when the Portuguese, having . . . taken possession of the whole western coast of Africa . . . and founded their Indian empire, that at this same time a negro king in the interior of the continent not only extended his conquests . . . but also governed the subjected tribes with justice and equity, causing well-being and comfort to spring up every where within the borders of his extensive dominions, and introducing such of the institutions of Mohammedan civilization as he considered might be useful to his subjects."[11]

❧

WHILE HE WAS in Mecca, Askia Mohamed apparently suggested to Prince Moulay El Abbas, who governed the Holy Places, that his empire would run even better with an adviser steeped in the lore and history of Islam, and petitioned him to send to Gao one of his sharifs, perhaps even his brother or a son, "to bring even more grace and benediction to the people of his country." Some evidence suggests that Timbuktu was more than slightly put out by this request, not having been consulted—and not being given the chance to put forward one of its own to fill the post. In any case, surely such a one would prefer Timbuktu to Gao?

Salem Ould Elhadj assembled a narrative on what followed, based mostly on legend and folktale and on references in the *Tarikh*s, sifting out most of the many dreams, tales of malevolent djinn, and minor miracles:

"More than 20 years later, in 1519, he sent the envoy Moulay Ahmed es-Saqli, son of his brother, to establish himself in the court of the prince of Songhai. This sharif was originally from Baghdad. That he would leave for Timbuktu he knew from a prophecy that came to him in a vision." By suggesting that Timbuktu and not Gao appeared in this prophecy, the *Tarikh*s neatly inserted their city into the capital's place, courtesy of a holy vision. "Soon afterwards, he left Baghdad for . . . Cairo, then to Alexandria." For the next few years the story has the holy one wandering all over North Africa, with stops in Benghazi, Tripoli, Ghadamès, Tunis and Sus, among other places. "Then he went to Fez . . . to Tindouf, then to Arawan. In each town he was given a certain sum of money. As the sharif approached Timbuktu, the *qadi* of that city, Mahmoud ben Umar, saw the Prophet in a vision (May God give him benedictions and honor him). The Prophet said to him, today there will arrive among you one of my descendants, wearing green robes. He is mounted on a black camel and has a stigmata on his left eye. He will preside today over the prayers at the fete. You must install him in a place close to the water, close to a cemetery, to a grand mosque and to a market."

It happened as the prophecy had said. The sharif arrived, was taken in and given lodging. "Following this, the inhabitants of the city all walked to the place of prayer, and he presided over all the ceremonies of the day. That was in 1519."

A little later, the sharif ordered a monument to be built at the place where his camel had first left its tracks in town. "This monument came to be called Koulou Seko," Sidi Salem said. "It means, the Monument of the Circle. The people of Timbuktu thereafter used the monument to celebrate the Prophet."

Several versions of what happened next can be found in the histories. The blandest merely reports that Askia Mohamed was told of the sharif's arrival, went to Timbuktu to receive him and gave him gifts of various sorts: 100,000 dinars, 500 slaves and 100 camels. Afterward the sharif married, had three sons and passed his life peacefully in the city. Other versions say that Askia Mohamed couldn't bring himself to be separated from the sharif and lured him to Gao, offering him 1,700 slaves as incentive. A more common Timbuktu variant, another sign of fractiousness between the political power in Gao and religious rulers in Timbuktu, is that the askia kidnapped him and imprisoned him in the capital; what happened to es-Saqli after that is not known. The most plausible version, which fits the character of the askia best, is that es-Saqli was persuaded to go to Gao with the promise of rich rewards. From the people of Timbuktu's point of view, whether he stayed in the city, was lured to Gao or was kidnapped, they considered him one of theirs and remembered him fondly.

That is more than can be said for the prickly cleric who next caught the askia's ear, the zealot Mohamed el-Maghili, sometimes known as el-Baghdadi, or more formally, Mohamed bin Abd al-Karim el-Maghili, a native of Tlemcen. He was a firebrand, an irascible imam and an incendiary preacher. He made a name for himself in Tuat as a zealot; indeed, his preaching led to a pogrom against the Jews of that region. But the austerity of his code, and the disruption to trade caused by his harassment of Jews, eventually turned the people against him, and he was forced to flee. He spent some time in Katsina and Kano, in Nigeria, and then ended up in Gao. Whether this was at his own initiative, having heard of the great askia, or whether the askia invited him in his continuing search for spiritual enlightenment, no one knows.

His primary advice to the askia was to be bold, and ruthless in policy: "Kingdoms are held by the sword, not by delay. Can fear be thrust back, except by causing fear?"

It was at Maghili's urging that the askia, normally so tolerant, briefly turned against the Jews. He also tried, briefly and unsuccessfully, to impose some fundamentalist discipline on the freewheeling Islamists of Timbuktu, trying to compel women to adopt the *hijab*, for instance, and setting up a posse of religious police charged with "exercising a constant vigilance, and to arrest and imprison any man found talking to a strange woman at night."

None of this went down well with the more worldly imams of Timbuktu. Then, when Maghili heard that his son had been killed by Jews in Tuat in revenge for the pogrom he had instituted, he apparently persuaded the askia to arrest all the Tuatis in Gao, Jews or not. When he attempted the same thing in Timbuktu, the *qadi* refused to acquiesce and forced the askia to back down.

It is not known when Maghili left Gao, though some stories suggest it was after his son was murdered. But as soon as he was gone, Askia Mohamed set about courting the religious leaders of Timbuktu; in the end, the departed firebrand had been more trouble than he was worth, and Askia Mohamed needed to repair relationships with his commercial capital. He was never going to actually live in Timbuktu, but it was already far and away the most important commercial center of his empire, and he badly needed to get the ruling classes of Timbuktu, especially the uléma, on his side. He therefore undertook to ostentatiously undo much that Sonni Ali Ber and his son had created, and equally ostentatiously abandoned the garments of zealotry he had donned during Maghili's tenure. He stopped harassing the remaining Jews and gave them back their confiscated property. The *hijab*, so scorned by the Tuareg and the notables of Timbuktu, was no longer to be obligatory for women. He liberated men and women who had been unjustly imprisoned. He put a stop to the deportation of scholars. Wealth that Sonni Ali had seized he returned. He took the advice of the city's savants to arrest those of-ficials of the old regime who had been most oppressive, confiscating their goods, their apparently numberless concubines and even their children. He freed all those slaves unjustly enslaved.

In an inspired gesture, he even humbled himself to the *qadi* of Timbuktu, Sheikh Sidi Mahmoud ben Umar. He made sure to pay a formal visit to the *qadi* when he returned from his travels, and he never passed through the region without visiting the sheikh's residence at Sankoré.

The *Tarikh al-Fettach* recounts a typical visit.

> After resting [at his camp] for a while, the king mounts his horse to take him to the house of the *qadi*, who awaits him attended by his assistants, his auxiliaries and his servants. When the prince arrives, the *qadi* rises to meet him at the gate. He has prepared food and drink for his visitors, who, wishing to participate in divine favor, consume the repast after ad-dressing numerous invocations to God. The king then proceeds to the grand mosque, where he is received by the venerable uléma of the city and the principal imams, who have preceded him there. In procession with the *qadi* and his assistants, he enters the grand mosque, where he receives the homage due to him. After which he returns to his camp outside the city to receive delegations of city notables. Not one night goes by in which he is not offered a splendid meal by the people of the city, who also present him with numerous gifts.[12]

The askia's brother, Omar Kumzaghu, governor of the province of Tindirma, also assisted Timbuktu when he could, for example, dispatching masons from Tindirma to help repair the mosque of Sidi Yahiya, damaged by rainfall.

Timbuktu's intellectuals could barely contain their delight at the transfor-mation and clasped the newly moderate askia to their collective bosom. Never mind that he remained in his capital at Gao; he was (now) a godly man and left them pretty much alone, and that was enough.

You can pick the encomiums out of the *Tarikh al-Fettach* to see their de-light: "It is not possible to enumerate all his virtues, his benevolence to his subjects, and his solicitude to the poor"; "It is not possible to find his like, not among those who preceded him or those who came after"; "He had a living af-fection for the *uléma*, and holy persons"; "This was a man of great intelligence and wisdom"; "He banished all those Sonni Ali Ber introduced to reprehensible iniquities and bloody savagery"; "He established religion on a solid basis, he re-installed the imams and *qadis*." Alpha Kati of Timbuktu even attributed to him several miracles and said his entourage was always made up of people of culture and religion.[13]

For his part, the emperor was a touch more cynical, once complaining that no two of the uléma ever agreed with each other on a single point; they were, he once told Mahmoud Kati, like little tributaries that never quite succeeded in joining to make a river.

෮

ONCE HIS EMPIRE was secure and his relationship with Timbuktu more cordial, the new hajj did something truly unusual: he disbanded a large part of his army and released many of his subjects from their onerous, expensive and time-consuming obligations to provide military levies. Barth, who is quoting a history of Songhai written by Ahmed Baba, puts it this way: "The first thing which this great Songhai king felt it incumbent to do was to give his subjects some repose by reducing his army and allowing some part of the people to engage in pacific pursuits, all the inhabitants having been employed by Sonni Ali in warlike purposes."[14] It had the desired effect: the newly liberated energy was indeed channeled into pacific pursuits that included trade and learning, and Timbuktu, especially, flowered once more.

As Sidi Salem puts it in an informal history of Timbuktu: "Strangers flocked into town from up and down the river and from the desert to do business in the town. In the markets, one could find all the plenty of the Maghreb and the Sahara, as well of goods from the Middle East, the Southern Sudan and the West African coast. Many Sudanese, Wangara and Songhai from Gao came to live in the city. With this influx of foreigners, the city grew enormously to the north and the south. In the period, Timbuktu was certainly the most populous city in West Africa."

Gao was still the political capital, the source of the empire's power and its military muscle. But Timbuktu was where business was done. The city's commercial flowering was fertilized by a trio of commodities: salt, gold and slaves. Other goods were traded too, of course. Copper paid plenty of taxes, luxury goods made their way to the south in return for leather, kola nuts and other southern produce, and esoterica such as civet (a substance extracted from the anal glands of civet cats and used as a basis for perfume) going north and books coming south paid many a wage. But in general those three, "white gold, yellow gold and black gold," represented the basis of all trans-Saharan trade. The demand for salt made the flowering possible; gold financed it; slaves made it work. Slaves were both the workforce and a luxury good in themselves.

CHAPTER TWELVE

c/o

The Underpinnings
of Wealth

WE SPENT A morning with a salt miner from Taoudenni at his home in Timbuktu. When he was in the city he lived in a small two-room dwelling belonging to his wife's family in the Walatakunda, the Walata quarter; it was surrounded by a large sandy walled enclosure, in which there was a covered shelter they used for socializing. He was in town this time, it seems, mostly to see if he could start a family, being newly married and needing children. In the course of the average year, he said, he would spend four months in town and eight months at the mines. He lived, in point of fact, very like the miners did in medieval times, at the time of the askias or farther back, during the long reign of Mali. He hewed the salt by hand and sent it in from the desert on the camels of itinerant caravanners, just as miners did in the long-ago past. Halis, our interpreter, is one of those whose camels take it to market.

The miner received us hospitably, spreading a carpet on the ground under the shelter and offering us tea. He himself was drinking a murky-looking water; it was, he explained (in Tamashek, through Halis) salty water from Taoudenni; he was readjusting to salt-free town water, but it was slow going.

We sniffed at the water; it had a faintly muddy smell, though not unpleasant. "It really is salty?" I asked Halis.

"Taste it," he said.

Everything at Taoudenni, it seems, was salty. Ibn Battuta had been right about the miners' houses being made of salt. He was writing about Taghaza, but the same applies to Taoudenni. The fastidious Battuta hadn't been impressed. "It is a village with no attractions. A strange thing about it is that its houses and mosque are built of blocks of salt and roofed with camel skins. There are no trees, only sand in which there is a salt mine. They dig the ground and thick slabs are found in it, lying on each other as if they had been cut and stacked under the ground. A camel carries two slabs. The only people living there are the slaves of the Massufa, who dig for the salt and live on dates brought to them from Dra'a and Sidjilmasa and camel's meat and *anli* (millet) which is imported from the country of the blacks." His caravan spent nearly ten days in Taghaza, "under strain for the water is brackish and it is the place with most flies. Here water is taken in for the journey into the desert which lies beyond. It is ten days travel with no water, or only rarely . . . Lice are plentiful in that desert, so much so that people wear around their necks string necklaces containing mercury, which kills them." Taoudenni, about ninety miles south of Taghaza, was worse; there was nothing there but grim slaves who lived in salt houses and ate salty food and drank salty water and breathed salty air.

All this is still true, the miner said. The whole town of Taoudenni is salt. All the houses are still made of slabs of salt, except for the roofs, which are reed mats supported by poles, instead of Battuta's camel skins. Even the furniture, what little they have, is made of rock salt. Everything tastes salty. The miners' clothes are saturated with the stuff. And of course the water is salty. How do they adjust?

"It takes some time," Halis said, after listening to the miner's rapid-fire exposition. "For two or three days after he goes back to Taoudenni, he is violently ill every day—his body cannot accept the water. Then, after a while, it adjusts, and he is all right. The same thing happens when he comes back to town: he is violently ill for several days until he can drink this water again."

The Taoudenni mines are only about thirteen feet deep. Below that the salt starts to get damp, and at twenty feet there is groundwater. They are open pits, and the salt is layered in slabs, almost as though they were precut and stacked there for the taking, just as Battuta had described.

Still, the "taking" is not so easy. Each miner can cut three 110-pound slabs a day, working with a hammer and a long iron bar like a crude chisel. The slabs are laid up in piles, loaded onto camels, four to a camel now, for transportation to Timbuktu. The salt is rough and often tears the animal's skin; many a salt slab arrives at market stained with camel's blood.

In the old days—no more than a generation or two ago—the actual mining would have been done by the Bella, who were either slaves or indentured labor, depending on your point of view, and the Tuareg, or to be more precise the Bérabiche (for they, rather than the Imagcharen Tuareg, were the true operators of the *azalaï*, the salt caravans), were the caravanners, polishing the slabs and hauling them to town. Now that the Tuareg and the Bérabiche have fallen on hard economic times, they do it all, and the Bella have been banished to the margins of what is already a marginal business. Our host was a Tuareg, though he had lost his desert ways and had abandoned the traditional Tuareg costume.

The salt trade is also how Halis makes a living, when he isn't in town looking after foreigners. He spends eight months a year in the desert, fetching salt from Taoudenni and selling it in town. Some of his compatriots take it directly to Kabara, where they sell it to Fulani middlemen or Bozo boatmen, who then ship it to Djenné or Mopti; Halis sells his in Timbuktu, as he always has.

I had once spent a morning in Mopti and had seen the stacks of salt slabs piled on the cobblestoned wharfside. The merchant I talked to didn't know, or care, exactly where they came from.

"The Tuareg bring them in from the desert," he said. "I don't care to go and see, myself. What does it matter?" He made more money fetching the slabs at Kabara, which took him four days, than he would have made spending three weeks going to the Taoudenni mines himself. Why should he go on that hazardous journey? "They always end up here, in the end," he said.

The price the miners pay the shippers is one slab in four. They get no money at the time but must wait, sometimes months, until the caravanner returns, and then they are generally paid in goods, not cash. Cash is useless at Taoudenni—there is nothing to buy anyway. Food and supplies, and sometimes clothing, are the trade goods. The whole trade is based, as it must be, on trust.

The mines at Taghaza, which is considerably north of Taoudenni, are worked out now, exhausted after centuries of activity. Many decades worth are still left at Taoudenni, provided the mining is done in the same way as at present. Modern earth-moving machinery and trucking would deplete it in months. Perhaps fortunately for an ancient way of life, no one has the means to invest in excavators; nor would the returns justify the investment. Still, the following day we saw a truck parked on a side street in Timbuktu near the main produce market, its bed piled high with slabs of salt. There must have been two hundred of them. Halis is a Tuareg with feet in both the desert and the modern world (he follows Tuareg custom but is skilled with machinery, carries a cell phone and is familiar enough with e-mail), but he still froze when he saw it. He shook his head and walked on without saying anything, but he was shaken, as though the sight was an ill omen.

ɣɔ

SALT HAS BEEN mined in the western Sahara for many centuries. At first, it was taken to the early hub cities of Koumbi Saleh or Audaghost to be redistributed to the salt-poor savanna or the even more salt-poor forest cultures of West Africa.

Ibn Battuta may have disliked the dreary little town of Taghaza when his caravan paused there in 1353, but he knew he was at one of the nodal points of the Saharan trade network. In those days the salt was sold, Battuta reported, "for eight to ten mithqals, and in the city of Mali for 20 to 30, sometimes 40. The blacks trade with salt as others trade with gold and silver; they cut it into pieces and buy and sell with these. For all its squalor, quintals of quintals of gold dust are traded [in Taghaza]."[1] A few hundred years later Leo Africanus reported that one camel load, four slabs of salt, could be sold for eighty ducats (more or less eighty dinars, or 338 grams of gold). The salt from Taghaza and Taoudenni is of uniformly high quality, fit for the human table. For their animals, the Tuareg prefer the salt that comes from Bilma, considerably to the east, in Niger east of Agadez, which is very bitter to the European palate. The nomads much prefer it to the synthetic diet supplements for sale in town; they believe camels grow strong because of it.

In classical times, when somewhere around three thousand tons was being exported annually, a slab of Taghaza salt traded for a bar of gold; now the profit margins are slimmer because salt is much more easily obtained and the competition is fiercer, but the profit still makes the trade go round.

Caravans of salt continue to come to Timbuktu, carried by Halis and his colleagues. But they are usually no more than fifteen or twenty camels, and their arrival excites little attention. At the time of the askias the arrival of a salt caravan was a major event; such a caravan was commonly five hundred camels, but it could be a great many more, up to ten thousand at times. Most of the caravanseries were located in the Sankoré quarter of town and contributed greatly to that quarter's wealth. One of the great merchant families of Timbuktu, the Baghayogho family, had its warehouses there. They supplied the caravans with camels, sold them water, food and lodging, bought the salt from them, hired Sorko or Bozo boatmen to take it to Djenné or Mopti, where other branches of the family traded it for gold—which they then took back to Timbuktu for transshipment to the north. The salt was taken on from Mopti by pirogue, by Wangara or Dyula traders, and redistributed throughout West Africa.

The Baghayogho family is still prominent in Timbuktu. One of them, Mahmoudou Baba Hasseye Baghayogho, has served as a director of the Ahmed Baba Center and has been a trustee of the Sidi Yahiya mosque. The great merchant families were commonly also prominent in cultural and religious affairs, and still are.

The Baghayoghos' historic connection with both salt and gold was predictable. The real reason salt reached such eminence as a trade good in the Sahara, and the reason the northern merchants were so eager to take it south, to "the land of the blacks," was the way it neatly complemented the gold trade: salt was in very short supply in the Sahel and points south, though it is a necessity for human life; gold, on the other hand, a commodity irrelevant to life, was in very short supply in the north. As a consequence, there was a seemingly insatiable hunger for salt in the south, and a similarly insatiable hunger for gold among the northern kingdoms and caliphates, and among the merchant houses of Europe. Indeed, salt and gold were intertwined from the beginning. Weight for weight, they were worth pretty much the same.

‹›

IT WAS THE sale of gold that helped build the cultures of the Sahel, and it was gold that sustained them after the collapse of Ghana-Wagadu and the rest of its immense industrial system. It was gold that financed the mansas of Mali, and the askias' later affluent benevolence. It was gold that was the engine of Timbuktu's expansion.

At the dawn of the Islamic period alluvial gold from the Senegal River and the Middle Niger was transported north via Ghana-Wagadu and Audaghost to Aghmat and Sidjilmasa, and from the Black Volta via Kukiya and Gao to Tunisia, Libya and Egypt. Later, the traffic shifted east from Ghana-Wagadu and west from Gao, and was funneled through Timbuktu and then to Tuat, as Maghreb merchants transported the gold north to the Mediterranean ports, and to the Spanish and Italians and, toward the end of the trade, to the Belgians, English and French. From the time of the mansas through to the end of the askias, so much of it trudged north on the backs of camels that the African gold traffic replaced that of central Asia and the east as the underpinning of the economies of the entire Middle East and the Mediterranean, the world financial system refocusing itself on the Maghreb and on the province of al-Andalus, or Spain. African gold became the essential lubricant of Mediterranean commerce. It's worth repeating: two-thirds of the world's gold supply in the late Middle Ages came from West African mines.

An anonymous Arab writer in the twelfth century, two hundred years before Battuta noted the amount of gold that changed hands at Taghaza, left this account: "In the country of Ghana is gold, treasure inexpressible. They have much gold, and the merchants trade with salt for it, taking the salt on camels from the salt mines. They travel in the desert as upon a sea, having guides to pilot them by the stars or the rocks in the deserts. They take provisions for six months, and when they reach Ghana they weigh their salt and trade it against a certain unit of gold, and sometimes against double or more of the gold unit, according to the market and the supply."[2] Leo Africanus had commented on the size of the gold vessels used by the king of Timbuktu; the seventeenth-century sea captain Richard Jobson, not the most reliable of sources, had described Timbuktu's houses as lined with gold, and the *Encyclopaedia Britannica*, in its 1788 second edition, was still reporting that "no other part of the world abounds with gold and silver in greater degree."

By the time of the askias, the gold business had been systematized—it had *become* a business—and the countinghouses of the great families knew to the gram what came from which field or which mine, for which trading house it was destined and how much profit it would bring. To outsiders, the source of the gold remained hidden, mysterious, giving rise to lurid rumors of how it was acquired, but in reality, the goldfields were not that well hidden and not that mysterious. The gold really wasn't, as one colorful legend had it, drawn to the surface by bird feathers coated in pitch, lowered into the mineshafts by a troupe of naked virgins. It was just that the rulers of Old Ghana and Tekrur, and later Mali and then the askias, made sure that foreign merchants didn't wander about in their territory, and thus kept their source secure.

The main gold-bearing strata were found on the eastern slopes of the Fouta Djallon Highlands (today located in Guinea), where many of the tributaries of both the Senegal and Niger rivers originate. The wash from these mountains was so great that for many centuries the actual source of the gold was believed (at least by the traders) to be on the floodplains of these rivers, below Bakel on the Senegal and Ségou on the Niger. When early Arab writers referred to the gold from "Wangara" or "Wanqara," they were probably referring to the area around Mopti where the Bani and Niger rivers join; in fact, there is no real evidence of gold as far downstream as that, not even alluvial deposits.

Among the most prominent real sources of gold were the fields called Buré in the western Niger floodplains and the Sankarani River. The earlier Ghana-Wagadu state never controlled this source, but Mali did, and so did the Songhai. The somewhat richer field called Bambuk to Buré's north, in the upper Senegal Valley between the Senegal and Falémé rivers, was controlled by both empires, Ghana-Wagadu and then Mali, and subsequently by the Songhai. A few smaller fields also existed in the Guinea uplands. South of Gao, in the modern country of Niger and more or less in the Niger River Valley, were the Sirba Valley gold workings, mostly shallow mines and not alluvial deposits. Available evidence suggests that gold from these mines actually made its way from Gao (or Kukiya) to Carthage in the early centuries before the present era.[3] Farther south, in the modern countries of Burkina Faso and Ghana, more deposits were being worked along the Black Volta River. Finally, there were the Akan fields, northwest of the present Ghanaian city of Elmina. Dyula merchants pioneered a route from Djenné to Akan.

Most of the gold from all these sources was easy to find. A Frenchman, Sieur Compagnon, reached the Bambuk goldfields in 1714 and remarked, "It is not necessary to take the trouble of digging. They need only scrape the Superficies of the Earth, wash it in a Bowl, and pour off the Water gently to find the Gold in Dust at the bottom, sometimes in large Grains."[4]

Even the few nonalluvial goldfields were generally fairly close to the surface; most mines were not much more than forty feet deep. Since each shaft generally yielded only a few grams of gold (the famous Ghanaian "rods of gold" notwithstanding), there would have to have been somewhere between 240,000 and 480,000 shallow shafts operating at any one time to meet the demand, a considerable mobilization of manpower.

Gold is still being brought to the surface in Senegal and Guinea in the way it was when Mansa Musa was alive. The miners work from shafts forty or fifty feet deep, less than three feet in diameter and about seven feet apart, connected at the bottom by lateral tunnels. The ore is mined with short-handled picks; the men work in tunnels less than three feet high, half filled with water. Ore is floated to the shafts in calabashes and pulled to the surface by women. Women generally wash the gold and guard it until it is collected by itinerant merchants who sell it in town.[5] Of course, the position of gold from Senegal and Guinea in the world market is greatly diminished, because of modern mining techniques and more productive goldfields in South Africa, Russia and Canada. The rods of gold of Old Ghana, once legend, then a sort of reality, have receded back to the storybooks.

ᙉᙣ

THE THIRD COMMODITY that underpinned Timbuktu's prosperity under the askias was slaves.

There had always been slavery in Africa, as there had been pretty well everywhere else humans made societies, but in Ghana-Wagadu and Old Mali it had been mostly a matter of captives or concubines—it wasn't really a *business*, with formal markets and published prices. The Arabs brought to it a new thoroughness and energy, unsurpassed in its rapaciousness until the mercantilist economies of the West turned their attention to Africa in their colonial period. Once the first phase of Muslim conquest was over, none of the newly protected subjects—People of the Book such as Jews, Christians or Zoroastrians, or of course Muslims themselves—could any longer be reduced to slavery, and slaves had to be sought elsewhere. Most were simply seized in punitive raids, many of them small though occasionally massive, but many were bought by Arab slavers from local chiefs, usually in weaker, less tightly knit societies incapable of defending themselves, like Nubia or Ethiopia in the east, and the more or less disorganized cultures south of the Mossi in the west. Cities like Gao and Timbuktu profited greatly from the trade.

The askias encouraged slavery and themselves frequently used gifts of slaves as incentives. Askia Mohamed, as part of his campaign to ingratiate himself with the uléma of Timbuktu, was generous with gifts of slave women, who were often turned into concubines. On the other hand, he encouraged the Muslim practice of freeing slaves after a certain period of service. For example, if a family paid a servant, not a slave, twenty ducats a year for wages, and then bought a slave for hundred ducats, the slave would work for five years, after which he was entitled to freedom. Of course, not everyone went along with this somewhat benevolent practice, but many did, and there were many instances when such a freed slave was set up in business by loans from his former master.

Many of the great merchant families operated slave pens on the northern fringes of Timbuktu. Some made slavery their principal business, buying slaves in the markets of Djenné and transporting them to wherever the demand was greatest. Aristocratic Timbuktu traded horses for slaves; horses were a sign of their eminence and material affluence, and were used mostly for display, for promenades about the city in the afternoons and for transport to Kabara.

ↄ

THE SLAVE PENS are all gone from Timbuktu now (though it's far from certain that the trade has altogether vanished from the more remote oases of Mauritania and Mali); and gold is no longer carried to or from the city, in any quantities. Only the salt trade is left, though a pale ghost of its former self. When Halis brings in his consignment of salt from Taoudenni, he takes it directly to the depot where the agents for the Mopti merchants have set up shop, a small shed on one of the main thoroughfares, the stock piled to the rafters inside, spilling onto the road. He is paid in cash, in piles of paper francs, not gold. Most trade in Timbuktu is done like this now, from small hole-in-the-wall shops, dealing with small entrepreneurs in a mix of cash and barter, seldom needing bankers, with equally hole-in-the-wall moneylenders papering over gaps in time.

Nothing is left in the city of the great commercial emporiums that existed under the askias. Then, commercial shippers from the north stayed, together with goods they brought for sale, in large warehouses called *fondacs*; these were privately owned establishments run by a class of entrepreneurs sometimes known, perhaps jestingly, as courtiers. These courtiers served as commercial agents and wholesalers, and sometimes acted independently as agent-in-place for the richer trading houses of Cairo and Tunis and Sidjilmasa and Tuat. They also acted as business boosters and touts, encouraging traders to come and spend money by offering three days of free housing, and receiving commissions on their guests' purchases in the market. Under the askias, these *fondacs* were also convenient places for the tax bureaucracy to do its measuring, assessing—and collection.

By the seventeenth century some of these warehouses contained upwards of forty apartments, and slavers kept a variety of slaves on hand, who could be had on short-term leases to do whatever chores needed doing. Typically, the apartments in a *fondac* were rented for three months, the accepted turnaround time for a caravan to sell its goods, assemble goods for the return trip and organize guides. Even native families sometimes rented *fondacs* to house their merchandise temporarily, before shipping it onward, either by pirogue to Djenné or via camel to the north.

After Halis showed us where his salt ends up, we went back to the main market to watch the smiths and the weavers at work, fashioning their crafts as they had for centuries, using much the same techniques. Then we wandered again through the produce stalls, wary this time of impish young boys with their quick hands. The same piles of produce we remembered from earlier visits were still piled high on trestle tables and on mats on the ground. The market looked much as it would have under the askias, with much the same mix of merchandise and cheerful people.

Askia al-hajj Mohamed had instituted an office of weights and measures in a corner of the market in his day; an inspector who found any cheating punished the offender by confiscating all his goods. (A document of the time refers to the common frauds being the "admixture of copper to virgin gold, the aeration of meat, and the baptism of milk . . . [by adding water].") Incentives to cheat were not strong, in any case. Profit margins were substantial in those days; imports from Morocco could earn a merchant 30 to 50 percent. The dinar was the main unit of currency, valued in 1510 at 4.23 grams of gold; Leo Africanus reported seeing "coin of Tombuto of gold, without a stamp or superscription." Among the ordinary people the cowry shell, imported from Persia, remained the currency of choice, four hundred shells to the ducat.

Barter was common. One could exchange salt for slaves, for example, or for other merchandise of high value. Occasionally leather was used as coin too. Barter is still used in the markets, but "cash is coin" as they say, and piles of well-used West African francs are now the normal commercial lubricant.

⁊

FOR ALL HIS vaunted tolerance and under the prodding of the odious Maghili, the first askia refused to allow Jews into his empire. Leo Africanus, who came to Timbuktu in 1510, in the middle of the askia's reign, remarked on their absence from the city. "[The king] so deadly hateth all Jews that he will not admit any into his city and whatever Barbary merchants he understands to have dealings with Jews he presently causes their goods to be confiscated."[6] This was not as true in Timbuktu as it was in Gao, and after a while it wasn't true even there. Both before and after the askias, Jews persecuted in North Africa did flee to Timbuktu and played a role in the city's trade; many of them set up stalls in the markets. In the open desert, many of them traveled as smiths with the Tuareg, fashioning some of the nomads' most intricate and beautiful metalwork.

Nomadic life was at its best then. The Tuareg were still a self-confident, even arrogant culture, with no threats on any horizon. They were still the facilitators (and operators) of the trans-Saharan traffic.

I thought of Halis's little caravan of twelve camels, another faint echo of the past, and remembered a description of a caravan brought in from the north in Askia al-hajj Mohamed's time: thirty thousand camels carrying dates, fabrics, weapons, ironwork, other metals like silver, incense and spices, tea and tobacco. Tobacco was coveted in Timbuktu but not grown there, and had to be imported. Swords and knives were brought in by the thousands, some of them originating in Mesopotamia, some in Germany (they weren't being made in Mema anymore). Dutch-looking glasses were favored by the rich, and camels were laden with those. Fish oil for lamps was imported from the Atlantic coast. The traders took back with them ivory, Guinea spices, honey, kola nuts, shea butter, cereals, cotton, baobab flour and calabashes, along with panniers of gold, leather and civet.

That was the time when Timbuktu's population swelled, though not yet to its greatest extent; that would happen under the first askia's son, Daoud. Many of the greatest caravanners, most of them Berbers or Tuareg, settled in the Sankoré quarter at the time; entrepreneurs and traders from Tuat, Tafilalt, the Fezzan and many other places settled around the Djingareiber mosque; after a while the Tuat people monopolized the mosque's imamate. Mossi traders, in town mostly to buy bolts of cloth and slabs of salt, stayed in their own quarter, the Mossikunda.

In those days it was rush hour between Kabara and Timbuktu; parking space for pirogues was at a premium. The *fondacs* were full. Even the rains seemed sweeter. No enemies were in sight.

The people of Timbuktu didn't think of it as the golden age, then. It was just the way things were.

CHAPTER THIRTEEN

ఴ

Travelers' Tales

SOMETIMES AT DAWN the sun comes up bloodred in a dusty haze. On mornings when the wind is still, it rises in a glaring yellow, already overburdening the desert with its animus. In either case, the city—if you are on the outskirts, waiting for daybreak—can be hard to see, for it casts no shadow and in color and texture, in hue and sky, it blends into the surrounding desert, being made of the same substance. All travelers approaching Timbuktu, especially for the first time, struggled with this . . . blending. "It lay close upon the sand about half a mile before us. My eyes might have missed it for some time to come, partly because it did not rise against the sky but more because it blended in color . . . the sunset was aflame, throwing a glow into the air . . . the fine dust of the sand was like a . . . veil; I first saw Timbuktu, faintly tinged with violet."[1] "At the end of the narrow canal . . . runs a bank of pale amber sand and beyond, silhouetted against the skyline, the old town, the Eyes of the Desert, walled, grey, crumbling, lies like some animal";[2] "in a slight depression was the town itself, a conglomeration of sandy brown buildings, with flat roofs, while here and there a minaret obtruded its pointed head. The sun was dying and as its last rays caught the somber-hued houses they were lit up and stood out more clearly from the desert that they so closely resembled."[3] There are dozens more like these, each visitor struggling to define the elusive. Even Bruce Chatwin, usually so fluent with a phrase ("lean aristocratic Tuareg of supernatural appearance . . . their faces encased in indigo veils which . . . dye their skin a thundercloud blue") was hard put to do better: "Walls of a spectral grey, as if all the colour has been sucked out of them."[4]

Since most of these descriptions were written, the city has sprawled out onto the sands, randomly dotted mud houses and straw huts colonizing whatever space is left between the dunes, and sometimes on them, so it is hard to know where a shepherd's camp ends and the city begins. The town is not walled. None of these travelers' tales, at least none in the last several hundred years or so, has mentioned town walls or gates, though casual mentions were common in earlier accounts.

This business of gates became a bit of a puzzle for us. More than one person in Timbuktu, learning that we were curious about the past, warned us not to take "Ibn Battuta's Seven Gates of Timbuktu" seriously; they were more a metaphor for the Gates to Paradise than a real description, and Battuta was more concerned with spiritual health than reportage. Several of our interlocutors told us we must distinguish between the myth and the hard history of Timbuktu—the hard history having to do with trade and battle—and that this notion of gates was part of the myth. I was curious about this; Ibn Battuta comes off in his journals as a worldly traveler, as much concerned with matters of sustenance and the pleasures of the flesh as piety, and when I went looking in his writings he nowhere mentioned gates, or walls, or defenses of any kind, except a privacy wall around the royal palaces in Melli and Djenné and Timbuktu. But at the time of the askias, it was said, the city's Albaradiou (or al-Bar'adu) Gates, facing the desert in the northern quarter, would welcome sixty thousand camels laden with goods every year, having come in from Taghaza and Taoudenni and the Great Ergs beyond, and the Mediterranean beyond that.[5] This gate was never described, however,

Heinrich Barth's view of his arrival at Timbuktu. (Heinrich Barth)

and neither was the wall it pierced; it may not have been a gate at all—the word *gate* is sometimes translated as "suburb of the caravans." The only really detailed description of city walls in all the literature is to be found in Shabeni, who was writing more than a hundred years after Moroccan invaders had finished off the askias once and for all.

The town of Timbuctoo is surrounded by a mud-wall. The walls are built tabia-wise, thus: they put boards on each side of the wall supported by stakes driven in the ground, or attached to other stakes laid transversely across the wall; the intermediate space is then filled with sand and mud, and beat down with large wooden mallets, (as they beat the terraces) till it becomes hard and compact; the cases are left on for a day or two; they then take them off; and move them higher up, repeating this operation till the wall is finished. They never use stone or brick; they do not know how to make bricks. The wall is about twelve feet high, and sufficiently strong to defend the town against the wild Arabs [Tuareg], who come frequently to demand money from them. It has three gates; one called Bab Sahara, or the gate of the desert, on the north [which could be the al-Bar'adu of earlier times]; opposite to this, on the other side of the town, a second, called Bab Neel, or the gate of the Nile: the third gate leads to the forest on the east, and is called Bab el-Kibla [el-Kibla signifying the tomb of Muhammad]; it faces Medina in Arabia. The gates are hung on very large hinges, and when shut at night, are locked, as in Barbary; and are further secured by a large prop of wood placed in the inside slopingly against them. There is a dry ditch, or excavation, which circumscribes the town, except at those places which are opposite the gates, about twelve feet deep, and too wide for any man to leap it. The three gates of the town are shut every evening soon after sunset: they are made of folding doors, of which there is only one pair. The doors are lined on the outside with untanned hides of camels, and are so full of nails that no hatchet can penetrate them; the front appears like one piece of iron.[6]

⁊

ALL THE MANY thousands of travelers who passed through these gates, or camped beneath these walls, or rented space in the *fondacs*, or had an agent buy them a house in town, or simply immigrated from the lost lands of defunct kingdoms to find a home in this most welcoming of metropolises—where did they come from, and what route maps did they follow? (See maps, pages ix–xi.)

The Sahara has been traversed by traders and adventurers since antiquity—indeed, since before the Sahara was the formidable barrier it later became. In the days when the old empires of Ghana-Wagadu and then Mali were the dominant political forces in the Sudan, there was already a skein of routes threading their way across the desert from oasis to oasis, from well to well. The two most venerable of these were the so-called Royal Road, and the diagonal crossing pioneered by Garamantes charioteers.

The Royal Road was, in the early days, the route of least resistance; for many centuries it followed ancient wadis and depressions and had only one truly arid stage, a perilous crossing in what is now central Mauritania. This was the most westerly of routes, beginning south of the Anti-Atlas Mountains and following, generally, the Dra'a Valley and its spur, Wadi Nul (sometimes Nun), along a string of oases roughly following the border between western Sahara and Mauritania, down to Ouadane and Chinguitti. From there the route went generally south and east, either to Tichitt and Walata, or to Audaghost and Koumbi Saleh, to do business with the people of the Senegal Valley. There was also a more westerly spur from the Chinguitti area to the mouth of the Senegal River for salt. The route's northeast extension paralleled the Anti-Atlas past present-day Biskra to Tunis on the coast. There are indications that wheeled transport used this route, too, in the first millennium BC.

The Chariot Route, so-called because cave drawings of Garamantes chariots have been found along its whole length, began at Tripoli, or Oea as it was called in Roman times. From there it skirted Jebel Nafusah in the direction of Ghadamès, and thence south through the massif called Tassili-n-Ajjer and west along the formidable northern perimeter of the Ahaggar. It curved around the Ahaggar, heading southwest and crossing to the southeast of the Adrar des Iforhas. From there it headed in a southerly direction to the Niger River, which it intersected at Gao.

The Fezzan, now a province of Libya but once the heartland of the Garamantes empire, lay at a crossroads of two more routes, a north-south one from Tripoli to the Lake Chad region, and a northeast-southwest route originating in Alexandria via Siwa, picking up the Chariot Route and terminating in the Ghana-Wagadu region. This was to become the principal route that Muslim pilgrims followed to Egypt and thence to the Holy Places.

Copper from the mines at Marendet and Takedda (southwest and north-west respectively of Agadez in Niger) found its way to the smelters at Gao, and also to Benin at the mouth of the Niger, where it was used to plate the roofs and walls of the palaces with brass.

The principal gold mines were at the Middle Senegal below the Falémé River, the Buré along the upper reaches of the Niger and the upper reaches of the Black Volta.

❦

THE WESTERLY ROUTES were already falling into disfavor with traders in the period of Timbuktu's founding. This had to do with increasing aridity, the fading of the Tichitt and Mema industrial heartlands, the politi-cal and ecological crisis that faced Ghana-Wagadu and turmoil resulting from the raiding of Almoravid Berbers. Timbuktu's increasing importance was partly a result of this decay; in turn, Timbuktu accelerated the decay.

During the golden age of Timbuktu, the principal trans-Saharan route was a direct north-south one across the great *ergs* of sand, through Arawan, Taoudenni and Taghaza. Its terminus was in the Dra'a Valley and at Sidjil-masa in the Tafilelt oasis. A slightly more circuitous route went east to Gao and thence via the west side of the Adrar des Iforhas, passed the pleasant oa-sis town of Tadmekka (renowned, apparently, for its hospitable innkeepers and even more amiable young women) and across the Tanezrouft to the Tuat oasis, with branches northwest to Sidjilmasa, north to Tlemcin or north-east to Qairouan.

The main trading routes to the south flowed through Djenné toward the goldfields of the Upper Black Volta; toward Melli and the goldfields of the Mali Empire; and toward the Middle Senegal River. That Djenné shifted its trade to Timbuktu from the more westerly town of Walata was a sign of Timbuktu's growing commercial power.

By the time of the askias Timbuktu had become the focal point of the Sa-haran trade, and by far the majority of commerce in the western Sudan was flowing through its trading houses, with Djenné, still, as its main distribution center and entrepôt. Merchants from the Maghreb gathered in Timbuktu to buy gold and slaves in exchange for the Saharan salt of Taghaza, for North African cloth and horses, and for luxury goods. To Timbuktu's north, the main distribution center was the Tuat oasis; Tuat had a large and influential Jewish community who served as the trade's bankers. (Islam forbade lending

at a profit, and traders delegated the business to non-Muslims.) Some of the
northern cities were at times receiving so much merchandise from Timbuktu
that they held fairs lasting three months. The town of Ghadamès, now in
Libya, received virtually daily shipments.

&

LONG OR SHORT, direct or roundabout, all the routes were hazardous. Desert travel left many a merchant's bones bleaching in the desert
sun, the victim of thirst, disorientation, bandits, illness or dangerous crea-
tures, like the ever-present vipers and the ubiquitous scorpions. Of all these,
simply becoming lost was the greatest danger. The routes were seldom straight
but wandered from well to well, wherever earlier explorers had found water;
these wells could be many days' march apart, and if a traveler missed even
one it could be perilous; you could wander in the desert for months and not
find water unless you had a skilled guide. A truism of desert travel was (indeed it still is) that selecting a guide is far more important than selecting even
congenial traveling companions or reliable transportation.

The merchant caravans traveled in the company of, and under the wary
protection of, and sometimes in spite of, the desert nomads: the Tuareg, the
Massufa, the Lamtuna Berbers, the Sanhaja, the Bérabiche, the names varied.
These nomads were the mariners of the sand seas and served as pilots,
protectors—and, sometimes, pirates.

We were having dinner one night on the rooftop terrace of the Timbuktu
house belonging to Shindouk Mohamed Lamine, and his wife, Miranda
Dodd. Tethered to a thorn bush in the compound were two camels, grum-
bling as camels do, while two men fussed about them, removing saddles,
adding hobbles, providing food. They were neither Tuareg nor Bambara but
French, and Shindouk had been educating them in the ways of the desert, for
they were determined to cross the Sahara by themselves, with only their
camels for company, traveling through Arawan and Taoudenni and so across
the *ergs* to Tuat until they reached Morocco. They would thereby be repeating one of the classic and venerable Sahara crossings; the sign in Zagora,
south of the Anti-Atlas Mountains in Morocco, still says, TOMBOUCTOU 52
JOURS (Timbuktu 52 days).

What Shindouk thought of this notion of theirs he kept to himself—
they were clients, for one thing. Other Saharan guides were less discreet
about the increasingly common practice of well-fed water-rich First

Desert expert Shindouk Mohamed Lamine Ould Najim. (Miranda Dodd)

Worlders blundering through the desert on their own, to their peril and the peril of those who often have to rescue them. Halis, who was at the dinner, told a story of a Canadian he had met in the desert, who had taken it into his head to cross the desert from west to east, from Mauritania to the Red Sea, a distance of more than three thousand miles, with only himself and three camels for company. "I told him he was mad," Halis said. "First of all, three camels is not enough. For safety, you need fifteen. And then you do not travel by yourself. You need a camel master, a companion in case you fall ill or have an accident. And he was filming his journey. He had all this equipment. He was moviemaker too. Really mad."

"What happened to him?"

"After six months he reached Walata, then went on, and passed north of here [Timbuktu]. I talked to him there."

"And then?"

"Sixty kilometers east of here he was found dead in the desert."

"What happened?

Halis shrugged. Whether he died of thirst or illness, or was bitten by a scorpion or was murdered by bandits for his film equipment didn't really matter. It was an inevitable death.

Another outsider, a Frenchman, wanted to run from the salt mines at Taoudenni to Timbuktu, a distance of more than 370 miles. He wanted to do this without a guide, on his own. To prepare for this senseless ordeal he hired Halis to take him to Taoudenni in a 4×4, planting caches of food and water every ten kilometers [about six miles] along the way, buried in the sand, sixty of them.

"What happened to him? Did he die too?" I asked, thinking sourly that the idiot probably deserved it.

Halis chuckled. "He had a satellite phone with him. After the first ten kilometers he called for me to come and get him. He had enough. He camped for the night and found a viper curling about his first night's cache, and that was enough for him." He made a face. "He wanted his money back. He said he hadn't got what he paid for." He shook his head—the logic of outsiders!

It was easy to understand the fascination these romantics developed for the desert. The immense parched emptiness of the Great Ergs has always attracted outsiders, as far back as the Arab invaders who were confronted by the terrifying mystery of the shifting rivers of sand, a boundaryless peril in which entire armies could disappear. Some of these outsiders, as we ourselves

Desert guide Mohamed al-Hasan al-Ag Moctar dit *Halis in a city square.* (Sheila Hirtle)

once put it in a book on the Sahara, "have crossed the portals of the desert as a challenge, or an adventure, or as prospectors, or simply to seek solace in a place as remote and empty and perilous as it is possible to be, hoping to find their center by becoming lost in the eternal, hoping, perhaps, that the soul can be healed there, in a place where it must perforce contemplate only the starkest of choices." Some of them came back to tell their tales, their lives greatly enriched. Many perished.

To the people who passed their lives there, to the nomads of the open desert, to the Imagcharen, the Tuareg of the Kel Ajjer or the Bérabiche of Taghaza, the desert was really none of these things. It was simply where they lived.

৩

SHINDOUK, CHIEF OF a small tribe of Bérabiche called the Oual-adnagim a few hundred miles north of Timbuktu, makes his living partly as a caravanner and partly as a guide, steering not only individual parties but movie crews, survey expeditions, prospectors and adventurers through some of the most difficult and hostile terrain on earth. He was born to the job, al-most literally; he comes from a long and illustrious line of desert experts, which is what his own business card calls him: GUIDE DE TOMBOUCTOU, EX-PERT DU DESERT, SHINDOUK MOHAMED LAMINE. (His full name is Shindouk Mohamed Lamine Ould Najim.) His father, Najim, was one of the most fa-mous Saharan guides of them all.

Najim's own father was one of the wealthiest, shrewdest caravanners to trade from Libya to Mauritania. Shindouk's great-grandfather had been an eminent adviser to the Tuareg sultan of Timbuktu, who protected Heinrich Barth from his multiple enemies. One of the documents in the Mamma Haïdara Library is a poem, part of a letter dated 1853, from the sultan, Sidi Ahmed al-Bakay, responding to demands of the ruler of Masina at Djenné, Ahmad Lobbo, that Barth should be killed out of hand. Lobbo had learned that Barth was staying in al-Bakay's home, and urged the sheikh to kill him because it was not normal for a Christian to live among Muslims. Al-Bakay and his advisers, including Shindouk's ancestor, responded with a poem in which they pointed out that Barth was a guest, had come in peace and had found safe passage through Egypt, Libya and Morocco, all Muslim coun-tries. "Why, then, should Timbuktu be less courteous?"

Tales of Shindouk's father are legion. One of his most famous exploits was to help save a lost convoy—at long distance, over a radio link. The convoy's guides had become confused and were disoriented. With only a few quarts of water remaining, they managed to get Timbuktu on the radio to ask for help. Someone called Najim. When he came to the military post where the transmitter was, he asked to speak to the most senior guide present.

"Describe the place," he demanded. "What does it look like, the horizon? What is its shape to the west and the north, to the south and the east? Are there any hills? Are there dunes, and what size and shape? Is the ground stony?"

The guide did as asked.

"Pick up some sand," said Najim. "Tell me its color. Is it clear, with white grains, or dark, with black particles? And its feel. How big are the grains? Is it sharp to the fingers?"

The guide obeyed once again.

Najim sifted the descriptions in his mind. Then he said, "You describe a small mountain ahead of you, to the north. Go there, turn west when you get there, travel for half an hour and call me again."

Three hours later the convoy reached the mountain and turned left as instructed. Najim came back on the radiophone.

"Do you see a large freestanding rock off to your left?" he asked.

"We do."

"Get the men to push it over. There is water beneath it."

Another tale concerned a military convoy that had been trying to map the tenuous and still-disputed boundary with Algeria. The military frequently used civilian freelance guides, who sometimes felt exploited and underpaid. Najim had taken this convoy into the desert, and one day deep into a most featureless part of the Sahara, he stopped. "I feel dizzy," he said. "I can't even tell where the west is, or where the north, I don't know what to do."

"But you must!"

"I cannot. I am confused."

The convoy leaders began to panic. "What can we do?" they asked.

"Two things might help," Najim said blandly. "More money and an honorary commission in the army."

An urgent phone call to Timbuktu military headquarters got patched through to Bamako, the capital, and a short time later the president of the republic himself called to personally induct Najim into the army and award him his officer's commission. He also got more money. The mapping survey continued amicably.

Another time Najim saved a lost convoy from the air. At first he was unable to help, because he had to fly to Bamako to have his eyes seen to. On the way back, despite his weakening eyesight, he was able to see a thin straight ridge, where the soil had been compacted and had slightly changed color. No one else noticed, and the wind had erased all signs on the ground, but Najim diverted his aircraft and found the convoy a short while later. When the aircraft flew overhead, the people in the convoy had just filled their tea glasses with radiator coolant, the only "water" they had left; they had been resigned to death.

Visitors would frequently bring Najim little bags of sand from various parts of the desert. He would look at the sand for a while, finger it, then dip his nose to smell it. Then he would tell them where it was from. He was always right. Or so the stories say.

This deep knowledge of the desert is a tradition that goes back into ancient times. Ibn Battuta, crossing the Tanezrouft from Morocco on his way to Melli, commented on this matter of Saharan guides: "A guide there is someone who has frequented it repeatedly and who has keen intelligence. A strange thing that I saw is that our guide was blind in one eye and diseased in the other, but he knew the route better than anyone else."[7]

The French explorer René Caillié had written in his journals in 1824, "Though without a compass, or any instrument of observation, they possessed so completely the habit of noticing the most intimate things, that they never go astray, though they have no path traced out for them, and though the wind in an instant completely covers with sand and obliterates the tracks of the camels."[8] What are these "intimate things"? Some of it, of course, has to do with celestial navigation: The Tuareg are as familiar with the stars and the angles of inclination of the sun and moon as any ancient mariner. But the Tuareg seldom travel in straight lines, and outsiders who have tried to keep track with a compass have found the instrument of little use. Any journey is a sinuous series of deviations and sidetracks; the nomads will use shifting shadows, wind patterns, blown sand, moonlight, the stars, the setting and rising sun, the incidence of scrub grasses, ancient erosion gullies, wadi traces, the now-waterless watersheds, the silhouettes of hills, mirages—and smell.

European explorers of the nineteenth century discounted the frequent tales of navigational miracles as scarcely believable, but early travelers knew about this notion of smell as a navigational aid. Leo Africanus described what happened to a caravan of merchants that had gotten lost in the middle of the Libyan desert.

The caravan had a certain blinde man in their companie who was ac-
quainted with all those regions: This blinde guide riding foremost upon
his camell, commanded some sand to be given to him at every mile's
end, by the smell whereof he declared the situation of the place: But
when they were come within fortie miles of this region, the blinde man,
smelling of the sand, affirmed that they were not farre from some place
inhabited; which some believed not for they knew that they were distant from Egypt some fower hundred and eightie miles, so they took
themselves to be nearer unto Augela [a bedraggled little oasis town on
the caravan route from Egypt to Mauritania, known to Herodotus as a
place to lay in supplies of dates]. Howbeit within three days they found
three castles, the inhabitants thereof wondering at the approach of
strangers, and being greatly astonied, presently shut all their gates and
would give the merchants no water to quench their extreme thirst. But
the merchants by main force entered and having gotten water sufficient,
betook themselves againe to their journie.[9]

Ask any of the Tuareg about finding their way in the desert, and they
shrug. It is either easy, and explanation is not necessary, or very subtle, and
impossible to explain. The driver of a 4×4 once told me he found his way to
where we were going by the feel of the sun on his left arm, the one he hung
out the window while he was driving.

Shindouk himself says that if you want to tell another Tuareg the way to
some place he has never been before, you "select a star that is steady in the
sky, the North Star, the Pole Star, and you tell him, for example, 'keep your
left shoulder to that star,' and he will arrive safely. At this time of the year, if
you keep the star on your right shoulder you'll be heading west. If it is on
your left shoulder you'd be heading twenty degrees north of west." The more
talented can even navigate by watching shifting or transitting stars or even
planets, knowing from a deep memory well where the star should be at what
time of night in what season.

Not every nomad has this gift of navigation, as they will readily tell you.
A caravan today will never set off unless it has at least one such in its party,
a guide who is treated with the utmost respect. Nor are all those advertising
themselves as guides quite what they appear. Some claiming to be guides
aren't; others have been bandits who would lead travelers deliberately astray.
In latter days, many who claim to be guides seem to know perilously little

about camels, being rather more used to the internal combustion engine, and sometimes are not very good with that either.

Caravans, small or large, were organized under the leadership of an experienced desert guide called a *khabir*. The *khabir* had full authority over the caravan, and could order its route and the timing of marches. He was also responsible for its well-being and liable for accidents and losses it might suffer. In addition, he had to pay the blood money for anyone lost in the desert through his error. "The proper *khabir* was a man of many parts. He knew the desert routes and watering places, and was able to find his way by the stars at night, or if need be by the scent and touch of the sand and vegetation. He had to understand the proper rules of desert hygiene, remedies against scorpions and snakes, how to heal sickness and mend fractures. He had to know the chiefs of the various towns and tribes with which the caravan had to deal along the way, and in this respect a responsible *khabir* might consolidate his position by strategic marriages in several localities, or into several tribes."[10]

He could also, if he was unscrupulous, sell out the entire caravan to Tuareg raiders.

అ

THAT NIGHT ON Shindouk and Miranda's roof, after the two Frenchmen had set out for the north and the open desert, the conversation wandered, mostly loosely attached to the notion of finetuning life in the desert environment, and little snatches of information stayed in memory, like patches of fine sand drifting through a camp late at night accumulating on a canvas screen. At this point Shindouk advised us to beware of legend masquerading as history in the long life of Timbuktu. "Reality is salt, slaves, gold, camels, caravans," he said.

His own family camp is 125 miles north of the city; Miranda showed us pictures of the well Shindouk had financed for the camp, more than three hundred feet deep, lined with what they called Dutch brick, interlocking stone that needed no cement but couldn't fall in; the water is drawn to the surface in a bucket pulled by a camel walking in a straight line away from the well. Discussion of the well led to how to find water in the desert (by a variety of signals, including the overall lay of the land, the fall of pebbles, even the direction in which camel dung is pointed, always toward water).

It was Miranda who told us of the subtle-to-outsiders differences between Bérabiche and the Tuareg of the high mountains, the Tamashek speakers.

"But both," she said, "still have the same moral values and traditions. All are Tuareg; all are fiercely proud and honorable. None accept shame. None would beg. None would refuse hospitality to whomsoever arrived at their camp. All would help any one of their fellows out of any difficulty. None would hesitate to expel any member of the tribe should he or she bring shame to the family—the worst possible punishment for the worst possible crime."

Other snippets I remember: Travel when you can by the stars; travel at night, rest by day. You need no money in the desert; everything is done by barter, the best mediums of exchange still being salt, fabrics, spices, tea. If you know the signals, you can sense the coming of the harmattan, the Hot Breath of the Desert, up to three hours before it arrives; you can even tell how long it, or a cold front, will last. Daytime meals are a porridge of millet, maybe some dates, meat only at night. Sheep's liver is "the Tuareg breakfast," as Halis had told us, but only in good times, for it's a luxury. The best caravan trail food is called *dognu*, a mix of steeped baobab leaves, millet, milk and sugar; after a draft of that, you won't need water for six hours or more. Or maybe that last advice was from Ibn Battuta. The eminent traveler had been giddy after his first traverse of the Tanezrouft. "This desert is luminous, one's chest is dilated, one is in good spirits," he wrote.[11]

It's the kind of phrase Shindouk would use, in his love of the desert, and its wide open spaces, and its free air, and the liberty it brings to free spirits.

એ

IT IS DOUBTFUL the nomad way of life in the Sahara, the long traditions that led to Najim and Shindouk, that allowed great caravans to cross safely, that led to Halis's yearning to live free in the desert, that had led directly to Timbuktu's prominence and wealth, will last much longer. One afternoon a day or so after our dinner at Shindouk and Miranda's, we spent an hour in the front room of the house Halis rented in Timbuktu. It was empty of furniture except for carpet on the floor; when he was in town he refused to sleep indoors but instead used a tent in the courtyard, which seemed more natural to him. In town you can't sleep—too much noise, too much dirt, too much activity. Cities are rife with disease and filth. People live from day to day, without forethought. Buy a little food, eat a little, sleep at night, live for the moment. "In town," as he put it, "they think money is beautiful." But money changes everything. Money is the root of all problems. It confuses thinking. In the desert it would be deadly to just live from day to day, as you can in the city with money in your hand. In the desert, you must plan weeks and even months ahead just to survive, and it forces on you a more philosophical view of life, a more thoughtful way of living. "Out there," said Halis, "it is impossible to be poor. You have your family, your animals, enough water to drink and food to eat, and a person needs nothing more; it is a pure and clean life, a spiritual life, or a life in which the spirit is free."

There's another thing wrong with money. It upsets the natural hierarchy. "The wrong people can become rich. Even blacksmiths can become rich; then they can lord it over you and get above themselves. This upsets everything. In the desert, everyone knows his place."

Halis's dream is to quit the guiding business and stay out of town for good. For that, he will need thirty camels. Thirty camels would make you independent of money, he says. Since he has only twelve at the moment, and camels cost 350,000 francs each, about $850, it could take him a while to reach this goal. Still, the camels he has are good ones, young but not too young, maybe three years old, each with a solid hump and strong in the withers, good breeding stock.

He mulled over this for a while, pondering the vagaries of fate. His father had once been rich, owning three hundred camels, but they had all died in the great drought of the late 1980s. His family was of marabout origins, he said, the religious and intellectual class, but later became part of the warrior class. Your class dictates who you can marry. The class system is still strict; you cannot marry up or down (unless, like the independent-minded Shindouk, you find your love outside the tribe altogether). Herders, for example, are lower-class people, and marabouts would never marry into a herder family. At the very bottom are the smiths. "No one would ever marry a smith," Halis said. Still, the smiths are important because they double as the news media of the desert, professional gossips, carrying information and messages. When Halis wanted to marry, a smith carried the request to the young woman's family to see if the match would be acceptable. "But . . . never let a smith know something bad about you, for the whole desert will know it soon enough."

Halis has a young wife in Arawan, and one small child, and one of each is enough for him, he said. This remark, made with some emphasis, reminded me of a conversation I'd had some years before with his uncle, Mohamed Ali, about this question of wives. Ali had been scornful about the common Islamic practice of having more than one wife. Education was the key, he thought. "You can't educate your children properly if they are scattered in too many tents."

"How many children, on average?"

"Only five, no more. The life is not easy."

I thought of the Tuareg women, so beautiful, "the most perfectly beautiful of women," as Ibn Battuta had put it—and so free. At least in theory, a Tuareg woman is still free to choose her husband and divorce him at will, though the husband cannot divorce his wife without her consent. So I had been curious about this matter of one wife. Was this because the women demand it be so?

"You're 'entitled' to four? Isn't that what the prophet allowed?" I asked.

"But only if you treat them all equally, and fairly," Ali said. He laughed. "And it's not just that *you* think you're treating them equally; *they* must think so, all four of them. The thing is impossible."

Halis had chosen his wife himself, which is not always the case. He saw her at the well, and they conversed. Whether she had any real say in the matter was unclear. She was very young, only thirteen, a fairly typical marriage age for the Tuareg; it's common to see newlywed couples where both bride and groom are fourteen. Halis differed with his uncle on this matter of the number of wives. Islam may allow it, but "among the Tuareg, only one wife is allowed." This is because the Tuareg place great store on happiness, he said, "unlike the Arabs." That the Tuareg women are not veiled, he points out, is a great advantage. "It is easier to choose that way," he joked.

"Why are the men veiled, then?"

This has nothing to do with the sand and the desert, or any protective device, Halis said. It has to do with what he called *pudeur* (shyness). "The mouth is the most intimate and personal part of a face, and you keep it covered until you are comfortable with the person you are with." This "veil" is not a trivial thing, but a twenty-foot length of indigo cloth wound in intricate fashion around the head and across the face. I remembered once spending a morning with Halis's cousin Ahmed in his tent, and even when we were seated drinking tea, he kept his *tagelmoust*, or *chech*, in place, passing the cup under the veil, keeping his mouth covered. The higher the Tuareg's social status, the more likely he is to remain covered when meeting strangers. When I first met Ahmed, he kept his *tagelmoust* hitched over his mouth and half of his nose; only his eyes could be seen, black and penetrating. As we'd become more comfortable, he'd allowed the covering to slip to his chin. His sister, by contrast, showed her face the whole time I visited them; she was in a green robe, with a headscarf that trailed down her back, held in place by a silver pin; she had bold black eyes and skin like cream, evidence of her Berber ancestry; around her neck she wore a single strand of blue beads and a *khomissar*, a fertility symbol. It is said that the People of the Veil, as the Tuareg are sometimes called, began the custom when they fled Yemen after incurring the wrath of its ruler, and wished to stay hidden, but no one can say whether this is true. It is a commonplace now, however, that the face veil for the men is deeply entwined with their view of their own nature.

Despite Halis's dream of living his life fully in the desert, he and his generation look to the future with foreboding. In a conversation we'd had a few days before on the dunes, a Tuareg man whose parents had been shot by government troops and who had spent three years in a Mauritanian refugee camp had suggested that the way of life wouldn't last more than another generation or two. "What do you think is the future of the Tuareg in the desert?" Halis had asked, mostly on our behalf, and the other man replied, speaking through his *tagelmoust*, "*C'est le malheur, c'est tout, le malheur partout.*"

For a long while after that they had remained silent, staring into the long distances as the sun went down in a sulfurous crimson, and the dunes turned violet in the dusk. Then the other man had said, "Two things have emptied the desert, war and the droughts." I asked him if the desert would have emptied (of Tuareg) anyway, without the war, but he never really answered, because they were twin halves of the same thing, and they happened together, one precipitating the other, and speculation was pointless. He was pessimistic. Despite the political rapprochement, the Malian republic has made it impossible to remain in the desert, really, what with its security concerns, and its need for documents, taxes . . . the whole panoply of bureaucracy militates against nomadism. To the modern state, life in the desert is a threat.

And the young? The young are either cosmopolites or more conservative and inturned than ever, dressing and thinking either in the ways of the West or . . . in some other way. Either they're more flexible, or they have been battered by an alien cultural invasion, depending on your perspective. Two such cultural invasions are present in the city. Sidi Salem Ould Elhadj, who is now in his seventies, sees the threat to his beloved traditions coming from the false cosmopolitanism of the West. Others see a different sort of assault, from a militant Wahhabism, which would hurtle the young into a very different kind of future. Either way, it seems, few Tuareg believe their traditional ways of laissez-faire personal relationships and intricate accommodation to the Great Emptiness will endure very much longer.

CHAPTER FOURTEEN

⁓

Life and Learning in
the City of Gold

A FRIEND OF Halis's called Tahara Baby lives with her sister in a rambling house in the oldest quarter near Sankoré, off a small twisty alley far too narrow for a car. To get to it you have to dodge small children playing in the alley's central gutter, which is also the conduit for wastewater, greasy and fetid, and also mounds of dirt, for workmen are (very slowly) excavating a trench that will be used for a sewer pipe. But once you pass through the gated wall into the house's outer courtyard, everything is neat and clean, swept to a fare-thee-well. Tahara conceived the notion of serving traditional Timbuktu meals to those foreigners who can be persuaded away from the standard grilled-to-a-crisp chicken beloved of the city's few innkeepers, using a large second-floor room for the purpose.

Tahara herself is a determined and, when we met her, newly separated young woman of somewhat exotic ethnicity; Halis describes her as "some Bambara, some Songhai, some Arab." Whatever the real mix, it wears well on her, for she is strikingly attractive, with an oval face the color of caramel and a shrewdly intelligent look. If this experiment of hers worked, she said, and if people liked her food and came back for more, she was considering negotiating with the city for the lease of the vacant house that had once been the Timbuktu residence of René Caillié, the first of the modern Europeans to have visited the city and lived to tell the tale. Caillié was there in 1827, and Europeans, even those who made it all the way to Timbuktu, always seemed more interested in other Europeans than anything else. That house has a plaque on the wall outside but has been empty for more than sixty years. She planned to start a small Caillié museum, which would attract at least the French tourists, and open a restaurant inside that served them meals. There really are no restaurants to speak of in Timbuktu; people perforce have to eat at the very few hotels or make do with what they can buy in the markets— plenty of produce but of uncertain standards of hygiene. Perhaps the French government would pony up a little money for the project? We suggested calling it Chez Tahara.

We were her first paying guests. Halis had kept promising to bring her customers, but we were the first, after months of nagging. She wanted to serve only traditional food, she said, so outsiders could get some small insight into how the people of Timbuktu lived their daily lives.

The food was just fine. (It is not always so in the desert or the desert's cities; the traveler's repast called *bouilli* is more or less repulsive, and the fly-blown "doilies" of dried meat that can be picked up at the markets as trail food can be hazardous.) Tahara herself hovered anxiously as a young relative brought the repast up from the kitchen downstairs, unloading it on a low table on the carpet, then joined us to eat. A large brass bowl contained *toucassou*, a dish of stewed goat and dumplings in sauce. The dumplings were massive, the size of grapefruit, though not at all leaden, and the sauce, called *almarga mafé*, was a peppery red, spiced with paprika and cinnamon. It was followed by fruit, bananas and oranges, and sweet mint tea. All in all, a meal rather better than those described by Ibn Battuta in the fourteenth century, but very like those eaten by later travelers.

Earlier that day we had wandered through the city's main market and had seen there heaping bowls of spices similar to those described by Leo Africanus as having come down from the Maghreb to flavor the food he was given. Some of the spices we saw had no doubt been brought up in commercial barges from Bamako, but much of it had followed the same route as Leo Africanus himself. Some of this was legitimate traffic, the importers having paid all the necessary "tea fund" moneys due the bureaucrats, but hardly any of the common people can afford the goods so imported. So the rest of it was "informally brought in." A thriving smuggling business has emerged— evading taxes but risking confiscation or destruction of the entire load, or worse: stories suggest that the Algerians, intent on interdicting the traffic, have taken to patrolling their borders in helicopters, and when they see a smuggler's truck, they will hover, demand the smugglers vacate, and bomb the truck from the air, leaving the smugglers to make their way as best they can on foot. Rumors also persist that they will occasionally do this to legitimate traffic too, even passenger buses.

Open-air marketplace with Djingareiber mosque in the background. (Sheila Hirtle)

After the meal was over and we had once more made encouraging noises about Chez Tahara, we walked downstairs into the courtyard and through the gate into the street. A man in a mustard-yellow robe with a donkey passed by, and we stepped aside, politely; going in the other direction were two elderly women, their bright blue *boubous* sweeping the sand, one carrying a bucket on her head. Otherwise the street was deserted, somnolent in the afternoon sun, the houses gray and dun, the street gray sand, the sky gray with haze. It wouldn't have looked very different five or six hundred years ago, except it would have been busier, much busier, for the population under the askias was double or three times as great as it is now, and except in the wet season the caravanseries and *fondacs* were jammed with visitors from afar. In the eighteenth century, when the city's decline had already begun, Shabeni estimated the population at "40,000 exclusive of slaves and foreigners, and there are perhaps 10,000 [more] from Fas [Fez] and Morocco."[1]

A busier city—and probably more agreeable too. It is not just nostalgia that attributes a joie de vivre to life in Timbuktu. Shabeni, for example, added, somewhat gratuitously after his comments on the size of the town, that "many of the merchants who visit Timbuctoo are so much attached to the place that they cannot leave it, but continue there for life. The natives are

Pedestrians passing Chez Madje, Salon des Princesses. (Sheila Hirtle)

all blacks: almost every stranger marries a female of the town, who are so beautiful that travelers often fall in love with them at first sight." The author of the *Tarikh al-Sudan* described it as: "[a] renowned, pure, delicious, illustrious, benevolent, luxurious and animated [city] that is my home and which I love more than the world." Mahmoud Kati, the author of the other *Tarikh*, compared it to Basra for its "animation, richness and sweetness of life." Ahmed Baba, during his Moroccan exile, sang of his city in a lament: "Oh you who go to Gao, make a detour to Timbuktu, murmur my name among my friends and take them the perfumed salute of an exile who yearns for the land, misses his friends, his family, his neighbors."[2]

"Even in our days," Sidi Salem Ould Elhadj told us, his eyes twinkling, "we in Timbuktu are so attached to our city and our land, that we consider the rest of the world, even New York and Paris, provincial by comparison."

Half a dozen markets existed in those golden days: livestock and camel markets, a market for horses for those who could afford them, produce markets, spice and foodstuff markets, a market for books and writing materials. But the streets were more crowded than that, for there were butcher stalls

Market seen from a second-story window. (Sheila Hirtle)

on each corner, selling butter, cheese, meat, milks and skins; the butchers were always Mandingo, with their own guild and arcane rituals. Streetside butcher stalls still exist and almost certainly look the same—the meat lying on tables in the glaring Saharan sun, clouds of flies ascending every time the butcher makes a swipe with his hatchet, the favored tool for the work. Bakers made bread and cakes in street-corner ovens, as they still do; the bakers were usually women, as they still are. Neither wheat nor barley was grown locally; bread was made from millet flour called *el bishna*. The rich, however, imported wheat from Morocco to make fine bread, considered a luxury item. Rice was the staple food, along with a corn called *callilila*.

Visitors to the Songhai kingdom often remarked on the energy they found in Timbuktu, the bustling nature of the city and its restless population. It was a commonplace in Leo Africanus's time that there was no charity in Timbuktu because charity was not needed. There was no unemployment, and even the meanest person with the most rudimentary skills could at least acquire a donkey or a mule and set up a small transport business; bringing goods up from the port at Kabara when the water was low, or from the nearby canal of Badjindé to the houses of the rich merchants all over the city. The lower castes found work as vendors of water, wood and charcoal. They generally lived on the outskirts of town and were on foot from sunup to sundown. Old women often took in washing and were paid by the piece. (Thursdays were wash days, in preparation for the Friday prayers.) Even wealthy women worked, frequently selling condiments, ornaments and rolls of cotton from their houses.

The livestock markets sold goats for eight to twelve cowries, chickens for four, camels for forty to sixty, depending on the quality and age. Ostriches were cheap, their feathers exported to Morocco. Slaves (usually listed in the inventories with other "livestock") were more expensive than goats and cheaper than camels, and had to be paid for in gold ducats—no barter there, except perhaps for horses.

The book industry (the copying and scribing business) was centered on Sankoré. Studios employed scribes, calligraphers, illuminators and illustrators, their products sold to wholesalers, who would either resell them in the local market or carry them to the Islamic world and resell them there; many pilgrims earned their passages to Mecca and Medina by selling manuscripts on commission.

Cloth was a major trade item in Timbuktu. In the sixteenth century the richer Timbuktuans could buy Italian cloth, Chinese silks, fabrics from England and from Morocco, especially the industrial towns of the Tafilelt region. Weaving, it seems, was done mostly in outlying villages, such as Goundam. The *Tarikh al-Sudan* recounts that at its apogee Timbuktu had twenty-six clothing studios employing around thirteen hundred people. Tailoring, along with its associated craft of embroidery, was considered art and was reserved for the literate. It was usually done by Arabs, who also made wool carpets called *telisse*. Thread, needles and scissors were imported from Fez.[3]

Of course, cloth is still a major industry, though not one necessarily monopolized by the learned. Later that afternoon we went back to the market, to a tailor Halis knew, who would run up, in just a few hours, the full Tuareg regalia: the pantaloons called *kartouba*, the under-robe or undershirt called *tanakabata*, the robe itself, the *anakabak*, and the head covering and veil, the *tagelmoust*. The design of this outfit quite literally hasn't changed since biblical times, except that the traditional indigo robes of the Tuareg nomads are now generally rayon from China, and they frequently contain a small pocket for a cell phone, mobile telephony having come to the city in 2004, and by 2006 being practically ubiquitous. A few yards from the tailor the weavers were at work on their looms, also a technology unchanged for more than five hundred years. Leo Africanus's description ("Here are many shops of artificers and merchants and especially such as weave linen and cotton cloth, and hither do the Barbary merchants bring the cloth of Europe")[4] is as valid now

as it was then. Leo added, "All the women of this region except the maid servants go with their faces covered"; clearly he was there when the askia was
briefly under the baleful influence of the visiting cleric Maghili, who persuaded him to impose the *hijab* on a reluctant female population, an imposition that lasted only a brief while before the women of the city shrugged it
off, in both senses of the word.

A later visitor to the city, Shabeni, was much more prolix on the subject
of cloth and clothing, so much so that his prose rather resembles the fashion
writing that these days emanates from the Rue St.-Honoré and the emporiums of haute couture in Paris. But then Shabeni was a teenager when he first
visited Timbuktu with his father, a merchant from Tetuan in Morocco, in
1787, and had nothing much on his mind except to watch what was going
on. In any case, he clearly had an eye for style. He remained in Timbuktu for
three years and then again later for seven more. He was making a living as
a merchant in Tuat when he was captured by English pirates and taken to England, where his story was recorded.

Here's Shabeni on the fashions of the time, a fair sample of his prose.

The sultan wears a white turban of very fine muslin, the ends of which
are embroidered with gold, and brought to the front; this turban comes
from Bengala. He wears a loose white cotton shirt, with sleeves long and
wide, open at the breast; unlike that of the Arabs, it reaches to the small
of the leg; over this a caftan of red woolen cloth, of the same length;
red is generally esteemed. The shirt is made at Timbuctoo, but the caftan comes from Fas [Fez], readymade; over the caftan is worn a short
cotton waistcoat, striped white, red, and blue; the fashion or the cut of
it comes from Bengala. The sleeves of the caftan are as wide as those of
the shirt; the breast of it is fastened with buttons, in the Moorish style,
but larger. The juliba [robe] has sleeves as wide as the caftan. When he
is seated, all the sleeves are turned up over the shoulder, so that his
arms are bare, and the air is admitted to his body. Upon his turban,
on the forehead, is a ball of silk, like a pear, one of the distinctions of
royalty . . . The sultana wears a caftan, open in front from top to bottom, under this a slip of cotton like the king's, an Indian shawl over the
shoulders, which ties behind, and a silk handkerchief about her head.
Other women dress in the same manner. They wear no drawers. The
poorest women are always clothed. They never show their bosom. The

men and women wear earrings. The general expense of a woman's dress is from two ducats to thirty. Their shoes are red, and are brought from Marocco. Their arms and ankles are adorned with bracelets. The poor have them of brass; the rich, of gold. The rich ornament their heads with cowries. The poor have but one bracelet on the leg, and one on the arm; the rich, two. They also wear gold rings upon their fingers. They have no pearls or precious stones. The women do not wear veils.[5]

෴

AS WE LEFT the market and walked up the street, we passed the place where the three Bella women had been pounding grain, then followed a couple of Tuareg men striding by, and saw in a doorway one of the tailors, on his haunches, picking away at a garment, and I was pondering Halis's notion that one of the advantages of the open desert life was that everyone knew their place, and that money gave people ideas they shouldn't acquire. In that sense he would have been comfortable in the Timbuktu of the askias, when the hierarchy was more clearly regulated than it is now.

At the summit of Songhai society, obviously enough, were the noble families of the imperial court. Leo Africanus referred to "the rich king of Tombuto," but the king lived in Gao, and Leo meant the *Tombouctoukoï* the provincial governor. Even so, this official was described as exceedingly wealthy, having "many plates and sceptres of gold, some whereof weigh 1,300 pounds, and he keeps a rich and well furnished court. When he travelleth any wither he rideth upon a camel . . . Whosoever must speak to the king must fall down before his feet and then taking up earth must sprinkle it upon his own head and shoulder." In this way, at least, did the Songhai emperors adopt the customs of their Malian predecessors. "He hath always three thousand horsemen and a great number of footmen who shoot poisoned arrows attending upon him. They often have skirmishes with those that refuse to pay tribute."[6]

Leo did visit the capital at Gao in 1510 and described the court: "Between the first gate of the palace and the inner part there is a place walled round where the king decides all his subjects' disputes, and although he is most diligent in this and performs all necessary things, still he has around him many counselors and other officers, secretaries, treasurers, factors, and auditors."[7]

Shabeni, who was writing sometime after the askia dynasty, had the "sultan" of Timbuktu reporting to the Hausa, which can't be correct; from 1600 until modern times the rulers of Timbuktu gave at least nominal allegiance to the sultans of Morocco. (However, it is possible he meant Gao, since he described "Hausa" as about five days' journey by land from Timbuktu, which would be about right for Gao.) This "sultan" nevertheless had a substantial army at his disposal, armed with pikes, swords, cutlasses, sabers and muskets. "At Timbuctoo, in time of war, there are about 12,000 or 15,000 troops, 5,000 of which receive constant daily pay in time of peace, and are clothed every year. They are all infantry except a few of the king's household. Sometimes he subsidizes the friendly Arabs [Tuareg], and makes occasional presents to their chiefs; these Arabs can furnish him with from 80,000 to 40,000 men."[8]

Below the *Tombouctoukoï* and his officials were the imams of the major mosques, a privileged class of generally well-educated men, and their associated savants. As Leo Africanus put it, "here are great store of doctors, judges, priests and other learned men that are bountifully maintained at the king's costs and charges." It was from their ranks that the city's *qadi*, or judge, was chosen. The *qadi* ruled on religious as well as civil matters, and at least under Askia Mohamed and his sons, wielded immense power—the emperors themselves usually deferred to the *qadi's* decisions. In theory, the king had no power to alter the laws. In practice, he could do so, but almost always "in council"—along with senior members of his administration, who could and sometimes did overrule him.

Under the askias the city's three medieval mosques were maintained by the *qadi,* who had ultimate authority over the three imams. The work was financed by the state and by voluntary contributions from the pious.

The most famous *qadi* of the city was also rector of the University of Sankoré, as well as imam of its associated mosque. In his time (1505–83) Aqib ben Umar set in train major reconstructions on all three mosques. From 1570 on he rebuilt the sanctuary of Djingareiber and enlarged the south and west façades. In 1577 he restored the crumbling sanctuary of the Sidi Yahiya, helped by a gift of five hundred masons from Askia al-hajj Mohamed and his brother Omar Kumzaghu, governor of Tindirma. In 1578 the *qadi* went on his pilgrimage to Mecca and brought back with him a cord that matched the exact dimensions of the Kaaba. He destroyed the sanctuary of the Sankoré to rebuild it to the exact same size.

A pretty little legend has the great askia, Askia Mohamed, helping in the work. One day, passing through the town, he asked the chief mason, "How much is the work costing each day?"

"Sixty seven mithqals [335 grams] of gold," the mason replied.

The sovereign emptied his purse and ordered that a thousand palm tree beams be sent to aid in the work. His brother Omar Kumzaghu sent a further thousand palm tree beams.

The next rank down in the Songhai hierarchy was "the nobility of origin," which is to say, the noble families of the native Soninke, Wangara, Sanhaja Berbers, and Tuareg.

Standing aside from the hierarchy—or perhaps with a somewhat sliding ranking within it—were the so-called Gabibi. Salem Ould Elhadj, the learned elder who had taken up our instruction, suggested that the syllable *Ga* might mean a rural Songhai encampment, and that the term's origin was therefore taken to mean a place in which non-Muslim Songhai congregated, or "animists, still plunged into obscurity," as he put it. On the other hand, he pointed out that at least in the twentieth century many Gabibi were indeed Muslims and were said to be possessors of magic. "Another theory, and now the most common, gives them an origin after Askia Mohamed. In this theory, they are the descendants of the slaves of Askia Daoud, who gave them to the Aqit family of Sankoré, who freed them. Still others believe they were always free men and women, but merely of an inferior rank."

Whatever the truth, the Gabibi are greatly respected in modern Timbuktu. As Sidi Salem put it, "In our day they are extremely proud and honest, and keep to their word absolutely. Ask anyone in Timbuktu who a Gabibi is, and he will answer, 'a person who keeps his promises and his word of honor.'"

Below, or to the side of, the Gabibi were the ordinary people and artisans. And at the low end of the scale were slaves and captives of one sort or another, who had—and still have—many derogatory names: *hosso, wosso, haribénéga, nikoï,* and others. They were the Bella, called *haratin* by the Tuareg. "They are known," said Sidi Salem with some delicacy, "to use language of a gross nature, even to the upper classes."

တ

MUCH OF THE manufacturing in town, and many of the crafts and trades, were controlled by guild monopolies, often ethnic-based.

The masons, as already suggested, were imported artisans, often Arabs or Moors, whose guild imposed a strong monopoly on building and carpentry. When in 1325 Mansa Musa brought with him the celebrated architect es-Sahéli, he also imported specialized workers for the construction of the imperial mosque and the royal residence. These masons settled at Djingareiber after construction was finished. Others, mostly Bambara, came from Birou (Walata) in the fifteenth century and settled in the quarter of Sankoré called Birinthié-kunda, the "quarter of the people from Birou."

These two groups of masons, from Mecca and from Walata, were widely thought to be practitioners of the black arts, and all levels of society feared them. Their women were the most dangerous, keeping their magic either in a *tawo* (an instrument made of iron for dressing hair) or in a small box made of stone.

A curious folktale shows how the masons (and especially their women) were regarded in those days.

A mason called Ali Willi Misra was married to one Aldjenna, a magician of great power. They seemed to live in perfect harmony, in the Sankoré quarter, with never any discord between them. In due time, they gave birth to a young daughter, who grew up and reached marriageable age. Her mother had great hopes for her, but her father, Ali Willi Misra, had other, more macabre, intentions. One dark night he led her into the bush and there ate her. Aldjenna was of course consumed with sadness, but little by little she got over it and in the end she was able to forget what had happened. Once more they had a daughter, a girl of rare beauty. She too grew up, helped her mother with the work of the household, and soon she, too, attained the age of marriage.

One day her father said to her, "I must tell your mother that you will no longer walk on the earth of Timbuktu."

The young girl of course reported his words to her mother, who responded, as well she might, with some vehemence, "Never! You will never be eaten like your sister!"

She immediately gathered up her sources of magic, the *tawo* and the small stone box. She sacrificed a black chicken. She scrutinized the heavens for the proper moment to enter her sacred chamber. She nailed the *tawo* to the wall. She took a small portion of *banco* and a portion of *alhor* and placed them carefully into the box, which she then sealed.

It was the rainy season. Nature was at her most beautiful. The sand dunes were caressed by the northwest wind and covered with fresh young grasses. The father, Ali Willi, with his three donkeys, left town for the north to get *alhor*. A day and a night passed, but he found none. He returned home depressed, saying nothing to anyone, but his wife of course knew what had happened. The other masons in Timbuktu had the same experience. None

could find *alhor* to the north, or *banco* to the south, either near the city or farther afield. Ali Willi Misra lost weight, for his wife, who prepared the meals,
would give him nothing because he contributed nothing. He grew more and
more depressed.

He hardly slept, and when he did, he had nightmares. "I can't go on this
way," he told his wife. "I obviously can't find *alhor* to the north; I'll go across
the river, to the south, and look for *banco*." His wife said nothing.

And so he did. He searched for *banco* all over but found nothing but pure
white sand. Nature had changed; everything was different. He returned home,
even more depressed than before. The other masons were just as badly off.

The whole guild was in danger. None of them could find work. Their wives
abandoned them and went home to their families, because they couldn't stand
the constant hunger. Some of the younger masons left Timbuktu for neighboring villages. Eventually the older masons of Birinthié-kunda and Djingareiber got together with the uléma of the Sankoré district to search for the
cause of the evil. Each group worked for three days and three nights, using all
their esoteric skills and all their arcane sciences, but without any luck. All they
could find out was that the disaster had been caused by a woman.

The miserable Ali Willi Misra told his wife of the calamity. She, of course,
knew the real cause, and she finally said to him, "If you leave my second
daughter alone, and let her live, you and the other masons will find *alhor* and
banco without any difficulty."

"I'll let her live," Ali Willi Misra replied.

"You must swear, on the graves of your ancestors."

"I swear on the graves of my ancestors that I will never, never ever, eat our
second daughter. May I be condemned forever if I break the word I have now
given."

And so the magician Aldjenna took down her *tawo* from the wall, opened
the sacred box and took out the piece of *alhor*, which she threw out to the
north. Then she took out the *banco*, which she threw out to the south.

The following morning Ali Willi Misra left for the north with his three
donkeys to look for *alhor*. In the immediate vicinity of Timbuktu he found
it, stone of the very best quality. The masons who went south found *banco*
without difficulty, large quantities of it.

From that day forward Aldjenna had great renown in the company of masons. She merited respect and obedience from all. Her husband carried out all
her wishes.[9]

This weirdly charming tale is supposed to describe the lives of the masons. In fact, it and dozens more like it more plausibly deal with the power of women and their relative influence over their husbands.

Whatever the power of masons, or their women, little of what they built in those days any longer stands. No stately houses remain in the city; nor does the royal palace. Only remnants can be found. The holy person (and rich merchant) known only as Sidi Mohamed was buried in his own house, and his mausoleum still exists, but it is one of the few.

☙

OF THE OTHER crafts, shoemakers tended to be Moroccans, jewelers Moors. The jewelers were connected, logically enough, to the gold trade and usually kept residences at Djenné too. The Songhai, for their part, generally disdained most manual work and monopolized the military and agriculture. Ironworking and blacksmithing were done by the so-called *garassas* (called *haratin* in the desert oases), who as already mentioned were plausibly in their own minds of Jewish origin. In Timbuktu these *garassas* were obliged to stay outside the city proper, and set up their forges in outlying quarters. They made kitchen implements and cutlery but were also weapons masters, turning out swords, sabers, spear points, lances and other gear; their women worked with animal skin to make the handles. This is another technology that has survived; very fine hand-wrought steel swords can still be bought from itinerant Tuareg, who often importune visitors to buy one, not knowing the more recent carry-on restrictions on airlines. Hairdressers and barbers, who doubled as surgeons, were mostly Mandingo, usually Bambara. They set up their stalls in the markets, but as with masons, wealthy families employed their own. They were greatly feared, given their arcane business practices, and were said to possess powerful magic, though not as powerful as that of the masons themselves. Physicians, on the other hand, were usually Arabs or Moors, and much less respected than surgeons; do-it-yourself medicine was commonplace, and the markets were filled with baskets of medicinal herbs. The population was generally healthy, and many people lived into their eighties or even nineties. Maladies treated included fevers and agues, the dropsy, headaches and consumptions. Snake and scorpion poisonings were frequent; they were treated with emetics but were often fatal.

☙

WE WERE SITTING one evening under the stars in a blackened courtyard listening to the sounds of the city. The courtyard was in complete darkness because the power had once again gone off, and our little table was lit by
a flickering candle. The upside of the blackout was the muting of the distant
rumble of Timbuktu's ancient diesel generator. In the quiet we could hear
the faraway bleating of goats and once, at the edge of audibility, the howling
of a dog or a jackal. Close by, we heard the murmuring of passing pedestrians, a sudden crystal welling-up of laughter, the abrupt braying of a donkey
and the occasional rumbling of a 4×4. For a while a woman sang, a gentle
sound there in the black, a *fait-dodo*, soothing and slightly melancholy, but
then she was drowned out by a blaring horn as a car passed in a cloud of dust,
and after that all we could hear was the treble of a zither of Arab-pop on a
cassette-playing boombox, presumably battery driven. By African standards
Timbuktu is not very musical, though Malian music is famous throughout
Africa for its complex melodies and layered lyrics. Earlier in the evening Halis
had invited us, only half seriously, to hang out at the local dance hall nightclub. "Ladies' Night tonight," he said. "Get in half price," and it probably
would have been a bargain, but jam-packed teenagers in a blackout wasn't on
our must-do list, and we declined, as he expected us to.

Apart from radios and cassette players (there are few CDs in Timbuktu),
public music-making is now infrequent. The Tuareg out on the fringes still
make their own music, poetic and extemporaneous, plaintive to the ear, songs
of the desert, songs of life, songs of history, songs of longing, but they are
seldom heard in town. On an earlier trip I had encountered a procession
marching through the street, headed by a tambour band and a dozen or so
women singing in counterpoint, but that was an exception. That procession
was leading a group of fifty or so hapless youths, all of them thirteen and
looking a little green in their white robes, to their ritual (and very much
group) circumcisions. These coming-of-age circumcisions are still taken seriously in Timbuktu. They are still performed by members of the barbers'
guild, "but very hygienic, careful for the boys' health," as Sidi Salem put it. In
the old days, however, they got cut, *chop chop chop*, all with the same knife,
one after the other, and were obliged to thrust their newly wounded members
into the desert sand to sterilize them. I recalled with a small shudder an anecdote from a writer called Mary Anne Fitzgerald, whose book *Nomad* contains
a splendid chapter on the people of the Turkana region of Kenya; she describes the cutter afterward, cheerfully "shaking antiseptic powder onto the

cut penises as though he were salting a stew."[10] I hoped the boys were brave; Sidi Salem said that tears would bring dishonor on the miscreant's family, so none of them dared flinch or cry. In any case, the tambour band escorted them to the affair, then escorted them home again, where (as well they might) they received munificent presents and held a party that lasted all night.

Female "circumcision" still exists, but girls are no longer routinely so mutilated in Timbuktu or much of the Sahel, although there are depressing signs that the practice is reviving, and the Fulani have never really abandoned it, considering uncircumcised women *bilakoro*, a disgrace, filthy and much too "emotional."

Music and dance were more common under the peaceful reign of the askias than they are now, Sidi Salem said. According to Leo Africanus, "the inhabitants [of Timbuktu] are people of a gentle and peaceful disposition and spend a great part of the night in singing and dancing through all the streets of the city." He went on to say, without missing a breath—hewing to a strict narrative line wasn't Leo's long suit—that "they keep great store of men and women slaves and their town is much in danger of fire. Without the suburbs there are no gardens nor orchards at all."[11]

Both the *Tarikh*s report on the prevalence of music and dance at the time. "The afternoons and evenings after work were an occasion for joyful celebration," the *Tarikh al-Sudan* points out, the music being made mostly by women on tom-toms, tambourines and three-stringed lyres. Military marches could be heard, music to celebrate great victories, religious chants, panegyrics to the great, amorous idylls, as well as songs on moral and philosophical subjects. Ahmed Baba, more piously, recorded the passion for music among "certain doctors of Timbuktu"; one of them, his mentor, the famous Mohamed Baghayogho (Muhammad ben Mahmud ben Abi Bakr al-Wangari al-Tinbuktu *dit* Baghayogho), "would listen to the violin which is his sole pleasure, though it doesn't prevent him from reading the Holy Qur'an and adoring God."[12] Music and popular dance were a part of all social life and its attendant ceremonies, especially baptisms, marriages and circumcisions, but also the arrival of caravans, or the docking of a large pirogue at Kabara. To an extent, this is still true. Halis's cousin Ahmed had once invited me to a family wedding in Timbuktu. I arrived too late, after the ceremony was over, but I remember that the night had been absolutely clear and the stars blazing hot in the desert sky; the tambours were already out, and the dancing had begun, formal but wild, intricate but improvised, every movement pregnant with symbolism, the music poignant and piercing, unchanged over the many centuries.

Some of the dances the *Tarikh*s describe as "vulgar," without specifying how vulgar or in what way. Apparently the slaves, the *hossos*, were wont to perform such a dance for the nobles to extract money from them, whether because the nobles liked the dance or were trying to get them to desist is not recorded. Shabeni noticed that too. Remarking on the people's love of music, "of which they have twenty four different sorts," he added, "They have dances of different kinds, some of which are very indecent."

Timbuktu at play wasn't always genteel. There was no theater, or set-piece musical concerts, "and they have no cards, but they play at chess and draughts, and are very expert at those games; [but] they have tumblers, jugglers, and ventriloquists, whose voice appears to come from under the armpits."[13]

Félix Dubois reprints a story told to him by a Timbuktu merchant in the time of the French.

> The people . . . liked to live well. They taught their slaves the art of preparing very elaborate and varied dishes, pastries, and sweets; so much incense was burned and attar of roses was sprinkled that you were seized with headache on the doorstep . . . The most costly fetes were those given to the women. The people from Djenné and Bamako rivaled the Arabs, but the people from Tuat were the most extravagant. On the other hand the Mossi did not squander their money in this fashion . . . Those who had mistresses gave feasts that lasted many hours, much intoxicating liquid was consumed and the men became as drunk as the idolatrous Bambaras. Musicians were sent for, dancing began and was prolonged throughout the night. Men would spend two or three hundred gold pieces disputing a mistress with a rival. A merchant . . . is said to have made his lady a present of five hundred blocks of salt. This man lived near the mosque, and having passed the night in feasting he wished to sleep during the day and had the audacity to say to the muezzin . . . "I am very tired, your voice will disturb me, if I do not hear you throughout the day I will make a rich offering to the mosque." . . . Many who arrived with a fortune went home ruined.[14]

Shabeni's recollections include a random potpourri of unrelated but occasionally tantalizing information. There was neither palm wine nor any fermented liquor, but "when [the Timbuktuans] wish to be exhilarated after dinner, they provide a plant of an intoxicating quality called *el hashisha*, esteemed for the extraordinary and pleasing voluptuous vacuity of mind which it produces on those who smoke it: unlike the intoxication from wine, a fascinating stupor pervades the mind, and the dreams are agreeable. *Kief* is the flower and seeds of the plant, of which they take a handful before a draught of water." Almost everyone was somewhat stained with henna, he observed, turning them a lurid orange, not so much for decoration but to allay the violence of perspiration in the part to which it is applied. "[Also] they frequently bathe the whole body, their smell would otherwise be offensive; they use towels brought from India." The Arabs also used henna to tattoo their hands and arms, but not the common people, who were "real Negroes; they have a slight mark on the face, sloping from the eye; the Foulans [Fulani] have a horizontal mark; the Bambara has a wide gash from the forehead to the chin."[15]

ↅ

FROM THE EARLIEST days, travelers had remarked on the freewheeling way of Timbuktu's women, and their lack of what Halis would call *pudeur*, traits they shared with Tuareg and Berbers everywhere. The photographer Angela Fisher had once remarked on "the strange wild beauty of the Tuareg women, unveiled and free," with their often startling blue eyes and fair skin burnished to old ivory by the Saharan sun, and their bold ways.[16] Travelers as far back as Ibn Battuta were fascinated—and occasionally repelled—by their extraordinary freedom. Of all the many things Battuta reported about the people of Mali and its cities, including Timbuktu, none had riveted him more than their famously relaxed view of human relations, their tolerance of unusual behavior. Of course, he didn't call it tolerance but laxity, and a scandalously immoral laxity at that. He was baffled at the coexistence of piousness and what he saw as sin.

Late in his stay, he made notes, headlining them carefully, as he always did.

Account of what I found good and what I found bad in the conduct of the blacks: Among their good practices are their avoidance of injustice; there is no people more averse to it and their sultan does not allow anyone to practice it in any measure; the universal security in their country, for neither the traveler nor the resident there has to fear thieves or bandits; they did not interfere with the property of white men [Arabs] who die in their country, even if it amounts to vast sums; they just leave it in the hands of a trustworthy white man until whoever is entitled to it takes possession of it. Their punctiliousness in praying, their perseverance in joining the congregation and in compelling their children to do so; if a man does not come early to the mosque he will not find a place to pray because of the dense crowd . . .

Among their bad practices are that the women servants, slave girls and young daughters appear naked before people, exposing their genitals. I used to see many like this in Ramadan, for it is customary for the *fararis* to break their fast in the sultan's palace, where their food is brought to them by 20 or more slave girls, who are naked. Women who come before the sultan are naked and unveiled, and so are his daughters. On the night of the 27th of Ramadan I have seen about a hundred naked slave girls come out of his palace with food; with them were two daughters of the sultan with full breasts and they too had no veil. They put dust and ashes on their heads as a matter of good manners. Many of them eat carrion, dogs and donkeys.

His fastidiousness spilled over into prudishness, and he was sometimes appalled at the lax morals he found, allowed by the idiosyncratic Islam practiced by the Tuareg and the people of Mali. The men, he wrote, apparently are immune to jealousy.

The women have no shame before men and do not veil themselves, yet they are punctilious about their prayers. Anyone who wants to take a wife among them does so, but they do not travel with their husbands and even if one of them wished to her family would prevent her. Women there have friends or companions among men outside the prohibited degrees for marriage and in the same way men have women friends in the same category. A man goes into his house, finds his wife there with her man friend, and does not disapprove. One day I called upon the *qadi* [this was at Walata]. After he had given me permission to enter, I found him with a young and exceptionally beautiful woman. When I saw her I hesitated and was going to go back, but she laughed at me and showed no embarrassment. The *qadi* said to me, why are you turning back? She is my friend. I was astonished at them, for he was a jurist and a hajj.

On another occasion he called on Mohamed al-Massufi, in whose company he had traveled to Mali, and found him sitting on a rug. In the middle of the room was a canopied couch and upon it a woman with a man, sitting and talking together.

> I said to him, who is this woman? He said, she is my wife. I said, what about the man who is with her? He said, he is her friend. I said, are you happy about this, you who have lived in our country and know the content of the religious law? He said, the companionship of woman and men among us is a good thing and an agreeable practice, which causes no suspicion; they are not like the women of your country. I was astonished at his silliness. I left him and did not visit him again. Afterwards he invited me a number of times but I did not accept.[17]

Shabeni had noticed the same thing, though not with Battuta's obvious (or professed) distaste. "Men and women mix in society, and visit together," he noted, in an approving tone. He observed that rape was exceedingly rare and punishable by death. Seduction and/or adultery, on the other hand, was in no way an offense under the law and was not grounds for divorce. Abusive language was, but not adultery. The law was quite specific: "A woman's flesh is her own; she may do with it what she pleases." Prostitutes were common— and honored. Venereal diseases were apparently unknown. A man could have only one wife, but as many concubines as he could afford. If on his death the concubine had at least two children, she became a free woman and was entitled to inherit property; otherwise she remained a slave. A husband was not permitted to divest his wife of her entitlement.[18]

Otherwise, Shabeni paid little attention to the common folk. He was effusive, though, at the notion of hunting with the *Tombouctoukoï* who frequently went on three- or four-day hunting expeditions, and anyone who could afford a horse was free to go along. Anything killed was split between strangers and others present; animals taken alive were reserved for the king. "He has 500 or 600 horses . . . He frequently hunts the antelope, wild ass, ostrich, and the wild cow of Africa. The ostriches, like storks, place sentinels upon the watch: thirty yards are reckoned a distance for a secure shot with the bow. The king always shoots on horseback, as do many of his courtiers. The wild ass is very fleet, and when closely pursued kicks back the earth and sand in the eyes of his pursuers. They have the finest greyhounds in the world, with which they hunt only the antelope for the dogs are not able to overtake the ostrich. There are no lions, tigers, or wild boars near Timbuctoo."[19]

Just as the forests are gone today, and much of the standing water, so too have the animals. No game is found anywhere near Timbuktu anymore. Only the hippos in the Niger, wallowing and bellowing, the sole survivors of what once was.

⟡

SOME OF THE girls and boys winding home from school at the end of the morning carried small satchels, as children do elsewhere. Others carried nothing, having nothing. A few carried smooth wooden boards about eight inches wide by sixteen long, some of them covered with Arabic script. I had seen these unusual copybooks before. Some years earlier, in Djenné, I had come across two Fulani boys, about ten years old, sitting on a mud ledge outside a doorway, in a small alleyway. I still have a photo of the scene: a couple of other children were walking in the alley at the time, one of them a small girl balancing a basket of boxes on her head. A woman sat on a chair, her orange dress a startling contrast to the dun-colored street and houses. Beside her on the ground were two large bowls of fresh peanut butter for sale. The two Fulani boys had across their knees these same wooden boards, and each had a small copybook. They were copying Qur'anic texts onto the wood, using an ink their class had made that morning. These were the school's star pupils, sent outside for independent practice of their art. I heard chanting and stuck my head through the doorway to hear more clearly. Inside a small room about twenty other children were sitting on the floor. At the head of the class was a graybeard, their teacher, leading them in their lessons. They were learning the sacred texts, as their fathers had before them. I leaned briefly against the doorway, feeling the tough-textured wood of the frame, scarred and pitted from the centuries. This school had been here, in continuous existence in this same building, since the twelfth century; for almost a thousand years, students had passed through this modest portal to study the esoterica of Islam and the mysteries of numbers.

In Timbuktu, all through the golden years of the mansas and the hundred-year reign of the askias, there were similar scenes. The very prosperity of the city meant that small children did not have to be put out to work; the rulers, pious Muslims themselves, encouraged such study. As al-Sa'adi said in his *Tarikh*, rather optimistically: "Timbuktu was never seduced by the worship of idols. None of its people strayed from the true path."[20] Studying Arabic had two benefits. The first was to better understand the words of the Qur'an and the sayings of the prophet; then as now it was believed that Muhammad could not be properly understood except in his own language—mysteries are encoded in the syllables and very alphabet, it seems. The second reason was commercial; their world of trade was conducted in Arabic, analogous to English in the modern world. And so every educable child, which meant every child not born into slavery, took part in Arabic and Qur'anic studies. Most of the pupils were boys. Girls were educated too, in their own schools, but not as universally as boys. Schools for both sexes were seldom in dedicated buildings but could be anywhere: in a mosque, at the home of the master, out in the open, against a wall somewhere. Teachers were supposed to be men (always men, never women) of irreproachable character, a clear voice, having memorized all 114 chapters of the Qur'an. They were not allowed to hold other occupations but had to dedicate their lives to education. They were paid by the parents of the children and sometimes by the mosques. Every Thursday at noon, when preparations began for the following day of prayers, each pupil brought a gift, either money or goods. At each Muslim festival, another gift was brought. And again every time a pupil finished a section of the Qur'an. A good teacher could do well financially. A sixteenth-century *Tombouctoukoï*, Sheikh Mohamed ben Ahmed, once visited the celebrated school of Ali Zakaria and reported that on that day the teacher had received 1,725 cowry shells from his pupils.

Teachers were always more important than schools. No one ever boasted *where* they had studied, only *with whom* they had studied. A respected teacher took on other roles, presiding over marriages, baptisms and funerals. Teachers were the learned elders of the community; they represented the public and regulated public affairs. When in need, these uléma could marshal considerable resources and help to mobilize the population.[21]

If a pupil achieved mastery of the Qur'an, which meant knowing all 114 chapters, these gifts could be much more substantial: money, fine clothes, livestock or slabs of salt.

The wealthy made a substantial ritual out of this graduation. The graduate donned a white robe, a shirt and a pair of shoes, mounted a white horse and headed to the school preceded by a band of singers and musicians. They paused along the way at the mausoleums of the principal saints. It finished with a grand fête, paid for by the parents. The boys, though not the girls, were also given presents: money, salt, a house or gold. The gold was kept in trust until the boy married, then it was used to finance his first business trip, either to Djenné or to Taoudenni.

Literacy was the point, and the curriculum was simple. So was the equipment: this wooden board, made of date palm wood, and locally made ink, the same recipe as that still used—a mix of water, ground horsehair, gum Arabic and charcoal. The ink could be erased with water. Then pens were stalks or twigs sharpened to an oblique angle. The only text was the Qur'an. Education began at the age of five.

This First Degree—mastery of Arabic, and the ability to read—was all many pupils received. The Second Degree consisted of language studies, grammar, poetry and literature. There was no Third Degree, but those who could and would went on studying, in a collection of informal schools that in the end agglomerated into the University of Sankoré. They would gather around well-known scholars or theologians, studying questions of law or of social order. Ahmed Baba, for instance, concerned himself with the rights and role of women, questions of Islamic law, justice and the role of the secular under Islam. Others taught algebra and arithmetic, still others astronomy, advanced grammar, theology, history and prophetic traditions. Other courses included the sayings of the prophet, philosophy, medicine, physics and chemistry.

The daily routine of these savants kept them busy. Ahmed Baba recounts the life of Mohamed Baghayogho: "In the first hours of the day, he applied himself to study, until six in the morning; then he went to the mosque for the prayer of Duhà; after that, he worked in the office of the *qadi* for the affairs of his clients, and to render judgments; after the midday prayers, Zuhur, he studied in his house until three, then went to the Mosque for the prayers of Asr; then he taught at his local academy until sundown; then after sunset he finished his day at the mosque for another series of lessons; then he entered his own house at nine."[22] Like many others of his kind, he also found time for several trips to Cairo, Mecca and Medina.

❧

THE INSTITUTION KNOWN as the University of Sankoré was founded, according to the legends, by a group of Berber savants who immigrated to Timbuktu and installed themselves in the northern suburbs that came to be called Sankoré—a corruption of the Songhai words *sane koraï*, or "white master," since the Berbers were widely regarded as white people. A second group of scholars came to the city under the Tuareg, between 1433 and 1468, before the askias; as already recounted, it was at this point that the two great families, the Aqit and the Anda Ag-Mohamed, came to the city. A third great wave of intellectuals came to Sankoré under the first of the askias, primarily from Tichitt, Takkeda, Tuat, Djenné, and Masina, and yet another under Askia Daoud, a generation later. Contacts were established with the great minds of the Islamic world, such as es-Sayouti of Cairo (who had given Askia al-hajj Mohamed advice on how to govern his country in a Muslim way). Sankoré, though less a real university than an assembly of small schools, became a sister institution to the universities in Cairo, Cordoba, Fez and Damascus. Studies were primarily theology, Arabic, Aristotelian logic and rhetoric, astronomy, geography and history. A typical degree course would consist of two kinds of studies. The first was itself divided into several strands: Qur'anic exegesis, traditions of the prophet (the *hadith*), jurisprudence (*fiqh*) and the sources of the law (*usul*). The second category consisted of grammar, literary style, logic and spoken rhetoric. Optional were astronomy, history, mathematics and medicine.

☙

CLASSES ARE STILL held in and around Sankoré, and there is still schooling for the first few years here and there in town, but the glory days are gone. The academically minded now make their way to the secular or religious schools in Bamako; the extra-pious are instructed at the madrasas of the newer imams. Here and there, young boys and girls still inscribe their Arabic letters on boards of date palm, and it matters, because it keeps the traditions flickering. Alas, it matters now in no other way.

CHAPTER FIFTEEN

❧

The Second Golden Age and the Intellectual Tradition

THE DIRECTOR OF the Ahmed Baba Center (more properly the Institut des Hautes Etudes et de Recherche Islamique—Ahmed Baba) received us formally in his office, sitting behind a huge desk and apparently barricaded in by an enormous briefcase parked on the desktop. Sidi Mohamed Ould Youbba, the director general, is himself a very large man, formidable of girth, grave of mien, speaking slowly for our benefit in unaccented French. (He speaks several languages: Tamashek to Halis, Bambara to a casual drop-in, Arabic to his chief conservator, French to us.) His office is down an open-air corridor from the main conservation laboratories and oddly bare for the custodian of such treasures as the center possesses; apart from a cheap schoolroom map Scotch-taped to one wall and two locked wooden cabinets (presumably housing some of the treasures themselves), the walls are bare, painted a utilitarian bureaucratic gray.

But after the formal part of the interview was over, he took us next door to the office of Djibril Doucouré, chief of the conservation and restoration division, where he kicked off his sandals, hauled his robe up to his knees and plunked his bare feet on his colleague's desk. The boring part over, he could now relax and chat about his life's consuming passion, the extraordinary intellectual resources of Timbuktu, left over from the glory days. This was in any case a much more agreeable office to hold such a conversation; shelves lining every wall, each jammed with books and piles of manuscripts, some of the more precious behind glass doors.

The center was founded around 1968 or 1970, he wasn't sure of the exact date, when UNESCO agreed to fund Mali's notion that what Africa needed was a center for the study of precolonial African history, and a place that scholars could use to research North Africa and West African history in particular, building on the long tradition of scholarship in Timbuktu. Its founding director, Mahmoud Zouber, spoke six languages and wrote his dissertation on Ahmed Baba while at the Sorbonne.

All this, Sidi Mohamed said, was part of an overarching ambition to construct a proper history of black Africa, one that recognized colonialism but was not imprisoned by it, a history that could transcend the sterile intellectual debates so common in the academic literature. It's a notion that caught the attention of eminent people at the other end of Africa, especially Nelson Mandela and his successor, Thabo Mbeki. On a state visit to Mali, Mbeki was taken on a tour of Timbuktu's intellectual resources and was astonished. He agreed at once to help, and South Africa's Timbuktu Project, run out of the University of Cape Town and the National Archives in Pretoria, is part of the result. The real benefit, however, is that South African money is building the center a properly air-conditioned home in which to do its work. The Ford Foundation helps with the annual budget, which is around 500 million francs a year, a little over one million U.S. dollars. The Timbuktu Project is also helping to pay the cost, and so is the University of Oslo. The Andrew Mellon Foundation helped finance the building itself.

"It is urgent," the director said, "to conserve what we have." Just as no one knows how many manuscripts and books still exist in Timbuktu and its environs, so no one knows how many have been lost or stolen. Thousands went missing in the colonial era, many ending up in museums in Britain, France and the United States, others in the hands of private collectors. Mali is so poor that black marketers still troll the population buying up family archives, usually for trivial amounts of money, and selling them abroad. Other documents simply molder away in homes across the city. The center now has some 21,000 manuscripts in its collection, dating back to the early twelfth century. The Mamma Haïdara Library has another 12,000 to 14,000. The extraordinary Kati collection has yet another 7,000 or so, and there are thousands more in private hands, still owned by the Timbuktu families that created or bought them so many hundreds of years ago. Estimates of the total reservoir in the region range from a further 30,000 to an extravagant 300,000. It's possible, of course, that there are even more: one estimate has asserted that there are over a million manuscripts still in the Sahel, in collections from Mauritania to Nigeria.

The best known of the surviving Timbuktu collections are those of the Ahmed Baba Center, the Mamma Haïdara Library, which we had already seen, the Fondo Kati, or Kati Library, the al-Wangari Library, and the Mohamed Tahar Library. The es-Sayouti family (the oldest brother, Abderrahmane, is imam of Djingareiber) also has a closet full of perhaps 2,500 ancient texts, including an extraordinary astronomical and optical treatise dating back to the 1300s, which contains drawings of the motions of the planets in red and black inks. (By way of comparison, Copernicus did his major work early in the 1500s.)

Timbuktu was not the only city in the Sahel to have extensive libraries; it shared its traditions of learning with dozens of other communities across the southern fringe of the desert. And it was a part of the larger Islamic world too. It is a truism that extensive literary collections were a part of Islam from the beginning, unlike Christianity, where writing was generally reserved for a small cadre of the scholarly, a phenomenon encouraged by the hierarchical nature of the Church of Constantine. Muhammad's famous dictum that the pious should "seek knowledge, even as far away as China," always translated in Islam as a general support for learning and education. "Islamic society fostered such a respect for book learning and scholarship that rulers and the wealthy opened their doors to the learned and lavished large sums of money on them. Caliphs, governors, courtiers, gentlemen-scholars and physicians sponsored new books as well as the translation of Christian and Jewish works written in Syriac or Greek . . . People wrote books simply because they wanted to, or because patrons and rulers suggested they do so. Writers expected to be paid with honors, presents and often cash. Others, such as secretaries or judges in state chanceries or offices, wrote books in their spare time."[1]

Muslim scholars advanced every field of science: mathematics, astronomy, medicine, optics and philosophy. "Al-Razi's and al-Khwarizimi's seminal work in the 9th and 10th centuries laid the foundation for modern clinical medicine and mathematics (the word algorithm derives from the name al-Khwarizimi)."[2]

The numbers of books mentioned are so huge that their accuracy has often been doubted. Mary Minicka, a book and document conservator at the South African parliament, cites several extravagant cases: The historian al-Waqidi, who died in 823, was said to have left six hundred trunks of books on his death, each requiring two men to hoist it. The essayist al-Jahiz was

notoriously crushed to death under a cascade of his books in 868. A nameless
tenth-century courtier apparently declined a new post on account of the difficulty of moving his library, which is said to have included four hundred
camel loads of books for the theology titles alone. By contrast, the largest-
known library in Christendom at the time was at the Sorbonne, which held a
total of 2,066 titles.

Even so, books weren't always treated with the greatest respect in Islam,
especially by the young and the careless. The noted scholar and educator ibn
Jamaa, a thirteenth-century imam, once cried the classic librarian's lament, is-
suing an irritated denunciation of his useless students who, instead of "keeping a book up the sleeve, thereby bringing wisdom to the heart," used their
books as pillows, as fans, or to squash bedbugs.[3]

☙

IN THE NORMAL way of libraries everywhere, the Ahmed Baba Center acquires its inventory through bequest or purchase. A fair amount of time
is spent in persuading families in small villages to part with their collections,
which they regard with some justification as family heritage. The director told
us a story, which we had already heard from Sidi Haïdara, of a widow in the
little town of Rharrous who had refused to sell her manuscripts for money
but was persuaded to part with them for two cows, on the grounds that cows
appreciated in value by multiplying, unlike cash. This little transaction was
in fact done by Abdel Kader Haïdara himself, who had helped the center get
going by doing some prospecting on its behalf (before deciding to set up his
own library).

No complete catalog of these various holdings has been achieved, though
an Arabic text is almost finished, and a list of the first nine thousand items
has been published by the al-Furqan Islamic Heritage Foundation, in London. "First we want to preserve them, then to catalog them, then, if possible,
to digitize them and make them available to scholars for translation or other
purposes. But digitization is difficult and expensive, and the bright light it
needs is destructive of old papers," Sidi Mohamed told us. By 2005 the
Ahmed Baba Center had half a dozen trainees generating digital images of important manuscripts and assembling them into a searchable database, and had
completed almost nine hundred of the center's most important holdings. The
Mellon Foundation, through a grant to a company called Aluka, is helping
fund the digitization and cataloging. "Putting those documents on flatbed

scanners can be destructive," says Aluka's Rahim Rajan. "So we're using pho-
tography. It's not so much the bright light—Timbuktu's light after all is
bright enough—but the laying them flat that causes the damage."

The content of these volumes is partly literary (including religious tracts
and commentaries) and partly purely documentary, records of commercial
transactions and legal documents. Hundreds are fatwas—legal opinions of
scholars or jurists. Hunwick, who has combed through thousands of these
manuscripts, says they deal with a wide array of topics, most of them advice
to the pious on their daily lives. He found, for example, fatwas on topics like
"On dwelling with the Christians." Others were considered opinions on what
to do about lost camels, on ritual purity, on a wife's rejection of her husband's
authority, on a slave who committed a crime against a free boy, on the pur-
chasing of plundered goods, on the division of inheritance, on cutting down
trees to feed goats, on a man and woman who befriended each other, claiming that they were related through milk kinship, on a married couple who
were told after many years of marriage that they were related through milk
kinship, on a man who married a woman without anyone telling him she was
within the prohibited degrees of marriage and on the failure of women to observe *hijab*.

Not all are serious-minded; food and recipe writing was popular in the
city, and dozens of examples survive.

Virtually none of these manuscripts have been translated into other languages, the director said, though a few exist in French. They are generally in
Arabic script, though many used the script to record ideas in languages such
as Tamashek, Bambara, Fulani and Songhai. Most were produced in Timbuktu itself and deal with the long history of the Mande empires of Ghana
and Mali, and the whole history of the Sahel, though there are a sprinkling
from Andalusia, Turkey and Saudi Arabia.

Many of the scholars who settled in Timbuktu under the askias brought
their libraries with them and purchased more hand-copied books from North
Africa and Egypt. There was a significant trade in books. Leo Africanus, when
he was there, noted "the numerous judges, scholars and imams, all well paid
by the king, who shows great respect to men of learning," and added, "Many
manuscript books coming from Barbary are sold. Such sales are more profitable than any other goods."[4] It was the local production industry, however,
that enabled Timbuktu scholars to build up their own libraries. Askia Mohamed often funded scholars by gifts of cash and kind, and once presented

two complete copies of the Qur'an to the Djingareiber mosque; there are stories that his son, Askia Daoud, actually funded public libraries, but the evidence for this is thin.

☙

"WE NAMED THE center after Ahmed Baba," Sidi Mohamed was saying, "because he was the most famous Timbuktu scholar of them all." As already recounted his personal library contained more than sixteen hundred books and manuscripts. (He himself said that his library was actually the smallest in his family, the celebrated Aqits, the eminent scholarly family that provided the city with *qadis* throughout the sixteenth century.) He also had written an extensive history of the region, alas now lost, the only fragments to survive in the writings of Heinrich Barth, who was able to scribble notes from a copy he saw in Timbuktu in the 1840s. Baba had written dozens of books, many of them during his long Moroccan exile, on diverse subjects such as Islamic law, history, medicine, natural history, science and politics.

He clearly admired piety, but he also admired bookishness. Baba wrote about his mentor and teacher, Mohamed Baghayogho, in a biographical dictionary, one of his most famous works of which only fragments still survive, calling him "a pious and ascetic man of God, a man given by nature to goodness and benign intent, guileless, and naturally disposed to goodness, believing in people to such an extent that all men were virtually equal in his sight, so well did he think of them and absolve them of wrongdoing." And he added a note about Baghayogho's bookish habits: "He was free with his own library, lending most rare and precious books in all fields without asking for them back again, no matter what discipline they were in. Thus it was that he lost a [large] portion of his books—may God shower His beneficence upon him for that! Sometimes a student would come to his door asking for a book, and he would give it to him without even knowing who the student was. In this matter he was truly astonishing, doing this for the sake of God Most High, despite his love for books and [his zeal in] acquiring them, whether by purchase or copying. One day I came to him asking for books on grammar, and he hunted through his library and brought me everything he could find on the subject."[5]

John Hunwick suggests that the kind of books that would have been found in Baghayogho's library, as in Ahmed Baba's own, would have included the texts that were to be taught to his students: commentaries on the

Qur'an, books of hadith, theological treatises in the Sunni tradition, works of jurisprudence and works on Arabic grammar. "But Timbuktu scholarship went beyond the teaching of basic texts. We know, for example, that Ahmed Baba had access to the great *History* of Ibn Khaldun, a work which he quotes from in one of his writings."[6]

"Do you have anything by Ahmed Baba himself here?" I asked.

Sidi Doucouré reached into a glass-fronted cabinet and withdrew a vellum folder, placing it carefully on his desk. "This is a copy of a manuscript by Ibn Khallikan, copied by Ahmed Baba in his own hand in Marrakech, in 1599," he said.

"What of his own writings? Anything that he actually composed himself?"

He shook his head. Ahmed Baba was the city's most illustrious scholar, but not a single volume of his writings has survived, except as fragments or as quotations in the works of others. We know of his eminence only because so many other scholars said it was so.

"What do you consider your most precious possession?" I asked.

He wouldn't, or couldn't, say, but motioned us down the hall to the conservation lab. In a small glass case a number of other manuscripts were on display: a treatise on traditional medicine dating to 1658; a glorious illustrated and gilded Qur'an dating to 1241; a compilation of Islamic laws from 1204; and a biography of the prophet illustrated and with marginal notes by its owner, bought at Arawan for 24 grams of gold (one fourth of a mithqual) and brought to Timbuktu. Such importation wasn't unique, as I later discovered. The Kati Library has a copy of an eleventh-century manuscript by the Moroccan scholar Qadi Iyad, undated, but with a marginal note that says it was purchased in Tuat in 1468 by a man emigrating from Toledo in Spain to Timbuktu. A note says, "I bought this illuminated book . . . from its first owner Mohamed ben Umar in a legally valid sale for the sum of 45 mithqals of gold in cash paid in its entirety to the one from whom it was purchased." The purchaser was the elder Mahmoud Kati.[7] Also in the glass case were a letter from the *qadi* of Timbuktu, Ahmed al-Bakay, to the king of Masina; an astronomical text by Ahmad al-Biruni (who is most famous in Timbuktu as the author of the much-quoted aphorism "that Allah is all-powerful does not justify our ignorance"); and a sixteenth-century exposition of the medical writing of the Iranian physician and philosopher Abu Ali al-Hussain ibn Abdullah ibn Sina, known in the West as Avicenna, who lived in Bukhara from 980 to 1037. Ibn Sina's monumental contribution to medical knowledge (his

Qanun fi al-Tibb, or Canon, ran to over a million words) included the first description of meningitis and significant contributions to anatomy, gynecology and the human circulatory system; the Ahmed Baba's manuscript is a gloss, or digest, of the great work.

We were back in Djibril Doucouré's office as school let out next door, and a procession of small children came into the room, one after the other, each receiving a small biscuit from a stash kept in his drawer. While he was busy with this work ("The children are sometimes hungry," he said later, by way of explanation), I thought of another medical treatise written by another of Timbuktu's eminences, the sixteenth-century scholar Sheikh Sidi Mahmoud ben Umar, *qadi* of the city, who was born in 1463 and lived to 1548. He was buried in the west end, not far from the lycée named for Mahaman Alassan Haïdara. He was an eminent man of letters still much venerated in the city; his early biographers called him a saint and attributed many miracles to his piety. His major book, *The Treatment of Maladies Interior and Exterior of the Human Body,* was recently translated by Salem Ould Elhadj and his colleague Mahmoud Mohamed Dédeou *dit* Hamou, and Sidi Salem gave us a copy. The purpose of his translation into French, he said, was to help focus attention on this work, "which reinforces the riches not yet explored by Malian medical science."

⁊⁊

FOR THE NEXT hour or so we hung around the conservation labs. About ten people were working at various tasks, all of them men. A few years ago a workshop had been held in Bamako to train local artisans in the arts. Stephanie Diakité, a consultant hired by the Ford Foundation, said many of them were descendants of the gilders and binders who worked on the originals generations ago. One trainee had found in a box inherited from his ancestors tools he was unable to identify; Diakité recognized them as tools for bookbinding and showed the trainee how to use them. "These are artisans of many generations standing, but in many cases the skills have been lost," she said. "It's fascinating to see them make those connections again.[8]

Later the trainees had been sent variously to South Africa—Thabo Mbeki again—and to China—the Chinese paying careful attention to Africa these days; Mali has no oil, yet, but one never knows . . . Mostly the work consists of painstakingly attaching the ancient documents to an acid-free linen backing, then mounting them in neatly made cardboard folders. The trickiest part is to make both sides of a double-sided document visible. One of the conservators, a man who had been in both China and South Africa for training, explained a Chinese-invented technique of sandwiching a document between two thin sheets of what looked like plastic but were apparently organic, perhaps a form of rice paper. The finished products are beautiful in their way, little boxes intricate in a rather Chinese fashion, which stack neatly in cabinets.

Mary Minicka spent some time in Timbuktu examining the procedures used there. She and her colleagues were able to change some well-meaning conservation habits that were making things worse rather than better, such as the careful use of white gloves by the staff while they were handling documents. (These gloves were often not very clean, but worse, they had picked up sand and grit over time and acted rather as fine sandpaper would, abrading the document surfaces.) She had them wash their hands frequently instead.

One of the conservators showed us a manuscript he had finished, perhaps a hundred pages neatly assembled in a maroon box. He pointed to a page at the start. At the bottom was a colophon, a kind of early logo, denoting the copyist. "See here," he said, "that shows which workshop produced this book. Not just the author, but the transcriber too, and also the person who verified that it was correct." A kind of early copy editor, in fact, and necessary, for accuracy was part of the contract. Often these colophons went even further, naming the dates of copying, from whom the paper was purchased and its price, and the fees paid the copyists and verifiers. John Hunwick reports seeing a colophon in Morocco, on an Arabic dictionary produced in Timbuktu, that gave the copyist's fee as 1 mithqal of gold per volume; a copyist would be expected to produce nine folios, or about 170 lines of text, per day. It was a full-time job.

The Timbuktu studios only rarely made their own paper. In the early centuries paper was imported from central Asia; in later times, from Europe. This sometimes caused curious problems. As Mary Minicka put it, "Muslims were often troubled about using paper produced by non-Muslims. Some papers even bore images in watermarks that they found objectionable, such as crosses, or representations of living beings." In the end, their misgivings were neatly finessed by a jurist in the northern city of Tlemcen, Abu Abdullah ibn Marzuq, who delivered a fatwa, a decision, called *Decision on the Permissibility of Writing on Paper Made by Christians.* His decision framed the question in terms of ritual purity and argued that writing in Arabic over the idolatrous designs rendered them invisible; therefore, in writing God's name and message on such papers the copyist replaced falsehood with truth, a situation analogous to transforming a Christian church into a Mosque.[9]

Some of the early books were simply copied by the person who wanted to own them, from manuscripts borrowed from others. Ahmed Baba himself did this several times. Others were produced in guild shops, mostly clustered around the Sankoré mosque, where the university was, which employed leatherworkers, bookbinders, gilders, and others. I thought back to the closet in which the Mamma Haïdara Library was currently resting. Most of these documents were parchment or heavy paper imported from or through Morocco too, but some of it, Sidi Haïdara had said, was produced in the city itself.

During our meeting I had wondered if custody of this treasure wasn't something of a burden. He had inherited the collection from his father, Mamma Haïdara himself, when he was only seventeen, and looking after it was turning into a lifetime's work. He is helped by South Africa, by the Ford and Andrew Mellon foundations, and the Smithsonian Institution brought a small collection of twenty-three manuscripts to Washington, D.C., for an exhibit, but most of the responsibility is his alone. I already knew that others were most definitely feeling the weight of their responsibility. The es-Sayouti family, for example—six brothers, ranging in age each side of fifty, have been left the family's library by their ailing father. Over the centuries, some of the artifacts have been damaged by fire, or insects, others by humidity in the wet season. Alpha Sané es-Sayouti, who makes his living as an engineer, admits it is not easy. "These manuscripts are very expensive for the family," he says. "But we fear the judgment of our sons and grandsons if we let them disappear." He added, "When we speak, the words disappear. But what is written should remain for all time."[10]

Sidi Haïdara had told us, just before we left his house, that he and a few other local collectors were trying to shed the burden somewhat. Rather than assembling everything into two or three large institutions, they wanted to develop a network of smaller collectors whose owners would keep custody but share resources and speak collectively. By 2005 this Association for the Safekeeping of Ancient Manuscripts included a few more than twenty private collections in Timbuktu.

Still, he denied it was an imposition, and indeed his eyes lit up when he talked about some of the collection's treasures. "Their range is so wide! Not just the Qur'an and the hadiths. Those, of course, but manuscripts on medicine, mathematics, astronomy, geography. Legends, poems, tales of magic. Judicial opinions, records of buying and selling gold. Even some on the rights of women and children. On how to treat animals. On music. On travel. On every aspect of life."

☙

IN A WAY, the most interesting light shed on the period by any of these collections is the Kati family's library. Partly this is because of the family's political and social connections. The first African Kati was Ali ben Ziyad al-Quti, who came from Toledo before it was captured by Muslims, in 1468. He was no doubt a Muslim and seemed to be fleeing growing religious intolerance, but he still called himself "Quti," the Goth, which is what the Andalusians called the Christians of the time. In any case, he settled in Goumbou, a city in the northern part of Mali, and a year or so later married Askia Mohamed's sister. Their son, Mahmoud, became friends with the askia and later his chief financial officer, and directed the empire's first census. He also served as *qadi* in Timbuktu. It was Mahmoud who wrote most of what is now known as the *Tarikh al-Fettach*, sometimes known as the *Chronicle of the Seeker of Knowledge.*

The other reason the Kati collection is so interesting is because it is personal; it was his own library, not an assemblage of documents collected by others over generations. It gives a unique insight into how the scholarly classes of Timbuktu dealt with ideas and what they considered worthy of passing on to their heirs. The Mamma Haïdara and Ahmed Baba collections focus on the study of individual texts collected by many people over time; here is the body of work that a single scholar used.

Albrecht Hofheinz, a German researcher who examined the collection, puts it this way: "The study of libraries as collections helps us gain insights into the composition of learning, the spread and 'popularity' of certain texts, which allows us better to understand the intellectual formation of educated people at the time. This makes the Kati library a unique treasure for the intellectual history of the Middle Niger region."[11]

That such a library has survived the ravages of more than five hundred years of warfare, conquest, pillage, jihad, drought and pestilence is a miracle. When Mahmoud Kati died, he bequeathed his library to his son Ismaïl, who in turn passed it to his son Mahmoud, and so it went. By the nineteenth century most of it was still intact, though in the custody of several branches of the Kati family. It was reassembled by a family member, Ismaïl Haïdara (no relation to Abdel Kader), along with cousins Thié and Kirchamba. Ismaïl is himself a writer of histories. ("I come from a family of writers," he once told the Saharan Studies Association. "We have been writing for 15 generations, so writing comes easily to me. The harder challenge I face is how to catalogue, restore and digitize the manuscripts my ancestors have left behind.") The library is now owned by two branches of the Kati clan in the village of Kirshamba, about a hundred miles to the west of Timbuktu. The intention is eventually to move it to Timbuktu, into its own building, where it can be properly cataloged and restored.

Up to 1,700 of the possibly 7,000 manuscripts have been examined by Sidi Haïdara; a few were brought to Timbuktu in 1998 for John Hunwick to take a look at. He professed himself astonished at what he found. "I saw a beautiful copy of the Qur'an in a fine eastern script with a copying date equivalent to 1420," he told a conference on the Arabic writing of the Sudan. "The final page was, in fact, written in Turkish, and recorded the fact that the copy had been dedicated . . . [to] a woman named as Sharifa Khadija Khanum. How this manuscript got to Timbuktu we do not know. Perhaps it was purchased by Mahmoud Kati, or some member of his family, whilst on pilgrimage."

He was particularly struck by the fact that Mahmoud Kati had used the sometimes generous margins on some of the manuscripts for notes in his own hand. Perhaps this was because paper was precious; or perhaps he was just being thrifty, the librarian's equivalent of keeping large balls of string. Sometimes his notes were a reader's scribbles—comments on the text itself—but mostly they were just records of events and objects that had caught his attention, thus giving insight into what he thought worth recording. The weather was one: "In that year God caused prices to fall," he wrote. "Rains were abundant, and wells filled up. As soon as rain began to fall, people began to plant, and God facilitated harvesting of the crop. He sent successive rains to His servants following the year 910 [1504–5], and people continued thus for five years." He also recorded a meteor shower: "In the year 991 [1583] in God's month of Rajab the Goodly [August] after half the night had passed, stars flew around the sky as if fire had been kindled in the whole sky, east, west, north and south. It became a mighty flame lighting up the earth, and people were extremely disturbed about that. It continued until after dawn." And he added his full name: "Recorded by the humble servant of his Lord,

Alf 'al Kati Mahmud ben Ali ben al-Mutawakkil bi'llah ben Ziyad al-Qutial-Wa'qarō, in the year 991." Other events the scholar had seen as worthy of note include a family wedding, the death of a scholar and brief accounts of some of his journeys in the region.[12]

☙

WE LEFT SIDI Abdel Kader's house at dusk and wound our way through the darkening streets toward the Hendrina Khan Hotel, where we were staying. In every street and alley, children were playing, shrieking cheerfully as children do. Here and there small twig fires burned brightly, boiling water for tea, and families squatted on the sand or small stools in the friendly dusk. The power was on again (it had gone off the night before as the city's creaking diesel generator sputtered to a halt, one more time), and as we passed we could see into courtyards where families were busy with the things families do at day's end. Mali was poor, Timbuktu was poor, everything we could see had the cobbled-together and makeshift look of poverty, and yet we wondered what other treasures some of these homes held, preserved in boxes and trunks and cupboards and bags for so many hundreds of years. For Timbuktu had not always been poor, and many of these families had been here for seven hundred years or more, and they had not always been poor either, and under the askias, especially Askia Mohamed and his son Daoud, only the Bella were without learning; and poverty—it's a truism but not always obvious—does not mean ignorance, or meanness of spirit. Sometimes, indeed, heritage and a notion of a glorious past are what keeps the spirit going.

Our Toyota Land Cruiser rumbled across the sand-filled depression where the young men were still playing soccer, the ball barely visible in the light the French call *entre chien et loup*, neither day nor night, then we decanted at the hotel and walked into the lobby. The director, Abderhamane Alpha Maïga, spotted us coming in and asked us what kind of a day we had had. When we told him, his face lit up. We plopped on the sofas in the lobby while he told us a story about Ahmed Baba and his long Moroccan exile, and asked us whether we had seen the honorable one's grave. (We had.) "The people still go there to venerate him," he said. "He was not a saint, perhaps, but he was a great man." Then his face darkened. The new people don't always appreciate people like him, he said. By the "new people" he meant the Saudi-financed imams, the Wahhabi Sunni at the new mosque. Like their mentors in Saudi Arabia, the local version of Wahhabism is strict and humorless, concerned mostly with matters of form, from wearing the veil to enforced prayers five times a day. It is an aggressively intolerant Islam that, as the Egyptian novelist Alaa Al Aswany once put it, "institutionalizes Islam as a state religion rather than allowing people to interpret it in their own individual ways."[13] It seems that "the new people" are suspicious of the restoration and conservation work going on; too many of the ancient texts are heretical, old-fashioned, impious, *loose*. Then the director said what we had heard so often in Timbuktu already, from Tuareg like Halis and others. "*We* are not like *them*," he said, meaning the fanatics, the intolerant and violent Muslims of al-Qaeda, of Afghanistan, and of London, New York and Madrid.

To the new intolerants, history is not something to be remembered but shaped, put to a purpose. I wondered what Ahmed Baba or Mahmoud Kati, or Askia al-hajj Mohamed himself would have thought of this notion. It would probably have been familiar; Islam's history is full of quarrelsome schisms, and they would have known of the activities of Yasin and his ilk, and would not have been surprised by the Fulani jihads of Usman dan Fodio and others. But Timbuktu under the benevolent rule of the askias was a beacon of tolerance in a darkening world, a true oasis in a spiritual desert, and in these days of clashing ideas that's a part of history worth remembering. I thought of telling the director this, but it probably was something he already knew.

CHAPTER SIXTEEN

&

The End of the Askias

FOR ALMOST A century, between 1492 and 1582, the Songhai Empire was the greatest, and most benevolent, power in West Africa. But toward the end, internal quarrels and palace revolutions seriously wounded the body politic, as contending brothers deposed or assassinated one another with a rapidity that kept the scribes scrambling to keep up with the news. There were too many brothers, as it turned out, and their loyalty to each other was, to put it politely, rudimentary. As Heinrich Barth expressed it, having studied the histories of Ahmed Baba: "It was certainly a great advance in the scale of civilization that, although their rulers were absolute, it was not customary among the Songhai to murder the younger brothers of the newly elected king, or to render them incapable of aspiring to the royal dignity by depriving them of their sight, or in some other manner disabling them; so, on the other hand, it was no doubt very prejudicial to the stability of the empire that so many royal princes were constantly installed as governors of powerful provinces, some of them situated at great distances from the capital. There is no doubt that polygamy, with its consequent intrigues in the harem, was the chief cause of the speedy decline of the Songhai empire."[1]

Then, in the last part of the century, drought and plague ravaged the country, and the population was almost halved. The "low people," the chronicles record, died in large numbers. Timbuktu split from the capital, Gao, and asserted its own tenuous independence.

All these calamities were caused, so the wise men of the madrasas said, by the actions of evil kings. In the reign of one of the last of the askias, Askia Ishaq II, religious war roiled the society. As an expostulation from Timbuktu's Sankoré mosque put it, "the inobservance of the laws of God, the unrest of the slaves, the greed and arrogance of the rulers, caused the town (Gao) to reach its limit of immorality, of the gravest crimes, of acts the most unpleasant to God and the committal of the greatest acts of turpitude possible."

The empire, disintegrating and consumed not with politics but with turpitude, was ripe to be plucked.

And up north, in Morocco, newly installed in his palace in Marrakech, his ego already casting a shadow across half of North Africa, was just the man to do it.

ೋ

BUT IN 1528, still seventy years before their Marrakech nemesis put an end to the askias once and for all, Askia al-hajj Mohamed, the first emperor of his line, was eighty-seven years old and going blind; and "the old lion no longer has his teeth," as the saying goes. He had lost his two beloved brothers, Omar Kumzaghu, who had helped him stabilize his rule in the early years, and the other Omar, Kondiago, who had become *Tombouctoukoï* and had run that turbulent city on his behalf. For some years he had been secluded in his palace, no longer going abroad, his orders forwarded through his sons (by some estimates more than a hundred of them), and rumors had swirled around the empire that he was no longer really in charge but had become the plaything of his turbulent family. Ali Foulan, his senior counselor and the chief executive of the empire, entered the palace late in the year, to demand to know whether the orders he was carrying out actually came from the old man himself. He was chased out by a passel of sons and refused the right to return.

What was going on, it became clear, was that the sons were jockeying for power. Musa, the firstborn, who had accompanied his father on his pilgrimage to Mecca, eventually threatened to kill the old man. The emperor fled to Tindirma and placed himself under the protection of another brother, Yahiya, who was then running that province. Yahiya settled things down a little, brokering some sort of compromise, and Askia Mohamed returned to Gao the following year. But disputes soon flared up again, and Yahiya was summoned to Gao to see if he could sort things out one more time. Instead, "the rebellious children," as Barth put it, had him murdered. Seeing that his father was powerless, later in the year, during a fête, Musa forced him to abdicate and proclaimed himself emperor. He left the aging king in his palace but without any power to govern; Musa stayed in his own residence, and all the power flowed to him there.

Ahmed Baba, well after the fact, put it this way: "He was [in the end] too mild to govern a turbulent country like Songhai." But the old man had reigned for thirty-six years and six months, not bad for a mild-mannered king.[2]

It didn't take Musa long to show his true colors, which were those of a ruler in the Sonni Ali Ber mold, suspicious of Islam, critical of intellectuals, preferring to base his power on the peasants of the countryside and their traditionally animist ways, paranoid and wary. He began what was to be a bloody and restless reign by going against recent convention, launching attempts to murder all his many brothers. Many of them had taken refuge in Kurmina, but the new askia sent a task force after them and they fled. For the next few years, he pursued vendettas against whatever brothers he could lay his hands on; they, in their turn, launched numberless plots to assassinate him.

Timbuktu, which had been accustomed under the first of the askias to running its own affairs—and indeed, in Askia al-hajj Mohamed's later days, helping to run the affairs of the empire—was incensed. Waves of protest rippled through the city, encouraged by the mosques and the madrasas as the new askia set about wrenching the capital back to the paganism of the Sonnis. Flouting the precepts of Islam, he put it about that he was going to marry all the younger wives of his father, and indeed did so, installing them in a corner of the palace at Gao. *Vile* and *irresponsible* were two of the words the uléma bandied about; when the new emperor deigned to visit Timbuktu six months after his installation, he paid a call on the *qadi*, Sidi Mahmoud, but the old man refused to meet him, turning his back on him in public and walking away, treating him, as he said later, like an errant son needing to be punished.

As the increasingly fragile relations between Gao and Timbuktu continued to deteriorate, Timbuktu cast about for a solution. They found one in Musa's cousin Usman Yubabu, who had been installed as the governor of Tindirma Province to replace the murdered Yahiya, and less than a year later they persuaded him to try for the big prize, the emperorship itself, with their support (though mostly moral—the uléma weren't warriors, as they hastily pointed out). Early in 1530 Yubabu marched with a substantial army, drawn from the largely Muslim western part of the empire, toward Gao. The two armies met at a place called Acalal, and the rebels were routed. Yubabu escaped, but the vengeful askia caught no fewer than thirty of his close supporters and put them painfully to death, along with hundreds of his senior adherents.

In the end, though, it didn't help the askia. This "vile personage" (Sidi Mahmoud's phrase) had alienated almost everyone, including (not surprisingly) his surviving brothers, and one of them—it remains unclear which one—assassinated him in April 1531.

The *Tarikh al-Sudan*, which has an ambiguous attitude toward him, contains a dramatic account of the killing. The brother chosen to do the deed, Alu, said to the others: "I will throw a spear at him while he is mounted. If I miss, all of you attack me with spears so I am killed and you escape his anger." He didn't miss, not quite: the lance pierced the askia's shoulder, "but Musa neither turned nor acted as though the least thing had happened to him, so stout was his heart." Musa wanted to fight the rebels. But he couldn't extract the lance, so he went to the palace, had the weapon yanked out, cauterized the wound and prepared for battle. "So great was his rage that he slept not at all, and swore repeatedly that blood would flow." In the end, though, the combined might of his brothers overcame him, and he was killed. As the *Tarikh* dolefully puts it, "from the time he took power he knew not a moment's rest, because of the enmity of his relatives, which is the greatest misfortune in the world, since it is a continuous enmity that neither changes nor ceases."[3]

For a while the succession was unclear. Would Usman Yubabu, a son of Omar Kondiago, the first askia's brother, now succeed to the throne after all? Or would another son of Askia Mohamed gain the prize? There was a good deal of fighting, and at least one beheading, before matters settled out and Usman prevailed. It would be a sign of Timbuktu's resurgent power that their candidate succeeded, taking the title of Askia Mohamed II Benkan Toraï, and another sign that one of his first acts was to make a ceremonial trip to Timbuktu to assert his friendship with the *qadi* and the imams of that city. (Prudently, though, for he was a shrewd and careful ruler, he also was clear that the observance of traditional customs and rituals of the country folk were to be explicitly permitted.) As a sign of his legitimacy he was given the symbols of power his uncle had received from the sharif of Mecca, Moulay el Abbas—the white robe, the green bonnet, the ceremonial sword—that had been withheld from his predecessor.

Mohamed II Benkan, or Bonkana as he is more often called, was "a man of the west" as the phrase went in Tindirma and Timbuktu—that is, a cultivated man of Islam, an intellectual. He continued to live in Gao, the seat of imperial power, but considered himself a friend of Timbuktu. He was a graduate of the university at Sankoré and had the education, manners and comportment of a Timbuktu man of the world. He was said to be a friend of good conversation and of pleasure, and introduced new musical instruments and styles to Gao and Timbuktu.

This worldliness of his seems to have seduced him, toward the end of his reign, into wrongdoing. He did many favors for the professors and students at Sankoré despite the many rumors of improprieties and indiscretions there, always unspecified. He also liked military campaigning but wasn't very good at it, and an upstart chief of the little state called Kebbi actually defeated him in battle, to the askia's chagrin. (He told his chief councillor afterward that the defeat troubled him less than what the malicious gossips of Sankoré would say about him.)

Unlike even the bloody Musa, Bonkana had chased his venerable uncle, the first of the askias, from his palace in Gao and had him imprisoned on an island in the Niger, a degrading decision that was in the end to be his undoing.

The story goes that one of the old man's sons, Ismail, paid him a courtesy call on the island. When he sat in front of his father, the old man seized his arm, squeezed his muscles and exclaimed, "Good Lord! You're as strong as this and yet you leave me here to be eaten by mosquitoes and croaked at by frogs!" This was apparently what he hated most about his exile, the damned mosquitoes and endlessly raucous frogs.

"What can I do?" Ismail asked. "I have no power."

So his father said, "Go to so-and-so," mentioning a eunuch of his, "and pinch his body in a certain place, and if he recognizes that signal between him and me, tell him he should give you what I have deposited with him."

That something turned out to be a cache of gold, and Ismail used it to buy mercenaries, which in turn he used to seize the askia's inner circle and depose the king. The deed was done, so the stories say, in the same village on the same day of the week and the same month in which that king had taken power for himself. He had reigned for six years. The deposed king fled to Timbuktu, but that worldly city was no safe place for losers, and he took refuge farther west, in the rump state of the old mansas of Mali, "at the farthest edge of the land of the sultans of Kala."

A year later the aging Askia al-hajj Mohamed, back in his palace at Gao, finally expired; he was buried in the city, opposite the point in the Niger "where he had taken leave of his kingdom." The tomb and little mosque, built for him by his remaining sons, is still standing, though his palace has long decayed. The tomb is a squat, heavily proportioned building, pierced as so many of Mali's buildings are by a pincushion of struts, a rudimentary scaffolding for replasterers. You can still stand on its roof, via an external staircase, and stare down at the river below and the rose-colored dune opposite, the site of his death. Inside is a maze of small prayer rooms divided by densely packed mud pillars. The whole is a ziggurat in shape, rising in seven terraces to the roof. The faithful still come here every day to remember him and venerate his memory.

Askia Ismail's reign didn't last long, less than two years, mostly remembered for a terrible drought that ravaged the whole of the Niger Bend. A story in the chronicles dramatizes his reign with a premonitory anecdote: at the very moment of his accession to power, Ismail's heart split and he suffered a flux of blood from the anus. He knew immediately what had caused it, saying to his brothers, "That happened because of the copy of the Qur'an on which I swore loyalty to Askia Mohamed Bonkana. That is what seized me and pierced me. I shall not remain in power for long, so look to yourselves and behave like men." He had wished to depose Bonkana for only three reasons, he explained, not because he wanted the power himself. The first was to release his aging father from his island prison; the second was so that "our sisters could resume the *hijab*"; the third was because the askia had disparaged his family, asserting the superiority of his own with the phrase, "a single ostrich chick is better than a hundred hen chicks."[4]

Ismail was succeeded by his brother Ishaq, who became Askia Ishaq I. Sidi Salem called him a cruel tyrant, and this seems a fair judgment, for though al-Sa'adi did call him "illustrious," he also said he was "the one who inspired most fear and awe"; he executed those senior army commanders he could catch, and at the least suspicion of opposition he would have the offender killed. He had an apparently insatiable hunger for gold, and at his death, after ten years in power, his fortune was estimated at seventy-five thousand pieces of gold, size and value unknown.

Early in Ishaq's reign something happened that was an ominous portent of events that would come to pass fifty years later. A letter arrived in Gao from the Sa'adian sultan of Marrakech, Ahmad al-Araj (who was deposed in 1540 by his brother, Mohamed el-Mehdi). The letter, demanding that the Songhai cede to Morocco the lucrative salt mines of Taghaza, was given a dismissive response. "The Ahmad who would achieve [such an agreement] was not he, and the Ishaq who would give it ear had not yet been conceived," the askia wrote, and followed his reply with a punitive expedition of two thousand heavily armed Tuareg *meharis*, with orders to pillage the Dra'a Valley on the Atlas route to Marrakech, but not to kill anyone. The raid was supposed to demonstrate the askia's power, which it presumably did, though in 1556

Mohamed el-Mehdi briefly occupied Taghaza anyway, killing the askia's governor there.

✑

STILL, THE EMPIRE was in good shape when Ishaq died and was succeeded by his brother Daoud (or Dawud). As the *Tarikh al-Sudan* puts it, "his father Askia Mohamed and his brothers had prepared the ground for him, and he had nothing to do but cultivate what they had sown."[5] In a way, this statement is true enough: for more than half a century Askia Mohamed and his successors had preserved peace in the empire and were now the absolute masters of it, and Daoud had no external enemies nipping at his heels. In other ways it is unfair, for Daoud was perhaps the most cultivated and urbane of all the askias, and under his long and peaceful rule (from 1549 to 1583) the empire and especially Timbuktu blossomed once more. He had served a long apprenticeship in government, running several provinces for his brothers, and understood what needed to be done and how to govern with moderation. Timbuktu loved him. He had studied there, for one thing, and was interested in men of letters and the arts. He left the uléma alone to run the city. Sidi Salem says that of all the askias he is remembered most fondly in the city. In the course of his writings, Sidi Salem has collected a dozen or more adjectives applied to the askia by his subjects—among them *subtle, eloquent, wise, well-educated, redoubtable, competent, generous, liberal, gay* and *amusing*. The *Tarikh al-Fettach*, for its part, said that "he was a sultan held in awe, eloquent, a born leader, generous, magnanimous, cheerful and good humored, fond of joking. He was the first to establish treasuries and even libraries."[6] Adds Sidi Salem, "Many Songhai who live here today call themselves 'Daouda haama,' descendant of Askia Daoud. They often have the family name Maïga [Daoud's matrilineal line] and generally live in the medina, in the old town."

The population swelled, almost doubling during Daoud's reign. The markets bulged with trade goods and manufactured articles from the north. Setting off from Timbuktu during the period were some of the greatest caravans in history—said to be fifty or sixty thousand, the numbers perhaps inflated by pride, but substantial enough for all that.

As they had many times before, learned men flocked to Timbuktu from the farthest reaches of the Islamic world. The educational system burgeoned: under Daoud the number of Qur'anic schools collectively known as the University of

Sankoré reached 180, with nearly twenty-five thousand pupils, an astonishing number in a town with a permanent population of about one hundred thousand.

He was prodigiously generous to men of learning. Alfa Kati of Timbuktu once asked the askia for gifts for his daughters and sons. He wanted four carpets, four female slaves, two robes, two turbans, two mounts (one horse and one camel), a plot of land for cultivation with slaves to do the cultivating and seeds to plant, and finally forty milk cows and the price of a copy of a manuscript that cost eighty mithqals. He also asked that four of his theology students, whose clothing were in tatters, be properly dressed. All these things arrived without comment, a day later. Another of the uléma, Sidi Aqib ben Umar, gave the askia benedictions one day. The next week Daoud sent him a gift of a hundred slaves, which he divided among his family. Daoud set up a studio in town in which teams of copyists and scribes produced books that he distributed to scholars.

℆

NOT ALL WAS sweetness and light in the kingdom, though. A good ruler he may have been, but he was after all an emperor with absolute power, and on occasion he seems to have exercised it with the usual casual imperial brutality. One of his counselors had treated him disrespectfully before he became emperor, and was, by all accounts, a man of great ambition—and folly, as it turns out, for Daoud instructed his nephew Muhammad to kill him when he could, instructions that were duly carried out.

Occasional discords did erupt between the askia and the *qadi* of Timbuktu, Aqib ben Umar. The *qadi*, an ambitious and energetic man, completed the rebuilding of several of the mosques of the city, including, Djingareiber. The old building was pulled down in May 1570, and the rebuilding started at once. The *Tarikh al-Sudan* suggests that the askia not only approved of the project but also donated considerable sums from his personal fortune for the work. The *Tarikh al-Fettach*, however, suggests something rather different, referring to "certain calumnies" (unfortunately not specified) being spread about the askia, and to "discord between the king and the *qadi*," and to "harsh words [from the *qadi*] about the king." When the askia sent a message to Timbuktu asking about these calumnies and harsh words, "he replied violently, a response that a prince like Daoud could not possibly accept." In fact, the anecdote is told in order to demonstrate the humility and the forbearance of the askia, as shown by his supposed response: "Soon after-wards Daoud himself visited the *qadi* at the mosque in Timbuktu. The gate-keeper shut the door in his face. He waited outside the gate. The *qadi* refused to let him enter until the intervention of several notables of the city. Then, the prince entered humbly, and lowered his head in respect. The *qadi* re-mained seated with a stony face. In the end an accord was reached, but only after stubborn resistance by the *qadi*. A little later, he sent the *qadi* a gift of 4,000 bags of grain to distribute to the poor, and established for those poor a garden by the river, maintained by 30 slaves."[7]

And man of peace though he was, Askia Daoud continued the work of conquest begun by his predecessors, and expanded his borders to the very west of the empire of Mali. In 1588 and 1589 he defeated the remaining armies of the old mansas, incorporating their estates, partly by marrying the mansa's daughter, "dispatching her to Songhai with a magnificent train of jewelry, male and female slaves, furnishings and household goods all covered in gold leaf, as well as water vessels, mortars and pestles and other goods."[8]

On his way back, he stopped at the little town of Sama, west of Djenné and north of the Niger, where the former askia Mohamed Bonkana had fi-nally come to rest, by now blind and infirm. Daoud paused by the river and greeted two grandsons of the old askia cordially; the following morning "he ordered his musicians to greet Askia Mohamed Bonkana by sounding their instruments. When Mohamed Bonkana heard the sound, his heart broke and he died on the spot, but his children continued living there.[9]

ↁ

IN 1556 THE new sultan of Marrakech, Moulay Mohamed al-Sheikh, moved against the salt mines of Taghaza, killing the askia's governor there and a couple of prominent Tuareg. Daoud's early response was to avoid conflict; at the suggestion of the remaining leaders of the Tuareg *azalaï* (salt caravan), he opened an alternate source of salt that came to be called Taghaza al-ghizlan, Taghaza of the gazelles, in the same year. The impudent occupation didn't last, and the Taghaza mines reverted to Songhai within a few years.

Then, in 1577, a comet appeared over Timbuktu, and the following year the sultan of Morocco, Abd al-Malik, died on the field of battle against the Portuguese and was succeeded by the man who was to become Songhai's nemesis: Moulay Ahmad al-Mansur, or Mansur al-Dahabi, the Golden One.

Relations between the two sultanates were, at least briefly and after a rocky start, cordial. One of al-Mansur's first acts was to send a threatening letter to Daoud demanding that he dispatch immediately to Marrakech all the salt taxes collected at Taghaza, a year's worth at once. Daoud's response was to send not only the taxes but a goodwill gift of another ten thousand mithqals of gold, an open-handed generosity that confounded the sultan and apparently established a close relation between the two men, for when Daoud died in 1583, after a bout of fever, al-Mansur went into mourning.

∾

DAOUD'S DEATH CAME, as the deaths of all emperors properly should, after a series of ill omens. Daoud's eldest son, also called Mohamed Bonkana, set off an a military expedition against a people who had successfully resisted Sonni Ali and Askia al-hajj Mohamed, a Mossi redoubt near the Bandiagara cliffs. His army, lent to him by his father, was under the command of one Yasi. When they reached the Dum Mountains, where the enemy were located, Daoud's son ordered his army to ascend. Yasi refused. When the request was repeated, Yasi again refused.

"You pushy slave![10] You don't take any notice of anyone!"

"You addressed me wrongly," Yasi replied. "You should have called me, 'you wicked slave,' for that is what I am," and he continued to ignore any requests for action.

A little later, after a great plague in Timbuktu that killed many people, Fulani brigands attacked one of the askia's barges on the Niger and plundered its goods, something that hadn't happened for more than sixty years. The same son, Mohamed Bonkana, went tearing off to Masina, the home of said brigands, to exact revenge. Alas, he had consulted neither his father nor his brothers, and after news came back that he had laid waste to Masina, "killing many of its virtuous scholars and holy men, from whom emanated many manifestations of divine grace after their deaths," Askia Daoud was so spiritually sapped by these events that he went into a decline and died shortly afterward. He had reigned for thirty-four years and six months. He was buried in Gao.

∾

THE SUCCESSION WAS troubled. The eldest son, the same Bonkana who had caused his father's decline, was away (whether campaigning or in disgrace is not clear), and so the eldest of the remaining sons, Mohamed al-hajj II, "mounted his horse to demonstrate his resolve, his brothers riding behind him at a short distance." The *Tarikh* approved of the choice, saying that "there was no one more intrepid, courageous and steadfast among the Songhai folk, or having more stamina than he. Wise and knowledgeable persons, who were there at the time, said he deserved to be an emir, even in Baghdad."[11] But it was to be a difficult transition and a fractious rule.

Signs of discord surfaced almost immediately. One of the brothers riding behind, Hamid, spurred his horses to the front and started bending the new askia's ear, telling him whom to arrest and whom to have killed. The *Tarikh* says his other brothers, knowing his character, went forward and said, "Don't follow the advice of this slanderer. Do not disgrace anyone, since no one opposes you here. If Mohamed Bonkana had been here, you would not have got the succession. But if you hadn't been here either, we would never have allowed this wretch [Hamid] to succeed."[12]

Bonkana, for his part, surprised everyone. Initially, he reacted predictably, returning to his camp near Kabara, within striking distance of Timbuktu, and massing his army for a march on Gao. But first he paid a formal call on the *qadi* of Timbuktu, Aqib ben Umar, a man of formidable intellect and moral weight. So much so, indeed, that he persuaded Bonkana to give up his thirst for power in exchange for a life of contemplation and study, much to the fury and astonishment of his army, which had expected bloody battle followed by the rich spoils of power.[13] Prudently, his brother had him arrested anyway, and he remained locked up until the death of the askia several years later.

Askia Mohamed al-hajj II never campaigned himself. A short time after his accession his lower body became afflicted with ulcers, which remained with him for the rest of his life. His only military activities were massive slaving raids into what is now Burkina Faso, bringing thousands of Soninke captives to Timbuktu.

His brief reign was riven by internal revolts and religious strife. In Timbuktu, a crisis of authority was caused when the *qadi* died in 1583 and the new askia's nominee, Abu Hafs Umar, refused to take office, being opposed by many of the uléma. For a while two eminent scholars took on themselves the task of running the judicial and political systems: Mohamed Baghayogho ran the affairs of nonresidents and southerners; Alpha Moghoyo of Timbuktu took charge of native affairs, running his department from the Sankoré mosque. The matter dragged on for months, before one of the uléma, Salih Takinni, suggested a stratagem to the askia: "Tell Abu Hafs Umar that if he continues to refuse, you will appoint someone truly ignorant to the post; then, when he appears before God Most High on Judgment Day he alone would be held responsible for all the judgments that person made." Apparently, when Abu Hafs read the letter, he wept, but accepted, and the crisis was over.[14]

The same year one of his military commanders, advised by his brothers that the askia was ailing and unable to oppose him, marched on Gao to seize power. The attempt failed, though the askia was described during the campaign as sick and powerless, and terrified.

In Morocco, Moulay al-Mansur, his friend Daoud now departed from the scene, sent an emissary to the new askia with splendid gifts, his object being to spy out the land. Askia Mohamed al-hajj II responded as Daoud had done, by greeting the emissary with honor and sending him back with even more extraordinary gifts, including slaves, civet cats, eighty eunuchs and other items. This time al-Mansur wasn't deterred, and within a year news came that the sultan had dispatched a twenty-thousand-strong army with orders to "seize the lands along the sea coast [although Songhai had never reached the sea] and other territories, until they reached Timbuktu. At that, people were very afraid, but God dispersed that army through hunger and thirst, and they scattered hither and thither. The remainder returned home, having through the power of the Creator—Exalted is He!—accomplished no part of al-Mansur's plan."[15] Then he sent a squadron of two hundred musketeers to Taghaza, but the news got there first and the inhabitants fled; the *azalaï* instead opening up new mines at Taoudenni, closer to Timbuktu. (A nice Timbuktu tale, told to Shindouk by his father, who was told by his father, and so back many generations, says that the discovery of salt at Taoudenni was accidental. The people fleeing southward included contract workers, male slaves, warriors and female slaves to serve the needs of the army; one of the women left the group and went to pee behind a dune, and there discovered salt. She showed her find to a learned man among them, and the Taoudenni salt mines were in business.)

The Moroccan musketeers, for their part, returned home without booty.

❦

BUT BY THIS time, the askia's brothers had had enough of what they considered his indecision and dithering. They brought in one of them, Mohamed Bani, from his post as a provincial governor and bundled the askia from office. He had lasted less than five years and died shortly after being deposed, of natural causes.

But Bani's accession just made things worse. He was fat, boastful, impulsive and fueled mostly by anger. His first act was to assassinate two of his brothers. The others soon tried to have him deposed or killed, but the plot failed and they were all imprisoned.

It didn't help that his accession coincided with the fourth year of a severe drought and an epidemic of fever that almost halved the permanent population of Timbuktu; in that city, the calamities were laid at his door, and the city's leaders cast about for a solution. They found what they thought was an ideal one when Mohamed es-Sadeq, another of Daoud's sons, killed the askia's representative at Kabara, Alu, who was described in the *Tarikh al-Fettach* as "an oppressor, a despot, an iniquitous eunuch, overbearing, uncouth and a stubborn tyrant."[16] They found themselves urging es-Sadeq to save the empire from itself and march on Gao to eliminate Mohamed Bani. This turned out to be a really bad idea.

Having declared a revolt against the askia, es-Sadeq invited his brother Salih, governor of Kurmina, to join him; Salih was senior and should become askia, he said. Salih also had an army of six thousand men, an army he felt he could put to good use. But treachery was at hand: "certain prudent persons," as the *Tarikh*s put it, warned Salih that his brother meant him harm and suggested that he put him to a test: would his brother hand over the goods he had seized from the venal Alu, or would he keep them? It soon became apparent that es-Sadeq had no intention of turning over a single mithqal, and strife became inevitable. Salih lost the ensuing battle and was killed as forecast, es-Sadeq uniting the two armies.[17]

The Timbuktuans were aware of the treachery of their newfound savior but were trapped; they had no other recourse but to urge him to continue, hoping that success would smooth his rough edges and that flattery would work its magic. He was their only candidate, the only one who could save them from Bani's wrath. And so es-Sadeq entered Timbuktu and in the precincts of the great mosque of Djingareiber proclaimed himself askia under the title Askia Mohamed IV.

The rupture of the empire was complete. Two competing askias, Bani in Gao and es-Sadeq in Timbuktu, spent the next few months proclaiming their legitimacy and building up support. The city of Djenné seized its opportunity and declared itself free from Songhai rule—or Timbuktu rule, for that matter. Finally, in March 1588, at the head of a powerful army, Mohamed es-Sadeq left Timbuktu for Gao. Askia Bani was prepared with his own army but died suddenly, before battle could be joined. The rumor mill said he'd died at siesta time in a fit of anger, the evidence being that he had bitten his lip almost through, and only that afternoon had raged in his tent, *May God curse kingship! For it is a source of humiliation and degradation!* Most of the accounts, however, simply asserted that he had died because he was too fat, and went out on a hot afternoon wearing chain mail. His brother, Ishaq, was immediately proclaimed askia by the army generals and took the field under the title Askia Ishaq II.

Two askias thus confronted each other; Ishaq II and es-Sadeq, or Mohamed IV.

For a couple of pages the *Tarikh al-Sudan* describes the atmosphere at the new court of Ishaq II while it awaited battle. One of the askia's sons, Umar, was said to have galloped up and down in front of the king and his council. Not yet knowing that Salih was dead, he yelled to the crowd, "Salih is coming tomorrow, and when we meet in battle I will put this spear in his mother's you-know-what!"[18]

The following day es-Sadeq, the Timbuktu pretender, was routed and most of his army captured; the short-lived and self-styled Mohammed IV fled back to Timbuktu in complete disorder. He stopped there only long enough to tell the people of the city what had happened, putting a nice gloss on his own heroism ("a mighty army had enveloped them and they had fought from morning to sunset") and then fled, hotly pursued by the askia's men. When they caught up with him, he and his men were dragged back to Gao, where he was killed and his chief retainers sewn into a sack, which was then placed into a hole in the stable floor and filled in with dung until they died.

Dung and death, death in dung, a metaphor for what the empire had become. The last days of the Songhai of the askias were dominated by boastfulness and lies, prurience and violence, division and suspicion. The uléma were in despair. The *Tarikh al-Sudan* reported that "faith has been changed to deceitfulness; no single thing defended by God is not flouted by those people." Gao reached what the *Tarikh* describes as "the extreme limit of immorality," and a visitor from Tuat was horrified at what he saw: "[Even] among virtuous people, men and women mix in the streets and the markets; there are indecencies of free girls or slaves, to the point where it is the custom, among the free population of Djenné for example, for a young girl to hide nothing of her nudity, from the time she is a virgin until she is 50 years old, be she the daughter of a sultan or a magistrate." The *Tarikh*, whose author seems to have a some-what prurient eye for these things, went further: "[They] . . . left no sin against God Most High that they didn't commit openly, such as drinking fermented liquors, sodomy and fornication—indeed, they were so given over to this latter vice that it appeared to be nothing forbidden. Nothing gave them so much pride or social status as fornication, to such an extent that some of the sons of their sultans would commit incest with their sisters." (This had apparently once happened under the saintly Askia al-hajj Mohamed, though when that worthy heard of it he was horrified and cursed his son, praying that his male member should not accompany him to the other world, "and God Most High answered his prayer and Yusuf's member was detached from his body as the result of an illness, may God preserve us from such a fate!")[19] No wonder the later askias were blamed for the famines, pestilences and droughts that seemed to bedevil the era.

We had been talking to Sidi Salem about the disintegration of the Songhai Empire, and the sense of hopelessness and dismay that spread through Timbuktu under the last few of the askias. Ishaq II, he said, "showed himself piti-less, pitiless toward Timbuktu." The city had supported the rebellion, after all, and Ishaq had the *qadi* and the local Tuareg chiefs taken to Gao and killed. He disbanded the western regiments of the army, absorbing some into his own divisions and dismissing the rest.

"The empire was divided," he said. "Timbuktu and Gao no longer spoke the same language."

"You mean literally?"

"No," he said patiently. "The language of politics. There was tyranny but no government. Rule but no order. But also, the language of religion. The west, Timbuktu and the western provinces, was strongly Islamic, Gao and the Songhai still holding to traditional ways. The west was mostly non-Songhai. Arab and Berber, Tuareg and Bambara, Soninke and Mossi and others, just a few Songhai."

"What happened then?"

"Before anything could be settled, the Moroccans came."

CHAPTER SEVENTEEN

❧

The Coming of
the Moroccans

SOME YEARS BEFORE, on the other side of the desert, north past Taoudenni and Taghaza and the waterless Sands of Iguidi and then the barrier of the Atlas, in the Almoravid-Almohad city of Marrakech, the Red City as it is still called, we had gone one day just before dusk to see the tomb of the Sa'adian sultan Abu Yusuf Ya'qub al-Mansur, or Ahmad al-Mansur, the Golden One himself, buried with sixty-six of his relatives in a necropolis near the Kasbah Mosque. The Golden One was laid to rest next to his son and grandson in the Hall of Twelve Columns, twelve pillars of Italian marble in a room so harmonious, so elegant, so *complete*, that it stands as one of the great monuments to Moroccan-Andalusian aesthetics, one of the most perfect buildings in all architecture.

Al-Mansur was, and still is, ill-favored in Timbuktu, where he has become a synonym for decay and decline, and so it seemed to us from our Timbuktu perspective only right that outside his tomb a vendor tried to bully us into buying a carpet containing the putative likeness of al-Mansur himself. We declined, and he cursed bitterly. Timbuktuans would have appreciated the irony, we thought—their nemesis reduced to kitsch, the great sultan become the property of hucksters.

❧

MARRAKECH HAD BEEN founded in 1062 by the Almoravid generals Abu Bakr and Yusuf ibn Tachfin, who with Yusuf's son Ali conquered all of the Maghreb and then Spain, defeating the Christian hordes in 1085 at Toledo. The irrigation canals that still water Marrakech's famously perfumed gardens were built by Ali. Ghanaian gold, brought by camel from Tekrur, helped finance the magnificence.

The Almoravids were succeeded in around 1125 by the purist Almohads, who destroyed and then rebuilt Marrakech in 1147. The Almohads were fundamentalists in religion but not necessarily in architecture; their synthesis of simplicity and Almoravid opulence created some of the world's most beautiful buildings. They rebuilt much of the sultanate in their own image. The tallest and most magnificent mosque of Marrakech, the Koutoubia, was Almohad-built in the twelfth century to rival their other edifices in Rabat and Seville. The Almohads controlled all of North Africa for a brief but glorious time.

Marrakech fell into decay when the Almohad Empire collapsed in 1269, and the successor dynasty, the Merinids, moved the capital to the new city of Fez.

Moroccan politics in the following decades and centuries were chaotic. After 1428 a dynasty of viziers—the Banu Wattas (Wattasids)—attempted to rule the country but were obeyed only in parts of northern Morocco. The Portuguese showed up on the coast and after 1480 began to settle at various points. Sufism, an ascetic and mystical view of Islam intolerant of foreign influences, spread through the region; it was Sufi brotherhoods who resisted the Portuguese. From the fifteenth century the Sufi marabouts, as they called their religious leaders, challenged the power of the sultans, and anarchy resulted. Morocco essentially split in two, into the *Bled Makhzen* (land under control) and the *Bled Siba* (land of dissidence) where the mountain people organized their own lives while limiting their contact with the cities and the plains.

Marrakech became the capital of Morocco one more time, under the Sa'adian dynasty, a puritan sect of so-called sharifs that boiled out of the Dra'a oases in the sixteenth century.

The first of the Sa'adians, the brothers al-Alej and Muhammed es-Sheikh, took Marrakech in 1524. They took it by deceit and criminality, though "bathing themselves in myths of divine sanction," at least according to the Arab historian al-Ifrani (Muhammad al-Saghir ben al-hajj Muhammad ben Abd Allah al-Ifrani al-Marakkushi, as his full name is rendered), writing in 1724, after the Sa'adians were safely gone.

In those days Marrakech and its surroundings were under the rule of Nasser ben Shantouf, vassal of the Wattasid sultan, to whom he paid a small tribute. When the sharifs (the Sa'adians) came into his territory, to recruit men for their holy war, Nasser had received them magnificently, and when he heard they had been victorious against the Portuguese he initiated negotiations with them. The sharifs asked him to join them, and he accepted. When the sharifs returned to Marrakech, they were treated with the same regard as during their first visit. Yet, a few days after their arrival, Nasser was invited to join their hunting party, and when they had left town, his guests poisoned him with small breads called *kreichlat.* He died on the spot. As the sharifs were loved and admired by all in this province, they were quickly accepted as legitimate rulers.[1]

The sultan of Fez, who considered himself the only legitimate ruler of all Morocco, tried to wrest the city back from the Sa'adians four years later but failed.

For the next half century, while Marrakech remained the Sa'adian capital, North Africa was the squabbling grounds for a mess of empires and cultures: the Ottoman Turks, the Holy Roman Empire, the Sicilians, the Spanish and Portuguese. Spain and Turkey fought a series of inconclusive wars. Then, in 1578, the famous Battle of the Three Kings was fought, in which Abd al-Malik, the ruling Sa'adian sultan and a poet of note, defeated a coalition of Portuguese forces and dissident Moroccans under a dethroned sultan, al-Mutawakkil. Al-Mutawakkil had in fact been deposed by two of his own uncles and had taken refuge in Portugal. The young Portuguese king, Don Sebastian, took it on himself to restore his protégé to his throne (and thereby increase his own influence), but the attempt was a fiasco. A mere handful of Portuguese soldiers escaped the battlefield at al-Ksar al-Kabir, leaving behind them some twenty-five thousand dead and all hope of further invasion of North Africa (and the dream of another crusade). Malik, though, was killed on the field of battle and was succeeded by his son, Moulay Ahmad al-Mansur, or Mansur al-Dahabi (the names shift with dazzling speed), the Golden One.

☙

THIS GOLDEN ONE was not short on ambition. His head was filled with the spiced dreams of empire, not necessarily for its own sake but with the even loftier notion of becoming a countervailing power to the Ottomans themselves and perhaps, God willing, supplanting the caliphs of Baghdad and becoming the preeminent figure in all Islam. First he needed money; controlling a provincial fiefdom, even one as wealthy as Morocco, wouldn't be enough. He needed to expand his domains, to capture places that had the money. To do this, he needed gunpowder, weapons and troops. Lots of troops.

His first opportunity came in 1582, when he received an embassy from Idris Alawma, the ruler of the eastern Sudanic kingdom of Bornu.

Bornu, or Kanem-Bornu as it is more often styled, was already venerable; Idris's Sef dynasty had founded the kingdom of Kanem sometime in the ninth century, and it was to last for a thousand years before it finally succumbed to the deadly technologies of the West, as exemplified by the French. Throughout its long history, Kanem, and later Kanem-Bornu, served as a point of contact between North Africa, the Nile Valley and the sub-Sahara region; the trade in salt, copper, cotton, gold and slaves brought the Sef kings to the attention of Muslim merchants, and by 1200 Islam was the dominant religion. The empire's first capital was at Njimi, northeast of Lake Chad. It was moved to Bornu, to the west of Lake Chad in modern Niger, in the late fourteenth century, driven there by raiders from the Bulala tribe. The empire languished there, dormant, until it was roused again in the sixteenth century, pushing out the interlopers and retaking Kanem.

Idris, who ruled from 1571 to 1603, was its greatest king. Under his rule, the empire was expanded and consolidated; he developed a strong cavalry force, complete with chain mail, quilted armor and iron helmets, and had a small force of musketeers trained in Turkey.

Under Idris, Bornu came face-to-face with the expanding Ottoman Empire. Suddenly, he was confronted with a world power whose boundaries touched his own and extended to the Balkans and even Persia. The Ottomans claimed to be his friends, but he prudently sought a countervailing force, and there on the horizon he found one: the ever-ambitious Sa'adian, al-Mansur, far enough away to be safe, but rich and powerful.

&

IDRIS'S AMBASSADOR TO al-Mansur was accompanied by a rich gift of male and female slaves, cloth and "other luxuries of the Sudan," and sought in return military aid in the form of troops, muskets and cannon, ostensibly to pursue the jihad against his non-Muslim neighbors but really as a protection against the Ottomans. It seemed like a good deal all around, because in return al-Mansur demanded that Idris swear allegiance to him as *emir al-mu'minin* (spiritual and temporal ruler), which would give substantial impetus to his notion of being declared supreme head of Islamic Africa, as a start. Then, if he could take Songhai, he would have the Ottoman African possessions essentially surrounded and could begin his campaign to drive them from Africa altogether. Taking Songhai and its golden emporium, Timbuktu, was necessary not only to consolidate his territorial gains but also to give him enough gold to finish the job.[2] Or so he thought.

✑

THE EXCUSE HE was looking for came from a runaway slave called Wuld Kirinfil, who had for some reason angered Askia Ishaq II and had been imprisoned at Taghaza. Somehow he escaped and made his way across the desert to Morocco. There, he represented himself as a brother of the askia and diligently spread rumors about the empire and its manifold weaknesses, its divisions, its corruption and its powerlessness, and urged al-Mansur to take action. For a while the sultan did nothing; he was diverted by an expedition against Fez, to which he took an army to blind all its leaders because (or so the Timbuktu historians say) "he begrudged them their worldly wealth." But when he returned, he addressed a series of letters to Ishaq, in increasingly menacing terms, on the subject of empire and allegiances; the primary demand was that Songhai abandon altogether the salt mines at Taghaza.

Askia Ishaq's response was very different from the approach taken years earlier by Askia al-hajj Mohamed or Askia Daoud. No conciliation for him. His letter was contemptuous in tone and was accompanied by a spear and two iron shoes (an old Bambara insult, meaning, "until you have worn out these sandals you will never be safe from our weapons.")[3] The second and third letters he ignored entirely.

The Timbuktuans' response was rather different. To them, Taghaza was not just a pawn of empire but a considerable source of wealth, for trade was dependent on a secure salt supply. Prudently, they sent explorers to the region and opened up alternate mines at Taoudenni, mines that are still in use. And which yielded, if anything, a superior quality of salt.

Al-Mansur's fourth and final letter was addressed to the *qadi* of Timbuktu, reminding him of his Islamic duty of allegiance. The *qadi's* reply, if indeed he did reply, is not recorded.

Invasion now seemed inevitable, but first al-Mansur had to deal with pusillanimous courtiers and fainthearted generals in his own employ, many of them still adherents of his dead brother, Abd al-Malik. The generals he fired, replacing them with men of his own persuasion. Those advisers who counseled prudence, fearing the awesome crossing of the great desert, he either fired or bullied into agreeing with him. The other objection—that Songhai was Muslim and should not be attacked by another Muslim state—he simply ignored.

"You talk of perils," he was recorded as saying. "You talk of fatal solitudes, barren of water and pasture. But you forget those defenseless and threadbare merchants, mounted or on foot, who regularly cross the wasteland. I can do the same with an army that will inspire terror wherever it appears."[4]

His plan was to have a light strike force cross the desert, relying on speed and superior weaponry to achieve their objective. How they would then govern the newly won province was never discussed. It was simply assumed that the allegiance of the conquered subjects would be effortlessly transferred. Wasn't al-Mansur, after all, an exemplar of an obviously superior way of life? It was the classical error of the powerful, the classical weakness of a self-centered culture.

☙

THE LEGENDS ALSO say that Askia Ishaq II might have had precise intelligence about the invasion to come, if only he had maintained better relations with the wise men of Timbuktu. In that city there lived one Abu Zeïk, known to the faithful as "the virtuous sheikh, the saint, the wise councilor, the confidant of God," who announced to his disciples at Timbuktu the ominous news of the Moroccan army's departure from Marrakech, on the very day the event took place, October 31, 1590.[5]

CHAPTER EIGHTEEN

❧

The Long March and the
Pasha's Conquest
of Timbuktu

THE ARMY THAT set off from Marrakech was indeed small for an invasion force, consisting of 2,000 foot soldiers with muskets, half of them renegades from other regimes and half emigrés from al-Andalus, 500 *spahis* (mounted musketeers), 1,500 Arab lancers and 70 Christian captives armed with blunderbusses, for a total of around 4,000 fighting men. (The commander had wanted more Christians, for it was considered unlucky to set off without a substantial number of these formidable fighters, but the sultan had refused to release any more.) In addition, there were 500 sappers and some 1,000 camel drivers, which likely meant there were about 15,000 camels.

In the hyperbolic reports of the time, this invasion force was sometimes said to be much larger. Ahmed Baba himself, the eminent scholar, put the number at 23,000 men. The historian as-Zayani said there were "20,000, with 20 corps of 1,000 men each." The Timbuktu historian and poet Ismaël Diadié Haïdara contented himself with suggesting that "they filled the horizon" and were made up of mercenaries from all over, a veritable United Nations, including "Muscovites, Bulgars, Poles, Hungarians, Czechs, Germans, Danes, Norwegians, Scottish, English, Irish, Flemings, Burgundians, Calabrians, Neopolitans, Romans, Tuscans, Genoese, Savoyards, Lombards, Venetians, slaves, Albanians, Bosnians, Greeks, Cretans, Cypriots, Syrians, Egyptians, the Abyssinians of Prester John, and the Indians of the Portuguese Indies, of Brazil and of New Spain."[1]

Still, 4,000 seems to be the real number.

The invasion force was led by a renegade eunuch from Spain, Jawdar (or Djouder as he is rendered in Timbuktu), and an epic invasion it was, long in the making, slow in the crossing and relentless in its armed conquest.

Pasha Jawdar, as he came to be known, makes a fascinating study. According to Haïdara's biography,[2] he came from a poor Christian family from Las Cuevas in the kingdom of Granada. He was said to be a short, blue-eyed eunuch (though as John Hunwick points out, the text of the *Tarikh* uses the word for blue, not blue-eyed, and in Arabic blue is also used for dark, or black).[3] He was captured and enslaved, then somehow "acquired" by the sultan. As the chronicles say, he was "relieved of his foreskin by a Jewish barber borrowed for the occasion," and relieved, too, of his testicles so the king could leave him free in the palace among his many wives. Obliged perforce to adopt chastity, he turned his attention and his naturally cruel nature to military matters instead. He prospered as the man who volunteered to hang any Christian who refused to adopt Islam; pacified many a rebel band for his royal master and was appointed *khatib* (governor) of Andalusia. He pleased the sultan by bringing under control one of the most rebellious provinces, that of the Bilad as-Sidi, in the southwest of the kingdom.

Jawdar's army left Marrakech on November 1, 1590, crossed the Atlas and Anti-Atlas Mountains through the Tizi n'Glawa Pass to Tifernine, then to Ouarzazate and the valley of the Dra'a, which they reached on December 2, 1590, pausing there for some weeks to provision.[4]

A contemporary account,[5] written by an unknown Spanish agent for King Philip II of Spain, said he loaded 10,000 camels with munitions (300 quintals of gunpowder, 10 quintals of priming powder, 4 small cannon, and 10 mortars), dates, biscuit, tents and personal effects of the soldiers, and water.

Reports still current in Timbuktu say that his sappers preceded the army to dig wells along the way; some accounts suggest that hundreds of them were constructed, many of them more than three hundred feet deep and lined with stone, a formidable undertaking. This may seem like hyperbole, but the evidence is there to be seen: five of the Moroccan wells are still in use four hundred years later (at Ina Lahi, 110 miles from Timbuktu, at Bou Djebeha, 155 miles from Timbuktu, at Foum el Alba, 310 miles from Timbuktu, at Bir Ounane, 385 miles from Timbuktu, and at Taoudenni itself, 450 miles north of Timbuktu). The Moroccan route is well known, and the people of the desert have not forgotten where the wells are; in his travels, Shindouk has discovered three or four others, and if he'd had the means could have excavated them and restored them to use.

Despite the wells, the army's camels would have carried water, because there is a stretch through the Tanezrouft with no wells or water at all for twelve days of travel, and another stretch of six days.

The pasha's army entered the Sahara itself on December 22, heading first for Taghaza. They passed east of Arawan toward the end of February, ignoring the town, but seizing several hundred camels from a local eminence, Abd-Allah al-Mumahdi, who later went to Marrakech to complain to al-Mansur and was recompensed. A few days later they were attacked by a wandering band of "wild Tuareg," who were easily driven off by the musketeers. "They are great robbers," the Spanish emissary to Marrakech wrote, and added, somewhat gratuitously, "as are naturally all Arabs, and normally they plunder the caravans that go from Timbuktu to Gao and back."[6] Another account says the entire crossing took 135 days, "and many died before reaching the Niger, [having] worn out their feet on the raw *hamada*, swamped themselves in the sands of the Great Ergs, braved the horrors of thirst and hunger in the improbable emptiness of the fearsome Tanezrouft."[7] When they reached the Niger, they camped there for eleven days to recover from the crossing.

☙

WHAT OF ASKIA Ishaq II and the Songhai defenders? What preparations were they making to deal with the invasion?

One would think, what with divinely inspired advance warning of the impending invasion, he would have gathered a massive army and begun preparing his defenses, or at least have done *something*. Instead, he seems to have done nothing at all (except, perhaps, fill in a few wells) and, obliviously, set off on two (unnecessary and in the end unprofitable) military adventures of his own, first against the Gurma district to the south and then against a renegade band called the Kala, west of Djenné. Timbuktuans' version of his inactivity (and needing, of course, to maintain the credibility of their divine's prophecy) was that while the news had spread through the city they curiously "forgot" to tell anyone from Gao. More plausibly, no one knew the pasha's army was on the way until they reached Arawan; the Tuareg nomads who spotted them in the desert outside the town raced down to Timbuktu to spread the news, and alarm and despondency followed, both in Gao and Timbuktu.

At last the askia was spurred into action. He called his council together and demanded advice. This he got in plenty, but no consensus. The *Tarikh al-Sudan*, a hostile witness to the goings-on in Gao after the split with Timbuktu, puts it this way: "Askia Ishaq assembled his commanders and the leading men of his kingdom to confer with them and plan strategy. Every time they offered him sound advice, they then went back on it, for God Most High had foreknowledge that their kingdom would wane and their state disappear, and none can reverse His decree or hinder His judgment."[8] In the end, there were only two choices: yield without bloodshed and forego the kingdom, or stand and fight. They decided to fight and devised a stratagem: they would herd large numbers of cattle before them, as a kind of moving living shield, behind which they could take cover and over which they could fire their arrows. Gao had no firearms; the kingdom spent large sums on weapons and weaponry along the Barbary coast, but mostly on horses for breeding, on chain mail, brass helmets and swords and lances. Two cannon were later found in the royal treasury, a gift of the Portuguese king to Askia Musa, but they seem to have been regarded as valuable for their metal, not for their firepower, and were never deployed.

✿

JAWDAR'S ARMY MARCHED steadily along the banks of the Niger, which they encountered east of Timbuktu, and headed for Gao. He was attacked twice by bands of Songhai, who were easily repulsed, though their poisoned arrows did cause some casualties. Some islands along the way contained villages, which the army plundered by building small boats from waterskins and other artifacts. Eventually they reached Tondibi, not far from Gao. From there, having learned from spies that an army was massing against him, Jawdar sent an emissary to Ishaq.

Many people will die in battle, the message said. Why not do of his own free will what he would be obliged to do by force? Why not submit to the will of Ahmad al-Mansur, seeing that he was a sharif, a descendant of the prophet, and to him legitimately belonged sovereignty over all Muslims? He promised Ishaq many honors and favors if he was to yield. Ishaq, of course, refused. His own spies had told him that the Moroccans were a small band, whereas the Songhai could muster many thousands more. He paid no attention to the muskets and blunderbusses carried by the Moroccans, simply assuming that they could be overrun by superior numbers. Jawdar was acting out of fear, he was convinced, having come so far with so few, and was bluffing.

Jawdar, apprised of this unsurprising reaction, readied his men for battle. He placed the army with the river at its back, so they could not be surprised by an assault from that direction. He rallied his troops by telling them they'd have a free hand to plunder Gao when it was taken; the Spanish envoy to Marrakech suggests that Jawdar offered them 24,000 ounces of gold belonging to him as an incentive (surely wrong, since this would amount to 5 ounces of gold per person).

Facing him on the morning of March 12 was an army variously described as 60,000, 80,000, or even 100,000 men, no doubt an exaggeration. (John Hunwick suggests the numbers were based on self-serving accounts sent back to Marrakech and points out that an eyewitness put the Songhai army at 18,000 mounted men and 9,700 foot soldiers.) They were fronted by a substantial herd of cattle. Behind the cattle was a line of elite warriors called *suna*, who prepared themselves for battle by bending one knee and hobbling themselves by lashing the thigh to the calf, to prevent themselves from being able to flee and thus stiffening the resolve of perhaps skittish troops behind them.

Alas for the askia's troops, the cattle stratagem failed miserably. The Spaniard maintains that Jawdar's people simply opened a gap in their ranks and let the cattle amble through peacefully; the *Tarikh al-Fettach*, by contrast, says that the first musket volley so badly panicked the cattle that they turned and ran, mowing down rank after rank of Songhai warriors before the battle even began. The *suna* either were killed in the first fighting or had their throats cut later; those who survived the fighting were found after the battle calmly sitting on their shields, cross-legged, waiting for death, for it was their honor not to flee when battle was lost.

One of Ishaq's senior commanders, Alfa Bokar Lambar (sometimes said to be from Timbuktu), leaped from his mount and gripping the bridle of the askia's horse, said, "Fear God, O Askia, and turn back."

Ishaq replied, "Would you have me flee? Have I not pleased God? I'm not a man to turn his back on his people."

"Flee then for your people," Lambar replied. "Don't kill all your brothers. God commands you, on account of the lives of all those who have perished here today, because it is you who have been the cause of their death."

At that point he grabbed the king's reins and dragged him away. And so the last of the askias fled ignominiously, dispatching a messenger to the people of Gao to evacuate the town, and another to Timbuktu, urging them to do the same. He regrouped with what remained of his army south of the river at Koraï Gurma, "amid tears and lamentations."[9]

There was more weeping and lamentation in Gao as the people packed

Heinrich Barth's drawing of Gao. (Heinrich Barth)

themselves into small boats and crossed the Niger. Many drowned, and as the *Tarikh al-Sudan* puts it, "God alone knows how much property was lost or left behind in the panic."[10]

It was low water at Timbuktu, and there were few boats at the port of Kabara. Only the Songhai governor of the town and a few officials left; the rest just waited.

As Jawdar approached Gao, the *khatib* Mahmoud Darami, the administrator of the capital, came out to meet him with all the remaining people of the town—just the poor were left, the notables and their womenfolk having fled. Jawdar ordered that the homes of those who had remained should be spared, but that his troops were free to plunder whatever they could from the houses of those who were no longer there.

It was at this point, as the victorious Pasha Jawdar entered the capital and occupied the palace, that reality finally intruded on the grand and avaricious dreams of Sultan Ahmad al-Mansur. The palace was bare. Where was the gold? Where was the treasury? The people of Gao couldn't have taken everything away, not in one day . . . and the palace was a mean thing, Jawdar thought, disappointed at what he found. He discovered, at last, that the gold that crossed the desert wasn't mined or minted in Songhai but came from another land far away; and that in any case little of it was now being transferred through Gao, but through Timbuktu instead.

❧

SO WHEN, AFTER a few days of disconsolately moping about the threadbare capital, a message came from Ishaq on the other side of the river, pleading with the conquerors to please go away, and offering an incentive of one hundred thousand pieces of gold and a thousand slaves, Jawdar was inclined to at least consider it. His solders were exhausted after their long march and savage though short battle; Gao's climate was not healthy for foreigners, and the food and water could be hazardous for those not used to it. Many of his people fell ill, probably to malaria, and many died. Reports reaching Marrakech minimized the trouble, but the reality seems to have been much more severe: some four hundred men died within a few weeks. Besides, the looting had been poor; what little wealth remained was hardly worth the effort.

In his note, Ishaq also suggested, somewhat disingenuously, that the climate in Timbuktu was much healthier for what he called "the white race"— why didn't the pasha go there? This would be a nice stroke; get the invaders out of the capital, let the ingrates in Timbuktu deal with them.

Jawdar decided. He would withdraw from the capital for Timbuktu and draft a letter to al-Mansur detailing Ishaq's offer; it was not the kind of decision he felt competent to take on himself. Perhaps the plunder in Timbuktu would be better; he urged the king to consider being bought off as Ishaq had suggested and wrote, provocatively, that there was nothing worth keeping in the Songhai capital, and that "the house of the donkey master in Marrakech is of greater value than the palace at Gao." He signed the letter along with his second in command, ibn al-Haddal, and dispatched a messenger to take it to the sultan. If the messenger moved rapidly using a team of *mehari* racing camels, he could be back in not much more than forty days or so with the sultan's reply.

Meanwhile, Jawdar withdrew his army from Gao and set off upriver to Timbuktu. They were in no hurry but wended their way along the riverbanks, eating off the land and plundering what few small villages they found. They left in late March and arrived at Timbuktu toward the end of April. Jawdar set up his camp east of the city, between the Sareïleina and Bellafarandi quarters, and waited there for a delegation from the city to greet them.

In due time a straggling party of apprehensive Timbuktu notables arrived at his tent. They made a brave pretense of welcoming him, prudently pointing out their own long-standing disagreements with Askia Ishaq and their own fidelity to the precepts of Islam, quite unlike the degenerates of the capital. But partly out of arrogance and partly out of ignorance, they made a crucial mistake. The *qadi*, Abu Hafs Umar, remained in the city and sent his personal muezzin, Yahma, out with the delegation with a greeting. A greeting only, however; unlike the *khatib* of Gao, Mahmoud Darami, he did not offer any hospitality or a place to stay in town or any gifts. Jawdar interpreted this as an insult and gave the muezzin a present of fruits, sugar and scarlet broadcloth to take back to his master; these were luxuries imported from Marrakech, and the gift was a symbolic humiliation of the errant *qadi*.

Jawdar and his commanders entered the city on May 30 and made a walking tour to see what they could find. The rains were coming, and they needed someplace to stay. The *qadi*, compounding his earlier mistake, said he could probably find something for Jawdar himself, but as for the rest, well, there was nothing he could do. Their inspection tour had shown that the merchant quarter had the largest houses, so Jawdar simply told the occupants to leave, giving them less than a week to do so. After that, he and his men moved in. Some of the houses they demolished, leaving only the exterior walls, which became the foundation of a casbah, or fort. Jawdar's sappers must have been efficient, for the fort was finished in thirty-five days: it consisted of heavy walls pierced by two gates, one opening toward Kabara and the other to the market. Inside was a prison, granaries, stores, a mosque and a public square in which the soldiers could parade or Jawdar harangue the populace. It was ostentatiously massive, ostentatiously foreign, ostentatiously central and ostentatiously *there*.

Of resistance, there was no sign. This didn't mean there wasn't fury and resentment in the academies around the mosques. It would express itself in due time.

CHAPTER NINETEEN

✌

The Long Decline

BACK IN MARRAKECH, Jawdar's missive had set off an uproar.

When news first came of the victory over the Songhai forces, al-Mansur was ecstatic. What a magnificent victory! He drafted a proclamation to his own people and to the notables of Fez, declaring that "the armies of God in this battle made the world tremble, even the mountains, and turned the enemy white with fear. The shock was so violent that the blacks, overcome by our sabers, fell to the earth in terror, stark naked. God has given victory to our armies."[1] Now this! What did Jawdar mean, there was no gold? How dare he simply depart from the capital without leaving behind a secure occupying force or taking hostages from the royal family? How could he possibly suggest being bought off for such a paltry amount?

Behind these superficial reactions lay a deeper worry. If it were true that the gold came from some unknown place a good deal farther away, of what use had been the conquest? And at what ruinous expense! He had dispatched his best and most loyal soldiers on the expedition, and there was little hope of any of them returning. Worse, it would always be necessary to send more to replace those who died or became old, and this was expensive—he had to pay their wages in advance, buy them supplies, send them munitions. And he had to send them in sufficient numbers, or they'd be picked off by Tuareg bandits along the way. He also had to pay for the construction of forts in both Gao and Timbuktu to keep his men safe. And in any case would four thousand men be sufficient to permanently pacify the Songhai, never mind the tributary tribes the askias themselves had suppressed? And even if everything went well, where was the profit? Saving the duties and taxes he would otherwise have paid on imported merchandise wouldn't nearly cover his expenses.[2]

Al-Mansur's reaction to Jawdar's letter was typically decisive. He fired his general on the spot and replaced him with another renegade eunuch raised in the palace, Mahmoud ben Zargoum, ordering him to proceed to Timbuktu immediately, to remove his predecessor, to drive Ishaq out of the Sudan altogether and to send back more sensible reports.

∾

THE NEW PASHA, Mahmoud, reached Timbuktu in August 1591. Following his instructions he deposed Jawdar, assigned a new governor to Timbuktu, one Mustafa al-Turki, and set about arranging an expedition against Askia Ishaq, still camped on the right bank of the river near Gao. What few boats remained at Timbuktu after the evacuation were confiscated, and he set about building more, cutting down all the large trees in the city and its environs (the last time such trees grew there) and ripping off the doors of houses for planking. On September 9 he embarked, taking Jawdar with him.

Ishaq and his remaining forces met the invaders near Bamba, about 125 miles east of Timbuktu on the left bank of the river, and once again Ishaq was routed. That was his end: the remaining commanders stripped him of his royal insignia (the ring, sword and green turban of Askia al-hajj Mohamed, twelve military standards and thirty fine horses); he wished them well, asked God to pardon him and departed with a small retinue "to the land of the Gurma pagans." He was there only a short time before he was killed, along with his entire retinue.

There was one last flurry of resistance. Ishaq's governor in Timbuktu, Yahya Ould Burdam, left the town and organized a small task force to attack the new casbah. But he was both foolish and foolhardy, and he led the charge yelling that he would enter through the Kabara gate and leave through the market gate; instead, he was struck by a stray musket ball and killed. Al-Turki cut off his head and paraded it around town on a pole, accompanied by a crier with the message: "People of Timbuktu! This is the head of the *mondyo* of your city. This is what happens to people who stir up trouble!"

This was just the most recent in a series of atrocities committed by the occupying forces, and at last the uléma had had enough. Muslims the occupiers might be, but they were killing and torturing other Muslims, and that had to stop. Taking advantage of Pasha Mahmoud's distraction with the remnants of Ishaq's army, Timbuktu rose in revolt against what was now being called the Arma (a Songhai corruption of *al-rumah*, the plural form of the Arabic *al-rami*, or musketeer). Al-Turki's forces were struggling against this unexpected defiance when the Imagcharen Tuareg, sensing an opportunity, invaded and pillaged the town. "Matters were becoming complicated," in Sidi Salem's nice understatement. Pasha Mahmoud was obliged to detach a force of four hundred musketeers under Mami ben Barun, with instructions to replace al-Turki and restore order at whatever cost in blood. Fortunately, Mami was more measured than this. He did pass on the pasha's condemnation of Timbuktu's *qadi*, Abu Hafs Umar, as the man who bore ultimate responsibility for the revolt, and "for the crimes committed by the people, and made worse because you are a servant of Allah and know His ways, and it is you who have broken the pact of the prophetic mission of al-Mansur" as the *Tarikh* put it.[3] But instead of repression, Mami brokered a compromise and got the citizens calmed down sufficiently to permit those who had fled town to return. The *fondacs* once again filled with goods, and caravans once again set off on the trail routes to the north. Life returned to something approaching normality.

ↄ〇

MEANWHILE THE REMAINING Songhai forces had regrouped around Mohamed Gao, another of Askia Daoud's many sons. The new askia sent word to free two of his brothers, Mustafa and Nuh, who had been locked up by Askia Mohamed Bani, but others of his brothers had defected to the Arma, and he decided to see if he could make peace with the pasha. His overtures were welcomed, and he was invited to Gao to take the oath of allegiance. A few of his councillors, smelling a rat, urged him not to trust the Moroccans, but he went anyway, and as they sat down to eat a meal prepared for them "the snares of deceit and treachery were sprung," and they were seized and disarmed. Askia Mohamed Gao and eighteen of his commanders were shackled, taken to an old house, which was then pulled down over their heads, becoming their grave. The only one who put up any resistance was crucified instead.

Mischievously, the pasha declared one of the turncoat brothers, Suleiman, to be the new askia, but no one in the former empire paid him any attention. Of the two newly liberated brothers, Mustafa and Nuh, Mustafa was the senior, but declined the offer of replacing Mohamed Gao, and Nuh became askia in his turn. For the next two years the new askia led the Arma and the pasha on a dozen fruitless chases through the old empire, to no profit. They could neither catch Nuh nor defeat him, and their resources steadily dwindled. Suspecting that the wily uléma of Timbuktu were propping him up with material aid and a network of informers, the pasha declared intellectuals everywhere anathema and decided to do away with them for good, especially the Tuareg (Sanhaja) leaders, whom he suspected of being ringleaders. At first, he tried to get some of them to sign a pledge of allegiance to the occupiers, but that didn't work. Mohamed Baghayogho, at that point an eminent scholar at the Sidi Yahiya mosque, told him, "I would rather have you cut my hand off, up to the shoulder, than to bear [such] a false testimony." Then Pasha Mahmoud dispatched a message to his governor in Timbuktu, Mami ben Barun, ordering him to arrest the scoundrel Abu Hafs Umar, the *qadi* of the city, and his brothers. Mami, who had been successful in keeping the peace through a delicate balancing act between occupiers and natives, declined. "Wait," Mami said. "Then do it yourself, but only when you are between these walls."[4]

When the pasha finally reached Timbuktu, he set out to strip the scholars and intellectuals of their goods. He did this, typically, through a ruse. He sent messengers through the city to say that on the following day, his men would search all the houses, and if any weapons were found, the owner of the house would have only himself to blame. The only exceptions were to be houses belonging to people directly descended from Sidi Mahmoud, by which he meant Mahmoud ben Umar, *qadi* of Timbuktu under Askia al-hajj Mohamed. Naturally, everyone suspected that this search for weapons would turn into a looting spree, and so everyone with anything to hide therefore took whatever it was directly to one of the excepted houses in question, those belonging to descendants of the old *qadi*. Alas, this merely concentrated all the goods for the pasha's men, who turned up the next morning to expropriate everyone, including the owners of the supposedly exempt houses.

☙

WHAT FOLLOWED WAS worse, far worse, and lives in Timbuktu lore as the Massacre of the Intellectuals. So much was it imprinted on the life of the city that some of the prominent Timbuktu families, such as the Baghayoghos, still remember it as though it were yesterday.

First, the pasha announced that everyone—everyone, that is, with any prominence in the city, which meant the *qadi*, the imams of all the mosques, most of the learned in the madrasas, all the scholars and some of the wealthier merchants, together with their families—should assemble at the Sankoré mosque to discuss a new oath of allegiance to al-Mansur. When the mosque was packed with people, soldiers ordered all aides and servants to leave, then arrested all who remained, dividing them into two groups to take to the casbah. One group was sent through the middle of town, the other skirting the city to the east. Among those in the first group were the *qadi*, Abu Hafs Umar, who was by then very old, and his brother, the saintly Sidi Abd el-Rahman. (They were the only two allowed to ride on a mule.) This group reached the fort safely. The second group had just reached the artisans' quarter east of the Sidi Yahiya mosque, when one of the prisoners, called Ndafu, grabbed a sword from one of the soldiers and stabbed him to death. At once the rest of the guards fell on the party to take revenge. The prisoners were in chains and could do little to defend themselves. Fourteen were killed, many of them grandees of the prominent families, including three imams and several jurists. Also killed were Ndafu, who had provoked the killing spree, a shoemaker, two tailors and even two *haratin*, or slaves. It was October 20, 1593.

After this the pasha lost control of his men, and they went on a looting spree, stripping the remaining great houses and all the *fondacs*. Those who resisted were killed, and their women raped. Those prominent citizens who had not been killed were dragged to the casbah and imprisoned. Commercial life came to a complete standstill. At the end of the year, the pasha was able to scrape together one hundred thousand pieces of gold to send to his sultan, but five times that disappeared in the chaos.

To break the power of the remaining religious leaders for good, after a five-month imprisonment the pasha sent them across the desert into a Moroccan exile. They departed their home city in a single long caravan, men, women and children, leaving Timbuktu, in the words of the *Tarikh al-Fettach*, as a body without a soul.[5]

The long journey was perilous, for many of the jurists were elderly. At one point the scholar Ahmed Baba fell off his camel and broke his leg.

Both of the *Tarikh*s, being Timbuktu-centric, suggest that God evened things up a little. At least one of the abusive guards died of a broken neck when his camel bolted, and the *qadi*, Abu Hafs Umar, was said to have hurled imprecations against Marrakech when it came into sight. "O my God, those who have so traumatized us and dragged us from our country, torment them in their turn, give them their own exile." Very soon an epidemic in town precipitated a mass exodus.[6]

This divine intervention no doubt satisfied the scribes, but there was a more practical revenge against the pasha too: just after the massacre, one Ahmed ibn Haddal had left Timbuktu in secret for Morocco, to inform the sultan of the atrocities, theft and blatant abuses committed by his representative. "He lives by his sword and knows no other way," ibn Haddal told al-Mansur, "even the sultan's friends sometimes have this sword wielded against them."[7]

This made al-Mansur angry—"have I become incapable of achieving victory in the Sudan without this wretch?" he is supposed to have said—but he became angrier still when the guards who had dragged the savants across the desert told him about the endless stores of wealth looted from the houses of the captives, only a smidgen of which had been sent to the sultan. He immediately dispatched Mansur ibn Abd el-Rahman across the desert with orders to arrest Pasha Mahmoud and put him to the most ignominious death possible. The captives, Ahmed Baba and his colleagues, were kept in prison until the epidemic was over; then they were released on parole, promising not to leave Marrakech.

Pasha Mahmoud had some inkling of his fate, for one of his patrons in Marrakech, al-Mansur's son, Prince Moulay Abu Fari, had high regard for the pasha and sent a messenger across the desert to warn him. Perhaps to prove his loyalty (though the *Tarikh* suggests he had suicidal intent and wanted to die in battle), he made another foray against Askia Nuh, accompanied by the renegade askia, Suleiman. After a brief skirmish, Nuh and his troops took refuge in an escarpment called Almina Walu. Mahmoud determined on a night assault, against the advice of his staff, and took a small party of commandos into the rocks just before dawn. There, he was killed by an arrow and his troops had to abandon his body. Nuh and his partisans cut off his head and sent it to his ally, the ruler of Kebbi, who placed it on a stake in the marketplace for everyone to see.

Early in 1595, Mahmoud's replacement, Mansur ibn Abd el-Rahman, arrived in Timbuktu and met with Jawdar, to whom Mahmoud's soldiers had once again rallied. Within a few days the new pasha took three thousand musketeers for a new assault on Askia Nuh, and this time the Songhai army was routed. Nuh fled and disappeared from the stories. Mansur returned to Timbuktu with thousands of captives and placed them in the hands of Suleiman the renegade.

Despite all this, Timbuktu embraced the new pasha, mostly because he was a strict disciplinarian who kept firm control of the soldiers under his command. The random acts of violence not only tolerated but encouraged by his predecessor had made daily life a severe trial. Now commerce was able to resume, and the markets returned to more or less normal activity. "He became beloved of the poor and the weak," the *Tarikh* says, no doubt overstating the case considerably.[8]

The fly in this balm of contentment was the old warhorse, Jawdar. The soldiers liked him and understood his style of command. For his part, he didn't see why he shouldn't reassume command of the whole province, and began to act as though he were in fact in charge. Eventually relations between Jawdar and the pasha grew so heated they both appealed to the Moroccan sultan, whose finessed solution satisfied neither. Jawdar was declared territorial commander—in effect, governor of the province. But Mansur remained commander of the army. Predictably, this couldn't be made to work. Within a few months Mansur fell ill on campaign and died; rumors implicated Jawdar, who was widely thought to have poisoned him. Earlier rumors of a similar poisoning, that of the sultan's emissary Bu Ikhtyar in 1593, resurfaced, and the rumors became an uproar when the fourth pasha, Mohamed Tabi, an experienced commander who arrived in Timbuktu in December 1597 with reinforcements of a thousand musketeers, also died within days of meeting Jawdar. Then another holdover from the days of Pasha Mahmoud, the former *khatib* of Timbuktu, Mustafa al-Turki, also died, in the middle of 1598, this time strangled on the road to Kabara. His death also followed a public dispute with Jawdar.

With his colleagues and supposed allies safely dead, Jawdar was once again in control, and he set off to consolidate and extend Moroccan rule. Djenné, which had watched the increasing chaos in Timbuktu with considerable horror, prudently yielded to Jawdar without a fight. Then Jawdar took the fight to the rebellious Fulani of Masina, who were supported by an army of Bambara, and defeated them handily, razing many of their villages and seizing their granaries. A small army from the old Malian kingdom was easily suppressed.

But that was the end of it. When Jawdar set off to take the ancestral homes of the Keita kings, and thus to control the goldfields, he ran headfirst into a massive army of Fulani from the west, under their military strategist, Hamdi Amina. For the first time since their arrival in the Sudan, the Arma were routed. After that, the Moroccan tide began to ebb.

❧

BY 1600, THOUGH, Moulay al-Mansur's Sudanic adventure seemed to have paid off. The Moroccans were in firm control of the Niger Bend, with garrisons in all the major centers and at key points on the river. On the maps, the sultanate stretched, in al-Fishtali's words, "from the Atlantic Ocean to the Maghreb until the country of Kano, and limited only by the existence of Bornu," that is, from the Mediterranean to the Niger, from the Atlantic to Lake Chad. It seemed all the sweeter because al-Mansur's great rival in Constantinople, Murad III, was facing revolts in Tunisia and Tripoli. The pasha of the southern provinces, once again the redoubtable Jawdar, lived in Timbuktu, which he established as the capital of what came to be known as the "Pachalik." He commanded the army of occupation; he named the commanders of the garrisons and the chiefs of police in all the towns under his command; his assent was needed for the appointment of any tribal chief, including the *amenekals* of the Tuareg; he even controlled the appointment of *qadis* and imams. For form's sake and administrative convenience he incorporated the turncoat askia, Suleiman, into his government, but Suleiman's functions were limited. As Sidi Salem put it, "He was not much more than a chief costumer."9

Jawdar's senior official was the *amin*, the tax collector and treasurer, and army paymaster. His main task was to funnel as much money as possible to Morocco. He controlled the customs collectors at the southern and northern termini of the trade routes, such as Sous, the Dra'a Valley, Tafilelt, Tuat, Tamini, Tamentil, Taghaza, Timbuktu, and Djenné. Substantial quantities of gold flowed into the sultan's coffers; before al-Mansur's death there were said to be 1,400 hammers at the gates of his palace constantly beating out gold coins; in 1594 a caravan reached Marrakech from Timbuktu that included 1,200 slaves and maybe 6,600 pounds of gold (some reports say up to double that amount). A British agent in Marrakech estimated that the gold sent by Jawdar in 1599 alone amounted to some £604,000 sterling.

❧

BUT IT WAS all an illusion.

The sultanate was overextended, and the profligate spending of money to prop up its far-flung provinces generated tax revolts at home, and then revolts in truth, as Fez reasserted its independence. Moulay al-Mansur urgently summoned Jawdar home to help, and in response to his master's orders the first of the revolts, led by Moulay as-Sheikh, was savagely suppressed. But shortly after that al-Mansur himself died, on August 16, 1603, and the kingdom he had built so eagerly began to disintegrate. His sons and courtiers struggled to see who would win power. Jawdar threw himself behind Prince Abu Fari, but it was the wrong choice, for Fari's forces were routed by Abd-Allah, the oldest son of the suppressed as-Sheikh, who proclaimed himself sultan and ordered his troops to cut off the heads of Fari's commanders. And so perished the first pasha of Timbuktu, losing his head in the turmoil of an empire in terminal decadence.

After a month of infighting another son, Moulay Zidan, emerged as victor in Marrakech, but it was a hollow victory because he had lost control even over Fez. Nevertheless, he found time to liberate the celebrated Ahmed Baba. The savant, after fourteen years of exile, returned home to a much reduced and shrunken Timbuktu (where he resumed his teaching and had as a pupil the future author of the *Tarikh al-Sudan*, al-Sa'adi). For the next few decades, incessant warfare was the norm in Morocco; three of the four succeeding sultans were assassinated. The last of the Sa'adian dynasty died in 1659, when the Alawites, who still run Morocco, succeeded to power.

The Arma were still nominally in charge of the southern provinces. But in charge of what, exactly? The Songhai empire had been torn to pieces and could never be put back together. Timbuktu, Djenné and Gao would never again see their old prosperity. Many of the peasants who grew the food that sustained them had fled, and the area under cultivation dwindled. The remaining forests had disappeared. The cities were drained of population. The University of Sankoré closed; the schools were emptied of scholars; the workshops that produced manuscripts shuttered their doors. Schools still operated, but their standards dropped; John Hunwick noted that the standards of grammar and rhetoric plummeted at about this time, and that even the author of the *Tarikh*, he says, committed many spelling and grammar errors in generally infelicitous prose.

Al-Mansur's successors, complaining bitterly of a venture that they maintained had cost nearly twenty-three thousand Moroccan lives, cut their losses and allowed the Arma, and the descendants of the Arma, to run what was left of the former provinces, paying only nominal tribute to Marrakech. The predatory Tuareg once again menaced the northern trade routes and levied tribute on caravans and pirogues heading for Timbuktu. The Mossi and Fulani were both resurgent. Control had slipped away. As Heinrich Barth put it, "During the age of anarchy which succeeded the conquest of the country, and owing to the oppression from the [Tuareg] on the one side and the Bambara and Fulbe [Fulani] on the other, the state of affairs could not be very settled; and Timbuktu, shaken as it was to its very base by that fearful struggle, with massacre, rapine, and conflagration following in its train, could not but decline greatly from its former splendor."[10]

The second-last pasha sent from Morocco was Mahmoud Lonko, who arrived in Timbuktu in 1604 with a mere thirty soldiers. He restored the treasurer, the *amin* el-Hassan, to his functions, but he really had nothing much to do. Lonko delegated his powers, such as they were, to a local man, Ali ibn Abdullah Telemsani, from Tindirma, but the latter deposed Lonko (who died in 1607) and proclaimed himself pasha in 1612, a year of ill omen— that same year there was an atrocious famine in Timbuktu, a great drought, a flood and an earthquake. Morocco tried one more time, sending one Ammar to Timbuktu as pasha, with orders to kill el-Telemsani. The new military chief arrived in 1618 and took power; he duly had el-Telemsani strangled, but then he used the money he raised in taxes to bribe "certain people," preached revolution against the sultan himself and was recalled.

In June 1618 the troops named Haddou ben Yussuf as pasha. He died the following January and was replaced by Mohamed al-Mas, who was assassinated after three years. He was replaced by Hamma in November 1621. In 1627 Ibrahim ben Abd al-Karim became pasha and lasted only a year. His successor, Ali ben Abdelkader, decided to visit Mecca but never got there; he was attacked by bandits at Tuat and obliged to return to Timbuktu. He was killed in July 1632 and succeeded by Ali ben Mobarak, who lasted only three months.

And so it went: the records show that no fewer than 155 "pashas" were appointed in 160 years, all chosen locally by the descendants of the Arma, now getting less and less "Moroccan" as they married local women, still professing allegiance to the throne in Marrakech, but in practice having nothing whatever to do with that distant place. Pashas were no sooner elected than deposed. Some lasted no more than ten days and a few less than twenty-four hours. At times, the same pasha popped up over and over again. Even the strongest of them controlled only a small territorial parcel, not even reaching as far as Djenné.

Timbuktu was well into its long, long decline.

CHAPTER TWENTY

☙

The Coming of Jihad

THE MORNING WE went to visit the salt miner from Taoudenni, our route took us past one of Timbuktu's main cemeteries, where Halis's mother is buried. He pointed out her grave as we skirted the cemetery gates and headed off into the southern quadrant of the city. The grave looked like a thousand others—there were no headstones and no markers—but of course he knew which it was. At the time we didn't pay much attention—Halis was telling us about his father, with whom the family was having some difficulties—but later, over another meal at Tahara Baby's, he asked whether we had seen the small parcels of food lying on a few of the graves.

We hadn't. "What are they for?"

He was silent for a moment. "They are trying to stop the practice," he said. "Who are 'they'?"

By way of answer, he told us the story of how he had taken his mother on her hajj, to Mecca. It was a long and expensive trip, and Halis didn't want to go, but she was insistent. They went first to Bamako, then flew to Casablanca and from there to Jeddah and Mecca, where his mother performed the appropriate rites. Halis had been offended by Jeddah. Not the city itself, or Mecca, but the people he found there. "Too many fanatics," he said. "Too many people who don't even care that they die there, as long as they are there. Islam should be peaceful, a gentle religion. It should not be for fanatics."

Of course, he was a Tuareg, and the Tuareg have always had an exceptional view of Islam. Of all the peoples of the desert, they resisted the proselytizers longest, and it wasn't until around the fifteenth century that all the clans professed Islam. Even so, instead of adopting the whole creed they grafted it onto their own already ancient matrilineal traditions, and as a consequence, they depart from Muslim orthodoxy in several subtle and not so subtle ways, and still indulge in practices that are eccentric, bordering on heresy. They are generally unrepentant about this, remaining convinced that the One Way has several paths for the righteous to follow, a tolerant view of devotion that was the very opposite of fundamentalism.

Among the most obvious of their religious eccentricities to non-Tuareg is their use of joyous music during their devotions, a frivolity (mostly) frowned on by the devout elsewhere, Sufis excepted. And they differ even more fundamentally from orthodox Arab societies in their treatment of women. The most obvious symbol of the difference is that Tuareg men are veiled, but the women are not. Tuareg women can divorce their husbands, but for a husband divorce is hedged around with so many restrictions as to be practically impossible.

More interestingly, many among the Tuareg don't regard Muhammad as the only, or even the most important, prophet. This is not new backsliding on their part, but a tradition of long standing. Heinrich Barth, who had gotten into some convoluted, and sometimes dangerously heated, religious disputes in Timbuktu 150 years ago (when unorthodoxy was hazardous to life, and Christians were routinely killed), had once pointed out to his hosts, rather tactlessly, that in addition to Muhammad himself the local Muslims acknowledged Musa (Moses), Aisa (Jesus) and many others as true prophets; "and that [though he was not the Son of God but merely a prophet] they seemed to acknowledge the superiority of Aisa by supposing that he was to return at the end of the world." The sultan of Timbuktu in return accused Barth of being a *kafir*, or unbeliever. Barth, of course, hastily denied it, and in any case he was probably wrong about Muhammad's lack of preeminence in Tuareg lore, but his point, derived in many other conversations with eminent Tuareg in his six years in the desert, remained that the nomads had adapted Islam, not adopted it; many of their own traditions had merely been given new names but had otherwise remained unaltered.

It was also evident, as we had discovered in many conversations in Timbuktu, that the brand of Islam that had animated the city over the long centuries had been as laissez-faire as that of the Tuareg themselves; it had gotten them into (and out of) trouble in the past.

These "fanatics" that Halis had found in Saudi Arabia were now making their way into Mali, he said. "People go there to work, on the oil fields or in the cities, and they come back with different ideas," he said. "Foreign ideas."

He pointed to a new mosque and madrasa perched on a rise east of the city. "Financed with Saudi money," he said. It was the same mosque that Sidi Maïga of the Hendrina Khan Hotel had mentioned earlier, governed by the same narrow morality, preached by the same "them."

In fact, there are several new mosques and madrasas in town, financed by the Saudis, preaching their more militant and intolerant Islam.

"What has this to do with the food on the graves?" I asked.

"We leave food for the dead on feast days," Halis said. "Of course, we know it is not really for the dead, but it is an old custom. And it serves a purpose: the food goes to the poor. That's what it's really for."

"And they are trying to stop this? Who?"

"The new imams. They say the practice is idolatry, un-Islamic." He paused again, looking for another way of putting it. "They want to drive the old imams from the old mosques, turn everything around." The new Saudi-trained imams won't let their people pray in the old mosques. They denounce all ancient customs, no matter how apparently harmless, as idolatrous or heretical; and on political matters generally side with al-Qaeda. The older traditionalists are fearful of the changes, as making life harsher for everyone. Taken along with the simmering Tuareg resentment of the Bambara, it makes for a volatile mix.

Another aspect of the new fanatics that offended Halis was their essential humorlessness, a trait that often accompanies fundamentalism.

One of the other eccentricities of the Tuareg and Massufa Berbers was their persistent belief in the efficacy of charms and talismans, also in violation of Muslim convention. The Tuareg of the twenty-first century don't take these matters too seriously, but some customs have survived. Women still commonly wear the fertility symbol called the *khomissar*; older women frequently hang around their necks an arrangement of camel's teeth whose therapeutic abilities are thought to be manifold. In earlier days some of the Tuareg nobles wore as many as twenty amulets pinned to the chest to ward off evil and disease. Not so long ago, by wearing, or sometimes swallowing, a sacred text, deep-desert Tuareg believed they were protecting themselves against illness and even against violent death. Certain charms were believed to make a man (and his camel) bulletproof, a belief that persisted into the early twentieth century despite ample evidence to the contrary. So effective were charms and amulets believed to be that the desert proverb "After death they hung an amulet on him" is the equivalent of the Western folk homily "to close the barn door after the horse has left." A belief in the often malevolent (but sometimes benign) spirits of the desert, the djinn, is still widespread.

Fetishes are forbidden in Islam, but certain of the marabouts to be found in Saharan towns offer them anyway, to protect against things as divergent as AIDS and unpopularity. It can be a fine line, Halis said, because it is customary, for example, to consult marabouts about matters of the heart, or about marital difficulties, and many will take advantage of the credulous to offer cures. "I myself was offered such a thing," Halis said, laughing.

The new imams are trying to stamp out the practice, the good along with the ludicrous.

ಌ

THE EVENING WE spent with Sidi Salem Ould Elhadj and Halis in the dunes, Halis had told a story about a Tuareg family at Arawan who were Muslim, but mostly denied it.

Sidi Salem looked dubious. We were curious. "Why?" I asked.

"Among the Tuareg to be religious is to have the reputation of being rather weak," Halis said.

Sidi Salem still looked dubious, but this time disapproving too.

"Not powerful enough," Halis amplified. "So even if you are religious, you sometimes hide it, or people will take advantage of you."

We contemplated this matter of Tuareg weakness for a moment. I'd never thought of the Tuareg as weak, though of course there must be weak people among them, or at least degrees of strength. Mostly what one notices is their public swagger. We weren't the first to spot this inbuilt arrogance, either: Ibn Battuta had compared them to scorpions as early as the fourteenth century, and Heinrich Barth, in the 1840s in the Nigerian city of Kano, described Tuareg nobles striding through the markets, uncaringly knocking people aside, the blind and the halt as well as the fit and furious, it made no difference to them, a living illustration of the curious fact that in the Tamashek dictionaries the words for bravado and freedom are the same.

We'd often wondered, in fact, how you could tell one Tuareg from another, since they were completely veiled and all dressed pretty much alike, and all seemed to have the same swagger, but Halis had said you picked out your friends by their gait anyway (and rather more subtle signals, like the idiosyncratic way they tied their *litham*, or *tagelmoust* [face veil]). You could pick out the poseurs, the phony Tuareg, the same way; the "real" Tuareg are scornful of imitators, calling them *daga*, a word whose origin is obscure but whose meaning is clear: a man who wears the indigo robes of the Tuareg without either looking or really being Tuareg. In an earlier conversation with Halis's cousin Ahmed, I had told him I had read somewhere that Tuareg poetry celebrated banditry. Ahmed had denied it ("it is the action, not its result, that is celebrated," he said, "the bravery, not the plunder"), but he didn't deny that the Tuareg had made their way through the great desert for millennia by preying on passing caravans, or, where there weren't any, on each other. And in our day, say what you like about Islamicist fighters—terrorists, guerrillas, martyrs, call them what you will—but *weak* isn't the first word that springs to mind. I wondered how this bravado could be reconciled with Halis's professed preference for a kinder, gentler Islam over that of his despised fanatics, but the conversation drifted to other topics and was never resolved.

℘

THE TUAREG HAD been Islamic for some centuries, but that had never stopped them preying on Muslim-run Timbuktu. In the aftermath of the Arma's dissolution, they became more of a trial than ever. As one pasha succeeded another at a dizzying pace, the defense of Timbuktu suffered. When their pay was behind, the soldiers would sometimes refuse to go into battle; the Arma itself developed split loyalties, based partly on region of origin, whether Marrakech, Fez, or descendants of native troops. All three of these groups sometimes appealed to the Tuareg for aid, though "aid" wasn't really what they got, and after 1650 or so there were frequent bouts of anarchy and pillage.

The deterioration of services caused by all this turmoil of course made things worse. A massive epidemic of plague, probably smallpox though it could have been yellow fever or cholera or even cerebral-spinal meningitis, ravaged the city from 1657 to 1660; and another in 1688. In addition, a severe drought hit in 1669–70, and many people starved. There was more plague and more famine in 1704, then again in 1711 and 1712. The drought over, violent rains destroyed crops in 1737. Timbuktu's population dropped by three quarters. Arawan was depopulated almost entirely.

Politics didn't help. Pasha Mansur *dit* Koraï, who ruled in 1712 and then again from 1716 to 1719, was an oppressive and authoritarian leader who managed to amass an immense personal fortune before retiring to Morocco.

In 1718 he attempted to fend off the Tuareg, attacking them near Gao, but without success. Koraï's personal troops were renowned for their brutality, and casual beatings and assaults in the streets were common. So much so that the city rebelled, led by one Sidi Bahadun of Sareïkeïna, who then took power in 1719. He attempted to quell the Tuareg by paying them off, offering three thousand mithqals of gold to their leader to refrain from pillaging the city. The Tuareg took the money but ignored the injunction; they severed the trade routes, cut the city off from the river and menaced travelers. For three years matters were so bad that no pasha could be found who wanted the job, anarchy reigned and the Tuareg seized the chance to pillage the city again. "Vile crimes" were once again committed, both *Tarikh*s say.

Finally, in 1737, an Arma commander called Ahmoud ben Seniber cobbled together a coalition of the willing of Moroccan leftovers, Berber and Arab partisans from the Bérabiches and the Kunta, and native Bambara and Songhai to deal with the Kel Tadmekket Tuareg under their *amenekal*, Aghomor. Seniber assembled this army, together with every able-bodied man he could scrounge from the city itself, and set up camp at a place called Toya, downriver not far from Timbuktu. The Tuareg chieftain, for his part, didn't wait to be attacked but crossed the Niger from the Gurma and marched toward Toya and Timbuktu. There was no one left in the city except the intellectuals, merchants, the infirm, women and children, but those who saw him pass—his cortege could be seen from the west gate—said his camels, his men, his slaves, his women and his herds filled the horizon.

The Tuareg attacked Seniber's army on the evening of May 22, 1737, broke for the night, then attacked again at dawn. Casualties were high on both sides, but the Tuareg prevailed, and Seniber fled into the river and was drowned with two hundred of his troops. Aghomor stripped the city of what he could but then, perforce being in charge, ordered the resumption of traffic between the river and the city. After a few months he even signed an accord with the *qadi* of the city, Ahmed ben Mohamed al-Tarzakini, who became pasha in his turn. Two years later Tarzakini's successor as pasha, Said ben Mansour Seniber al-Za'ri, managed to pacify the Tuareg with a mix of threats and bribes, and the city finally knew a little peace. One of the Tuareg leaders, the *amenekal* of the Awlimminden, Ghuman Ag Sheikh Ag Kalidan, even agreed in 1741 to be invested in office by the pasha at Timbuktu.

∽

WE SAT AND reflected for some time on this long and sorry history of conflict and decay. Not much of the city could be seen from where we were, but we could hear the bleating of goats returning to town as they did each night, here and there the braying of an ass or the occasional blatting of an un-mufflered motorcycle. Only the motorcycles gave a clue to the century; without them, it could have been any year in the last millennium. I wondered, without those decades of strife and warfare, would things have been different for Tim-buktu? By the eighteenth century the Dutch, the English and the French had established themselves in West African ports, mostly for slaving purposes, but their presence there and the ships they sailed would in any case have done away in the end with the trans-Saharan trade, the lifeblood of Timbuktu. At the same time, the economy of the Maghreb ports and of North Africa generally had fallen on hard times—Timbuktu was losing its important markets. Also, the climate was getting worse, possibly through natural cycles but partly be-cause the forests that once surrounded the city had been destroyed. In 1741 and 1744 famine and plague again ravaged the whole of the Niger Bend. In No-vember 1755 an earthquake shook Walata, Timbuktu and Djenné; damage was minor, though the minaret of the Sankoré mosque was toppled. Three more epidemics occurred before the end of the century, and another in 1805.

Somehow, the people survived, though they became more parochial and inturned than before. Foreigners were no longer welcomed, as they had been under the askias, but treated with suspicion. The central market served the whole city, but all the others were open only to residents of the quarter in which they were located. The *fondacs* had long since disappeared, and the car-avan traffic had ground to a halt. Through the influence of the imam of Sankoré, al-Aqib, a network of residential mutual-aid societies was set up in the late eighteenth century to deal with the destitute; these so-called *kondays* after a while became obligatory, and after circumcision every male was re-quired to join; women had their mirror groups. These were lifelong associa-tions, designed to give material and financial aid, and to manage the major social rituals, like marriages. If a member appealed for help, such help was obligatory. Any member who refused faced expulsion, and expulsion meant exile or death. It was a necessary closing of the ranks.

∽

TOWARD THE END of the eighteenth century the Kunta clan became more influential in Timbuktu.

The Kunta had arrived in the southern Sahara as far back as 1504, when the first head of the family, Sheikh Sidi Ahmed al-Bakkai, established a Sufi community in Walata. Over the next hundred years they expanded to Timbuktu, Djenné, Agadez and as far as the Hausa cities of Nigeria, and in the eighteenth century moved to the Middle Niger, where they set up a headquarters of sorts in a village called Mabruk. The sheikh of the time, Sidi al-Mukhtar al-Kunti, established an extensive confederation by uniting various factions, and under his leadership the Sunni Maliki school of Islamic law was propagated throughout the region and into Guinea and the Ivory Coast. More important, the marabouts of the Kunta, who were by now more Fulani than Berber, often served as intermediaries and negotiators between factions, and in August 1771 Sheikh al-Mukhtar, Sidi al-Kunti's father, had managed to reconcile the pasha of the time, Bahadu, and the *amenekal* Hammiyuk of the Tuareg, chief of the Kel Tadmekket, who had been blockading the city and exacerbating the famine. (The siege had been so complete that the people of Timbuktu were reduced to eating diseased animals and vermin.) Under the agreement, the city had to pay the Tuareg a tribute of 18 horses, 1,200 articles of clothing and 700 mithqals of gold. This was something of an achievement, as al-Kunti suggested later (in a document now in the Mamma Haïdara Library), because Tuareg honor forbade the taking of blood money. Later, this same "sheikh of peace" even ruled on an internal Tuareg dispute, with both parties assenting, and managed to put a stop to terrorist acts of Bérabiche bandits.

Not long afterward, Hammiyuk violated the agreement by seizing a party straggling up from Kabara, and the Kunta sheikh promptly cursed him and gave his blessing to a rival, al-Ghimayr. With the Tuareg thus split into two factions, busy fighting each other, the city had a breathing space during which normal life could resume, or what passed in those times for normal life.

ᘓ

IT IS SAID in Timbuktu that the Arma came under the control of the Peul [Fulani] in 1826.

The Fulani were the scourge (or one of the scourges) of the eighteenth- and nineteenth-century Sahel, and their exploits roiled Timbuktu over and over.

Sometime around the start of the eighteenth century their ideological puritanism, combined with their unhappiness at the constant taxation and vexations of the petty successor kingdoms that followed the disintegration of

Songhai, brought them to a boiling point. The precipitating event seems to have been the arrival in West Africa and the Sahel of a mystic and militant version of Islam, the *tarikhah*, based on a Sufi notion of the ineffable ideal, but which in its African incarnation also suggested that the conversion of pagans was for the glory of God and therefore an urgent duty. The *tarikhah* spread through Fulani society like a desert storm in the late seventeenth century, and the first of the Fulani jihads was launched by Karamoko Alfa near the source of the Niger, in central Guinea, in 1720. This led to a small theocracy that persisted until 1881, when it was finally brushed aside by the French.

These early skirmishes were only a taste of the agitation to come. In 1790 a Fulani holy man, Usman dan Fodio, who lived in the northern Hausa state of Gobir, began to preach sedition against the kings, whom he accused of being little more than pagans. His jihad charged through Hausaland and engulfed the three old Hausa kingdoms of Kano, Katsina and Zaria and the adjacent one of Daura, and swept up tribal chiefdoms in what is now northern Cameroon and southern Chad. Only the armies of Kanem-Bornu, secure against Lake Chad and trained in battle against the predatory nomads of the central Saharan mountains, were able to resist. After the old kingdom of Gobir was destroyed, two major military encampments, Sokoto and Gwandu, emerged as the twin capitals of a new Fulani empire. Sokoto, the more powerful, was the last of the empires of the Sudan.

The commanders of the jihad, Usman dan Fodio's brother Abdullah and his son Muhammed Bello, became the viceroys of the new empire, which combined the three former Hausa kingdoms of Katsina, Kano and Zaria with the smaller kingdom of Daura. Abdullah ruled the western half from Sokoto and Bello the eastern half from Gwandu. But they were too urbane and cultivated to sustain militancy for long, and when Usman died the standards once again decayed, the people seduced by the softer life of the Hausa, and the Hausa tongue, forbidden by the theocrat, returned as the language of state. Bello, particularly, was a gracious and urbane ruler; it was he who astonished the British explorer Hugh Clapperton by asking him cogent (and rather condescending) questions about British exploits in India, about which he seemed to know a great deal.

Neither of these first two jihads directly touched Timbuktu, but that was only an accident of geography, and it wasn't to last.

A few decades later, in 1818, a Fulani cleric called Agmadu ibn Hammadi launched another jihad patterned after the conquests of Usman dan Fodio. This time there was resistance even among the Fulani. The local chief called on his ruler, the Bambara king of Ségou, for help, but to no avail; the Bambara army was only a pale imitation of its former self, and Ségou was crushed. A new theocratic state was set up that included Ségou, Djenné—and Timbuktu. The Tuareg, summarily ejected from Timbuktu, waited in the desert for revenge.

The city struggled on. In 1844 the Tuareg drove the Fulani completely out of Timbuktu after a battle fought on the banks of the Niger River in which a great number of Fulani were slaughtered or drowned. This victory was to no avail either; as Heinrich Barth wrote afterward, "[It] only plunged the distracted town in greater misery; for, owing to its peculiar situation on the border of a desert tract, Timbuktu can not rely upon its own resources, but must always be dependent upon those who rule the more fertile tracts higher up the river; and the [Fulani] ruler of Masina had only to forbid the exportation of corn from his dominions to reduce the inhabitants of Timbuktu to the utmost distress."[1]

In 1852 yet another jihad, the third of the nineteenth century, was launched by a Tukolor cleric called al-hajj Umar Tal, who had been seduced by the puritanism of the Wahhabis in Arabia. He had been appointed the West African leader of a relatively new activist brotherhood, formed a community of his own and in 1852 came into conflict with nearby Bambara chiefs. A jihad was launched northward through the valleys across the Upper Senegal, then down the river. In 1857 he took twenty thousand troops to assault a French fort on the river near a place called Médine but was repulsed with huge losses, a blow to his prestige. After 1859 he sought to enlist the Fulani in taking on the once more resurgent Bambara kingdom of Ségou on the Niger, but they refused. He conquered Ségou anyway, established a "kingdom" there, calling it Masina, and continued downriver until he was able to assert control over Timbuktu. In 1863 he took possession of the city itself but couldn't hold it against Tuareg raids and was forced to retreat, leaving it once again at the mercy of the nomads.

The old established Muslim towns and Fulani communities regarded Tal's Tukolor, tribal cousins, as upstarts, and in a subsequent battle in 1864, attacked on three sides by Tuareg, Moors and rebellious Fulani, Tal withdrew to his capital of Hamdallahi, took refuge in a cave and was blown up by a massive bomb.

❧

ONE OF THE thousands of documents in the Mamma Haïdara Library—one of the bound parchments in those tottering piles in Sidi Abdel Kader's storeroom—is a memoir written by that same Umar Tal. It's one of his most famous works, *The Sword of the Truth*, which is still widely studied in the Sahel. Several translations from the Arabic are available,[2] and it makes somewhat disorienting reading, because its tone—conciliatory, generous, even wise—contrasts so vividly with his known actions.

He had lived more like a warrior than a scholar, waging war in the name of God, converting the unbelievers by fire and sword, killing heretics and apostates. Daringly, his life has even been compared to the prophet's; the Senegalese griots singing of his exploits cite the thousands he killed, and the thousands more he sold into slavery, as proof of his divine mission. At one point in his campaign against the Bambara, he executed three hundred hostages as a sign of his iron will, which can hardly be construed as a conciliatory gesture.

Umar Tal was born around 1797 in the Upper Senegal River region, the son of an educated man who instructed converts in the esoterica of Islam. On his way to his pilgrimage in Mecca he stopped in Sokoto to visit Usman dan Fodio's nephew, Muhammed Bello, who offered him his daughter, Maryam, in marriage. Tal settled for a while in Cairo; later, on a visit to Jerusalem, he succeeded in curing the son of Ibrahim Pasha, viceroy of Egypt, and in Mecca he was designated *khalif*, or representative, of a mystical brotherhood called Tijaniya. He subsequently returned to the Niger "to obey the voice of God" and convert the black pagans to Islam. It was the classic life arc of a jihadist.

What, then, to make of the self-professed Armed Prophet's own story?[3]

In his writing, he tells the story of how he passed through the territory of the Hausa kings on his way to Mecca and learned there of a long-standing dispute between the Hausa state of Sokoto and Bornu. He did nothing at the time—reaching Mecca was clearly the more important priority—but on the way back he talked to both parties and succeeded in papering over their differences, bringing peace to both kingdoms.

"We thought not to succeed," he wrote (his modest tone somewhat offset by his use of the royal *we*), "but we intervened in any case and our intervention bore fruit. We undertook these steps in the name of God who said in the

Holy Qur'an: 'It is created in you what you know not.' It was the word of God that pushed us to proceed, as God said: 'There is no greater good in their conversation, if one of them orders charity, an obvious good, or the reconciliation between two peoples. And to whomever seeks the approval of God, to him shall be given great reward.' "

Of course, both Sokoto and Bornu were Muslim countries, but still, the tone is hardly belligerent. Self-confident, yes, even self-satisfied, but not belligerent. Later in his life, Tal wrote:

Tragedy is due to divergence and because of a lack of tolerance. In the tradition of the Prophet, it is written that those who keep rancor in their hearts will not benefit from divine mercy . . . It is written by the Guide of mankind that he who associates himself with God and kills voluntarily will not be pardoned. Glory be to he who creates greatness from difference and makes peace and reconciliation. Purity, for those who repent, and find refuge in peace and in avoiding ruin. God, the good Guide, makes it a duty for men to support healthy mutual relations. The purity of relations and social cohesion are guarantors of peace. Who would dare to create havoc in that of his own, to thus mutilate himself? Not even the drunkard. You will never see a wise man purposely harm himself or harbor hostility. Conciliation and concord are immense sources of happiness and those who ensure their institution shall be showered in virtue. Such virtue will safeguard you from the hatred of men and the temptations of the devil.

༄

THE CONFLICT, OR apparent conflict, between Tal's words and his deeds is striking. How to square this circle?

How we would do it now is hard to say, but at the time the uléma of Timbuktu did it by the simple trick of cherishing his words and deleting his deeds from their collective memory. In this, they were entirely consistent with their own traditions. Conciliation and tolerance had always been for them the highest of virtues, praised in many a fatwa and argued into the heads of generations of pupils. I thought back to what I knew of the "sheikh of peace" of the Kunta clan, and the other story told by Heinrich Barth of the Tuareg Timbuktu ruler who protected him against those Fulani forces, Umar Tal's predecessors, who wanted to kill him. The poem written by Sidi al-Bakay in

Barth's defense was recounted earlier, but in the same era, al-Bakay discovered that the militantly theocratic Fulani ruler of Hamdallahi, Amadu Amadu, had infiltrated spies and saboteurs into Timbuktu with a view to conquest and more pillage—he had already taken Djenné by the same ruses. Sidi Haïdara asserted that al-Bakay was "one of the most charismatic figures of Timbuktu's political and spiritual history, a pious Muslim who, according to the manuscript entitled *Zakhîrat al-Sarmad*, 'fought as well with plume as with sword.'" That's as may be; Barth, who was grateful for his protection, nevertheless thought him indecisive and a bit of a ditherer. In any case, to Amadu he wrote, indignantly, "I will not be kept quiet about the shameful acts of the depraved. I will revile them, I will criticize them, their acts, their companions, and those that accompany them in their ideology!" Amadu was later executed by commandos sent by Umar Tal, the biter bit.

૭૭

ONE MORNING WE walked past all three of the city's medieval mosques, the Sankoré, the Sidi Yahiya, and the royal congregational mosque, the Djingareiber. They are in sad shape, though perhaps not as sad as they have been at various times in the past. Djingareiber's walls and minaret have been repaired several times, and its main doors rebuilt and rehung, and from the outside it looks sturdy enough, massive and impregnable. Inside, beams are rotting and the roof threatens to give way; a consultant from the Aga Khan Foundation told us the building needs great amounts of work; the foundation is fronting the money and is trying to prevent its being siphoned off in Bamako. Sankoré, the most venerable and also the closest in style to the traditional mud architecture of Mali, is crumbling, too, but has preserved its integrity. The repair work done after the earthquake in the seventeenth century can still be detected; much money is needed for ongoing maintenance, but it still looks substantial enough. The third, the Sidi Yahiya, was spoiled by careless work done under the French. They used concrete, for one thing, in violation of tradition; and during World War II they even converted the minaret into a crenellated tower of sorts, a grotesque error. Work done with World Bank financing in the year 2000 repaired some of these mistakes and also replaced roof beams and structural work, but of the three mosques it is still the least "authentic."

Under the mansas and then the askias, the financing of maintenance was the prerogative of the rulers. The Arma cared little for Islam, and the imams and the masons' union took on the work, paid for by wealthy individuals and by subscription. As the city passed successively under the Fulani of Hamdallahi (1826–62), Umar Tal (1862–64), the Tuareg (1864–93) and then the French (1893–1960), this repair work was institutionalized. All masons' guild members had to contribute work (or at least provide donkeys to help transport stone or mud), and all congregants were obliged to give something, however small, whether it be money or poles or *banco* (pounded mud) or maybe just food.

On the day of designated repair work, the guild leader sent a kola nut to each member, a symbol of his obligations. A town crier informed the whole population, including students and the military, that work was to be done that day. The two leading families of the guild hosted a breakfast for the workers, those working on Sankoré with the Haman family, those working on Djingareiber with the Koba family. Drums were beaten, a ceremonial bowl of mortar was mixed, and work began, accompanied by drum bands and female singers.

Work on the minarets and roofs had to be performed by Haman or Koba family members alone.

All this has faded now. After independence, there was neither money nor energy for repairs. The diva of the masons' choir, Fatouma Arafa, a great animator of tradition, died in 1966 and was never replaced, and with her departure the will for work seemed to seep out of the people. Then in 1989 the three mosques were placed on UNESCO's World Heritage List, and somehow even the imams expected that the UN would now supervise and pay for repair work. Nothing, of course, happened, though the World Bank got some work done in 2000, and the Aga Khan got involved in 2003.

℘

AND NOW? AFTER all these years, after all these centuries, the three medieval mosques still stand. After all those kings and emperors, all those *qadis*, all those grand clerics, all those saints and scholars, there they still are, enduring symbols—despite Umar Tal—of peaceful endeavor and scholarship. As Sidi Haïdara said, for centuries the mosques have been centers of mediation and arbitration between warring regional factions.

One of his favorite examples was the story we already recounted, from the days of the great Askia al-hajj Mohamed, a fine ruler but a man who had been briefly persuaded into political persecution of the Jews. The grand *qadi* of Timbuktu at the time, Sidi Mahmoud ben Umar, who lived from 1463 to 1548, was one of the great jurists of Timbuktu, and he vehemently disapproved of his askia's imprisonment of Jewish merchants. His arguments, sustained and elegantly put, obliged the askia to release those Jews he had locked up, restore their property and give them liberty.

"In situations of extreme conflict," Sidi Haïdara said, "where neither argument nor reason brought resolution, they even went to extreme measures to invoke the faith of the parties in dispute, by literally throwing their prayer beads at the belligerents, a symbolic gesture inspired by the Qur'an, they practically forced the parties to unify."

Ahmed Baba himself had a typically measured Timbuktu view of the intersection of religion and politics. The pious must deal with the powers-that-be with "distance and respect," he wrote, "but only when merited. Searching for modes of friendship with tyrants, or ways of friendship with them, or exchanges of hospitality with the masters of this transitory and ephemeral world, are to be condemned."[4]

❧

LATER THAT DAY, Halis took us out of town again, and on the way we passed that new Saudi-built mosque, with its blue dome and pencil-thin minaret in the Arabian style, out of place in Timbuktu. The drumbeat of emotion emanating from the mosque didn't seem to be one of conciliation, not even of the Umar Tal variety. It was bent for the moment against the men and women of the older mosques, with their seemingly soft and nonconfrontational ways, and their accommodation with the gentler traditions of the past. If they succeed in driving the old imams out and turning tolerance into a messianic narrowness, maybe it won't matter anymore if those venerable buildings crumble along with their traditions. They will have lost their meaning anyway.

CHAPTER TWENTY-ONE

⁊ი

Finally, the Europeans

NO MATTER HOW faded and down-at-the-heels Timbuktu has become, no matter how shabby and crumbling its streetscapes, how reduced its population, how depleted its schools and mosques and madrasas, how rudimentary its hygiene, its citizens are still illumined enough by the glow of their city's past glories not to wonder why outsiders want to come and visit. They take it for granted that the world is curious about them. They're an isolated people, but not cut off; they know a good deal about the world beyond the sands. Halis, when we first met him, boasted about some of the famous people he had shown around the city—Nelson Mandela, Jimmy Carter, the secretary general of the UN, Betty Ford—but then, seeing that his nonfamous visitors were less than impressed, said gracefully that "all are equally famous who come here, because they all come the same long way and they all come to see our city."

In past centuries, too, travelers were received equably and treated with courtesy. But after the long decline begun by the Moroccans, in the centuries of anarchy and strife, the city became closed and hostile to outsiders, and even when outsiders came, there was an incredulity that they didn't have some deep and necessarily sinister ulterior motive. Despite the long history of exploration by eminent travelers such as Ibn Battuta, in later centuries the idea of journeying for its own sake—just because the traveler wanted to see what was there—had become unknown and was greeted with skepticism. Such people must perforce be the outriders of conquest. Or spies. Or maybe they were just mad or sinners. Certainly they were infidels or, even worse, Christians. Better to kill them and be sure.

When the Scottish explorer Mungo Park first clapped eyes on the Niger, for example, he explained to the Bambara king of Ségou, then part of Masina, that he had come a long distance through many dangers just to behold it, a remark that was met with puzzlement. "He naturally inquired," Park wrote later, "if there were no rivers in my own country, and whether one river was not [just] like another."[1]

☙

THE FIRST EUROPEAN, other than the Granadan al-Gharnati, known to have crossed the desert was a Frenchman from Toulouse, one Anselm d'Isalguiers, who made it to the Niger Bend, married a "princess of Gao" and returned home with her in 1413. He left no word of his travels, or whether he had in fact seen Timbuktu, and his bride's fate among the sturdy peasant farmers of the Loire Valley is unknown. In 1447 a Genoese merchant, Antonio Malfante, landed at Algiers and penetrated the interior as far as Tuat and Tamentit. He never mentioned Timbuktu either; his reports were mostly account books, but he noted that the population was "generally negroid, with trade mainly in the hands of the Jews; the Tuareg controlled the open country." A Venetian in Portuguese service, Ca' da Mosto, made it to the Guinea coast in 1455, and in a later commentary on his travels he advises merchants to do business with the king of Timbuktu and of Mali, send their cargoes and their agents to those kingdoms, where they will be well received and cared for, "those kingdoms being at present so much civilized and so desirous of the merchandise of Europe, as may be read in this book of Giovan Lioni."[2] In 1469 a Florentine, Benedetto Dei, was reported to have reached Timbuktu, but if he wrote about it his accounts have vanished. The Portuguese were trying for some time to reach the interior, and some of them may have done so. Two Italian priests were rumored to have crossed from Tripoli to Katsina in Nigeria in 1711.

Europe had been somnolent during those centuries the Arabs were traveling widely, somnolent and isolationist, generally ignorant of far places and foreign ways. It was only after the Renaissance, and then the Enlightenment, that their curiosity wandered abroad, and their great age of discovery began. After that, the urge to explore the unknown came upon all the European nations for a time. The urge was a combination of venal and not so venal motives, like colonialism itself, in which curiosity and the desire for expansion were conflated with business. At first, the main impulse was avarice—those legends of the "cones of gold" in Old Ghana, and of cities whose minarets

glittered gold in the desert sun. Those legends kept many of the explorers going; as already recorded, fabulous tales had been circulating in Europe about
the Golden Kingdoms of the Sun, and they sometimes merged with the quasi-
religious mythmaking about the "lost Christian empire" of Prester John. In
the aftermath of the Enlightenment, knowledge came to be prized for its own
sake, and that there should be large tracts still unknown an affront to science.
For some explorers, like the Frenchman Henri Duveyrier, ethnographic studies were the prime rationale. (He popularized the Tuareg as romantic nomads
and until the end of his days refused to see the darker side of their culture.) In
later years, of course, exploring got tangled up with colony-making. Only a
few explorers resisted co-option. Some did, however, like the admirable Adolf
Krause, who refused to have anything to do with extending the German
empire into the interior of Africa.

In England, the need to scratch the itch of exploration was given concrete
expression by the formation, in the middle of the eighteenth century, of the
African Association in London (or more properly the Association for Promoting the Discovery of the Interior Parts of Africa). It was one of the earliest of
the geographic societies that have since proliferated in the West, and which
are still concerned with identifying areas of interest and sponsoring scientific
expeditions. According to the association's original prospectus, issued in
1788, "Of the objects of inquiry that engaged our attention the most, there
are none, perhaps, that so excited continued curiosity, from childhood to age;
none that the learned and unlearned wish so equally to investigate, as the nature and history of those parts of the world which have not, to our knowledge, been hitherto explored."[3]

The association's charter asserted that "as no species of information is
more ardently desired, or more generally useful, than that which improves
the science of Geography; and as the vast continent of Africa, notwithstanding the efforts of the ancients, and the wishes of the moderns, is still in a
great measure unexplored, the members of this club do form themselves into
an Association for promoting the discovery of the inland parts of that quarter of the world."[4] Unstated was another motive: a number of members of
the association were slavers facing ruin if their business was essentially abolished by government fiat, finding new sources of revenue outside of slavery
was high on their private list of priorities, and gold would suit admirably.

In their files were the usual well-worn anecdotes, among them Idrisi's notion of "the many civilized cities of Africa, among them Kaugha, a populous

City without Walls, famous for Business and useful for Arts for the Advantage of its People; Kuku, where the Governors and Nobility are covered with Sattin [sic]; and Ghana, where the King, for decoration, had a lump of Gold, not cast, nor wrought by any other instruments, but perfectly formed by the Divine Providence only, of thirty Pounds Weight." Then of course Leo Africanus's effusive description of Timbuktu was known to all: "The rich King of Tombuto has in his Possession many golden Plates and Scepters, some whereof are 1300 Ounces in Weight, and he keeps a splendid and well-furnished Court."

Some of the stories were disbelieved but were piquant even so. For example, Benjamin Rose, aka Robert Adams, claimed to have been shipwrecked somewhere on the Moroccan coast in 1820 and taken to Timbuktu by "Moors," where he was fattened up on coconuts, went on vast elephant hunts and generally had a wonderful time. (The core of his story might be possible, but it's more likely that he was a slave for three years, because he was ransomed by the British consul at Mogador, and that he never crossed the desert at all, spending his time in the oases of the northern Sahara.)

There was more. A report in 1790 from Tangier to the secretary for the Barbary States was quite specific: "The Caravan Trade from Morocco to Guinea proceeds no further South than to Tambuctoo, the Capital of Negroland. This town, I believe, is a general Rendezvous not only for the people of this country [Morocco] but likewise for the Traders of Algiers, Tunis and Tripoli." Caravans of up to three hundred people carried European products to the interior and brought tobacco and salt, gold dust, ivory, slaves and gum back to the north; as many as four thousand slaves were being marched across the desert to Morocco each year, among them eunuchs "of a Country called Bambara, whose king was said to be happy to exchange some twenty of them for a good horse." The region of Timbuktu, the report went on to say, "[is] inhabited by a civilized and quiet People and abounds with large unfortified Towns . . . The Country is fruitful and produces much Corn and Rice near the Rivers or Lakes, I suppose, for I am informed it never rains there. It abounds likewise in Cattle and Sheep."[5]

In the minds of these eminent persons, after reading Leo, listening to the tales of the person they called Shabeeny, about how "gold was found nearby, not by mining, for there were no mountains to excavate, but simply by digging up and refining the sand,"[6] Timbuktu became a symbol of this search; Timbuktu was one of the last mysteries, the path through the puzzle of Africa and the key to its treasury.

Henry Beaufoy, a member of the association, asserted that "their mines of gold (the improvable possession of many of the inland states) will furnish, to an unknown, and probably boundless extent, an article that commands, in all the markets of the civilized world, a constant and unlimited scale."[7]

Many a traveler perished in the search, victim of either the implacable desert or the ferocity of its inhabitants, or both. In the nineteenth century, all in all, some 150 European travelers lost their lives exploring the Sahara, a very high proportion of those who set out. Sometimes they succumbed to thirst or disease, in others to a hostile population suspicious (often with good reason) of European intentions. Daniel Houghton disappeared around 1791. Captain George Francis Lyon set out from Tripoli in 1819; his companion, Joseph Ritchie, died in Murzuq, and Lyon struggled on to Ghat, where he was forced to turn back. John Davidson tried to get to Timbuktu but was murdered six weeks out from M'Hamid, Morocco. Walter Oudney, who traveled with Dixon Denham and Hugh Clapperton to Lake Chad, never returned. By the time Clapperton set off on his second expedition across the Sahara (his first, to Lake Chad, had ended badly), desperate to beat Alexander Gordon Laing to discovering the secret of the Niger, the British government was no longer interested in exploration as such. Where the Niger went was no longer of much interest. Controlling it, headwaters and delta, was more the point. Laing himself got to Timbuktu but never returned; he was killed as an infidel by his Tuareg escort.

Heinrich Barth set out with two companions, expedition leader James Richardson and Adolf Overweg. Richardson died at Zinder, Overweg, the first European to circumnavigate Lake Chad and to map it, died on the lake's shores a short time later. Barth, a man of immense strength, stayed away six years and returned with massive journals packed with priceless ethnographic and geographic information, only to find celebrity passing him by. His contemporary, David Livingstone, was much more suited than the dour German to the life of the celebrity traveler and spoke much more eloquently at revival meetings and at conventions of geographic societies. Before Barth returned, another expedition under Edward Vogel was dispatched to find him, but Vogel was murdered by the sultan of Wadai; a subsequent explorer looking for Vogel was also killed.

The exotic Hollander Alexandrine Tinné was also murdered by her escort, probably for her wealth, though lurid rumors of her doings with changelings and familiars in the form of gigantic dogs almost certainly did her no good.

Gustav Nachtigal, another German traveler, who seemed both awed by and smitten with Tinné, escaped with his life after a harrowing captivity among the Tubu of Tibesti, but in 1870 two Frenchmen, Norbert Dournaux-Dupéré, from Guadeloupe, and Ernest Joubert, set out to cross the desert and were murdered by Chaamba Arabs between Ghadamès and Ghat. Another Frenchman, Camille Douls, tried to cross the Sahara from the western Mauritanian coast. He disguised himself as a Muslim, even to the extent of having himself circumcised. He fell into the hands of a wandering band of Moors. Believing him to be a Christian, they buried him in the sand up to his neck, but he escaped by repeating memorized passages from the Qur'an. He was killed on a second trip. In 1881 Colonel Paul-Xavier Flatters, exploring the Sahara northeast of Ahaggar for a possible railway across the desert, was killed when his expedition was wiped out by its Tuareg escort.

Yet, some adventurers survived and at century's end could still be found wandering in the deep desert. The young writer and adventurer Isabelle Eberhardt, Russian born and Swiss raised, spent most of her adult life in the Algerian Sahara. She became a Muslim, dressed as a man and spent most of her time traveling on horseback. She was drowned in a flash flood at Aïn Sefra, Algeria, in 1904.[8]

∽

THE AFRICAN ASSOCIATION'S first expedition aimed at crossing the Sahara was a disappointing fizzle. The "explorer" they chose was Simon (sometimes known as William) Lucas, the British vice-consul in Morocco who spoke a little Arabic, having had perforce to learn it when he spent three years as a slave. (He later parlayed this meager knowledge into a sinecure as oriental interpreter at the Court of St. James.) Lucas's notion was to cross the Sahara to Fezzan, or rather to travel to Fezzan, from Tripoli, and with this in mind, he set off in October 1788. He never got more than four days from town, and at Misurata he prudently turned back, deterred by news of a Tuareg revolt, which was stirring up the desert tribes to the south. He remained British consul until 1801 but never again ventured into the interior. This didn't prevent him from gathering stories about the desert, including distant Tibesti, from other travelers, and publishing them under the title *Historical Accounts of Discoveries and Travels in Africa*.

Next up was John Ledyard, who came to the attention of the association when he was arrested and expelled from Russia for apparently trying to walk to Canada without the proper permits—this seemed the right sort of spirit. Ledyard, however, perished in Cairo before he ever got to the desert, apparently of an overdose of self-prescribed medications. Next the association hired an Irish major called Daniel Houghton, who duly set off up the Gambia. There he was promptly robbed by a Mande ruler, inflicting a wound on himself when his gun misfired. He kept going but was never heard from again.

Finally, the association hired a young ship's surgeon called Mungo Park. He had some pretensions to being a naturalist (his treatise *Eight Small Fishes from the Coast of Sumatra* had commended him to the Linnaean Society), and he claimed some linguistic ability (he had apparently picked up some Mande while staying with a trade mission on the Gambia River). He offered his services to the African Association in 1793, and his offer was accepted. His task, he said in his *Travels*, was "to pass on to the Niger and . . . to ascertain its course and, if possible, the rise and termination of that river," as well as "to visit the principal towns in the neighborhood, particularly Timbuktoo and Houssa." (Shabeni had described "Houssa" or "Hausa" as a city "as large as London, with a palace whose walls were eight miles long," though he didn't have a clue where it actually was; it was probably Kano.)

Park seemed to get on well with the Africans he met, though he was subjected to a good deal of suspicion and, in some cases, bewilderment. The women of a Fulani king, he reported, "rallied me with a good deal of gaiety in different subjects, particularly upon the whiteness of my skin and the prominency of my nose. They insisted that both were artificial. The first, they said, was produced when I was an infant, by dipping me in milk; and they insisted that my nose had been pinched every day, till it had acquired its present unsightly and unnatural configuration." As David Mountfield pointed out, "Park was himself no mean hand at this kind of raillery . . . at one of his worst moments, when a captive of the Moors, he agreed to their demand that he should prove himself to be uncircumcised provided he was allowed to demonstrate the fact to the prettiest girl present."9

His relations with the Tuareg were very different. With them, he bristled with hostility. It is difficult now to sort out fault. He was convinced they were simply barbarians. "It is sufficient to observe that the rudeness, ferocity and fanaticism which distinguished the Moors from the rest of mankind found here a proper subject on which to exercise their propensities. I was a *stranger*, I was *unprotected*, and I was a *Christian*; each of these circumstances is sufficient to drive every spark of humanity from the heart of a Moor, but when all of them, as in my case, were combined in the same person, and the suspicion prevailed that I had come into their country as a *spy* [all these italics are Parks's own], the readers will easily imagine that in such a situation, I had everything to fear."[10]

But there is another side to the story. Later explorers discovered that the locals were as little fond of Park as he had been of them. In Timbuktu, Heinrich Barth was regaled with tales of "that Christian traveler Mungo Park, who had arrived on the Niger some 50 years earlier, appearing apparently out of nowhere, to the consternation of the natives." When Barth left for Gao, he ran into a party of Tuareg. "I counted not less than fifty of them, all decent-looking men. After a while I became very good friends with them, although the commencement of our intercourse was difficult. They had had some dealings with Mungo Park, whose policy it was to fire at any one who approached him with a threatening attitude; and having lost some of their tribe to his well directed balls, they kept at first some distance from me, viewing me with a suspicious and malevolent eye. But when they observed that I had entered into cheerful conversation with some of their party they convinced themselves that I did not belong to the class of wild beasts, or *tawakast*, for such, from the reception they had met with from Park, they had supposed all Europeans to be."[11]

Who started the animosity is unclear. When Park first reached Bambara country, he was taken captive by a Tuareg chief and kept for several weeks. "Never did any period of my life pass away so heavily," he reported; "from sunrise to sunset was I obliged to suffer, with an unruffled countenance, the insults of the rudest savages on earth."[12]

He was finally released, quite alone, speaking none of the languages of the region except for his rudimentary Mande, and with no food or clothes. He passed by Ségou but was forbidden entry. Hungry and depressed, he was taken in by a woman in an outlying village, fed and given a bed. "[I gave her] two of the four brass buttons which remained on my waistcoat; the only recompense I could make her."

He tried to reach Djenné but was forced to turn back, "worn down by sickness, exhausted by hunger and fatigue; half naked and without any article of value by which [he] might secure provisions, cloths or lodging."[13] He fell in with a slaving party, who saved his life by allowing him to march with them, and in June 1797 he reappeared on the Gambia, to the astonishment of the small British colony there, who had given him up for lost.

He returned to London, where his account of his adventures, *Travels in the Interior of Africa*, was published in 1799 to great acclaim. He returned to Scotland to savor his new celebrity, and there married a local girl. But it wasn't enough, and in 1803 he accepted another commission to lead an expedition to the Niger.

This time it was a quasi-military adventure. Park was given thirty-five soldiers to accompany him, and set off with the soldiers, a few local guides and his brother-in-law, Alexander Anderson, as second in command. However, it was the rainy season, and the soldiers soon sickened with fever, and before they had gone very far, half of them had died. On August 19 they reached the Niger, but Park found their prospects gloomy. By then three-quarters of his crew had died, and another two succumbed that very night. The carpenters who might have built their boats had died too. But he took comfort from the entirely mistaken notion that he had "always been able to preserve the most friendly terms with the natives."

Since they couldn't build a boat, they got several derelict canoes and cobbled together a serviceable vessel from the good parts of two of them, calling it, only half in jest, *His Majesty's Schooner Joliba.*

Just before they launched this dubious vessel, Park's brother-in-law died. The small party of five finally pushed off downstream. For a while, things went well. They were attacked by Tuareg below Kabara, the raiders rowing up in a series of canoes, but these were no match for his larger boat, equipped as it was with an immense iron hook for protection against hippos, and he fended them off. He seized on the notion of staying in the boat, heading as rapidly downriver as he could to prevent more hostilities (thereby depriving himself of the chancy notion of visiting Timbuktu), but at Ensymmo (now Tosaye), where the Niger narrowed to a gorge, Park's boat stuck fast. The Tuareg attacked again, this time with more success. The five men leaped into the river to escape, but they all drowned.

Years later, when George Lyon was traveling in the desert, he heard rumors that Park had not in fact drowned but was held captive by the sultan on account of his skill in surgery. Barth found that the Park story was still a sensation in the 1860s. "With what immense excitement the mysterious appearance of this European traveler, in his solitary boat, had caused amongst all the surrounding tribes!"[14] Soon "Mungo Park" became a generic insult hurled at European travelers; the lost explorer was passing into myth, and "it is said the legend exists to this day, and that the Emir of Yauri uses Park's silver-topped cane as his staff of office."[15]

☙

ALEXANDER GORDON LAING was next to try his luck, in 1825. A British army man stationed in Sierra Leone, he had been sent by his superiors into the interior to drum up business and do what he could to stamp out the slave trade, Britain having decided by this time that slaving was a bad thing in and of itself and wasn't that beneficial to business either. Laing believed the German theory that the Niger River flowed into the Bight of Benin, and wanted to be the first to prove it.

For reasons having more to do with army politics than geographic sense, Laing made his way to Tripoli, where he would cross the desert to the Niger, then take the river downstream. But there were delays in Tripoli. Not just the usual—the local ruler, despite his uncertain control of territory beyond the Fezzan, demanding ever-increasing sums to permit foreign travelers to cross his land—but more personal ones too: Laing met and was smitten with the daughter of the British consul, Colonel Hanmer Warrington. They were married in a civil ceremony, and only with the strict injunction from the indignant father of the bride that they were not, under any circumstances, "to co-inhabit till the marriage [was] duly performed by a clergyman of the established church of England."[16]

In July 1825 Laing finally set off from Tripoli in the company of a Tuareg chief from Ghadamès, who was taking a roundabout route that would lead him, eventually, to Timbuktu.

They reached Tuat without incident, but there matters started to deteriorate. The desert tribes were again in turmoil—Fulani jihads had stirred up Tuareg wrath. While Laing and his party were waiting in Tuat for additions to their caravan, a passing Tuareg spotted Laing and accused him loudly of being none other than Mungo Park. Laing at first found this rather funny, but the accusations mounted and fury against this pseudo-Park reached fever pitch. The caravan nevertheless set off but now began to blame Laing for its every ill. Rumors of marauding Tuareg swirled through the camp every night, and many times the entire caravan seemed on the point of turning back. "We were in a constant state of alarm," Laing reported. "Every acacia tree in the distance being magnified or metamorphosed by the apprehensive merchants into troops of armed foes."

A little later, in a letter to his wife in Tripoli, he reported that matters had improved. Friendly Tuareg from Ahaggar had joined their convoy as escorts. Surely, he wrote, "my prospects are bright, and expectations . . . sanguine."

Nothing more was heard from Laing for three months, and then a letter reached his wife, explaining that his bad handwriting was the result of a cut finger. The truth, related later by one of his camel drivers, was far worse. The Ahaggar Tuareg attacked Laing in his tent one night, having first gained possession of his ammunition. Laing was "cut down by a sword on the thigh, he . . . jumped up and received one cut on the cheek and ear and the other on the right arm above the wrist which broke the arm, he then fell to the ground, where he received seven cuts, the last being on his neck." His attendants were killed, but astonishingly he survived. He was rescued by another Tuareg from Timbuktu and provided with an escort into the city.[17]

Heinrich Barth's view, when he visited Timbuktu later, was that the attack on Laing had not been motivated by treachery alone, but instead by "a certain feeling of revenge for the mischief inflicted upon their countrymen by the heroic Mungo Park." Park's policy, remember, had been to fire on anyone who approached him in a more or less threatening manner, prompting Laing, in a letter he later sent to General Edward Sabine, to mention that he had met a Tarki [Tuareg] who had been thus wounded by Park. "How imprudent!" Laing wrote. "How unthinking! I may even say how selfish was it in Park to attempt to make discoveries in a country at the expense of the blood of its inhabitants, and to the exclusion of all after-communication! How unjustifiable was such conduct!!"[18]

Laing spent a difficult month in Timbuktu, despite being generally well treated by the inhabitants. His timing was execrable. The Fulani who governed Timbuktu at the time were still preaching holy war (and treating the inhabitants with a mixture of cruelty and contempt), and Tuareg raiders had isolated the city. As Heinrich Barth put it later, "these people [the Fulani], owing to the impulse given to [Usman dan Fodio], had become far more fanatical champions of the faith than the Arabs and Moors; and treating the inhabitants of the newly conquered city . . . with extreme rigor, according to the prejudices they had imbibed."[19] After a month in Timbuktu Laing set out again, this time heading for the Senegal River, territory which he knew well. He was accompanied by a "friendly" Tuareg chieftain. They hadn't gone far before he was murdered as an infidel. His skeleton and that of an unnamed Arab boy traveling with him were exhumed by the French authorities in 1910 and reburied in Timbuktu. The house he stayed in is marked with a small plaque. His journals were never recovered, though there were rumors they had turned up in Tripoli for sale and had been acquired by the French consul there.[20]

છ્ર

IN THE END, the African Association was trumped by, of all people, a Frenchman, René Caillié, the first European (Leo Africanus and the Granadans aside) to visit Timbuktu and return, more or less unscathed.

Caillié was born near La Rochelle, in southwestern France, in 1799, the year Napoleon returned from Egypt, bringing with him a fashionable yearning for antiquity and a romantic identification with faraway places. By Caillié's own admission, the bug got him early; in the introduction to his *Travels*, he said he had cherished a desire to become a traveler from "earliest infancy." He had, he admitted, absolutely no qualifications for doing so, but he always wanted to go to unknown Africa; "in particular, the City of Timbuktoo became the continual object of all my thoughts, the aim of all my efforts, and I formed a resolution to reach it or perish."[21]

This obsession took him a long time to realize. As a boy of sixteen, he managed to get to Senegal but was stuck there for several years without getting to the interior. He applied to join a British expedition up the Gambia in 1819, but Major William Grey, its leader, turned him down; he had after all, by his own admission, nothing to recommend him.

He was back in West Africa again in 1824, this time fired up by the cash prize offered by the Geographical Society of Paris to the first person to deliver an eyewitness account of the fabled city of the desert.

He prepared for his journey in the thorough and leisurely way of the time. For two years he learned Arabic and studied Islam, for he had seized on the idea, commonly adopted by wandering Europeans, to travel as an Arab to avoid the well-known hostility of the desert tribes; that he was fair-skinned and not a wonderful linguist troubled him not at all. While he waited and learned, he worked as manager of an indigo factory in Sierra Leone. When he had saved two thousand francs from his wages, he quit his job, moved up the river to Rio Nunez, where his evident Europeanness was not so well known, and spent his money on trade goods. At last, he made contact with a small caravan of Mande merchants who were departing for Timbuktu, and they agreed that he could accompany them.

He took with him a guide, Ibrahim, the guide's wife and one porter. He set out on April 19, 1827. He hadn't been on the road for more than a few minutes when Ibrahim announced gloomily that the Tuareg would never fall for the masquerade—Caillié's fair skin was too much a giveaway. The admonition, Caillié noted, was a trifle late.

In any case, Caillié had a story ready. He was an Egyptian Arab who had been kidnapped by Christians early in life and had been forced to pass his miserable existence among infidels in Europe. This, he hoped, would account for both his poor Arabic and (banking on the scant scientific knowledge among the heathen) his fair skin. It seemed to work, too. The party was joined on the road by a band of Fulani traders, who were entranced by this vision of an Arab rescued from certain perdition: "they shewed a sort of veneration for me, and were never weary of looking at me and pitying me: their extreme devotion rendered them charitable: they came and sat by me, taking my legs upon their knees, and rubbing them to relieve my fatigue. 'Thou must suffer sadly,' they said, 'because thou art not used to such a toilsome journey.' One of them fetched leaves to make me a bed. 'Here!' said he. 'This is for thee: for thou canst not sleep upon the stones, as we do.' "[22]

They reached the Niger in the Bambara lands, but there Caillié could go no farther. He developed ulcers and signs of scurvy. His teeth began to rot and fall out, and he took refuge in the house of a sympathetic local, who pressed on him remedies that may or may not have helped, but who was happy to take his "gifts" in any case. It wasn't until five months had gone by that he was able to resume his journey.

He reached Djenné, the old capital of Mali, where the emirs treated him with courtesy and curiosity, wanting to know something of the Christian lands, and whether he had been treated as a slave and forced to eat pork and drink intoxicating liquors. He responded with some creativity and afterward seemed ashamed of his lies, though they had kept him alive. Thereafter, he resumed his journey, this time in the kind of sixty-five-foot pirogue that still plies the river between Djenné and Gao, wrapped in a blanket to keep his fair skin from the sight of the Tuareg. He arrived in Timbuktu on April 20, almost exactly a year after he set out.

Despite Caillié's first exhilaration ("On entering this mysterious city, which is an object of curiosity and research to the civilized nations of Europe,

I experienced an indescribable satisfaction"), he was gravely disappointed in what he saw: Timbuktu was a typical desert town, low-built of mud, crumbling, its inhabitants scratching a living on the edge of the Great Emptiness, the roofs and minarets of gold conspicuous by their absence, its libraries meager and its countinghouses virtually empty. It was flyblown, shabby, a metropolis only of mud. Its security was precarious, entirely dependent on Tuareg goodwill—and the Tuareg were prickly to insult: "I was assured that if the crews dared but to strike one of these savages, they would forthwith declare war against Timbuktoo and intercept all communication with its port." Caillié nevertheless found the city orderly, crime minimal, the warehouses and markets full and tobacco smoking banned, except to visitors.[23]

Caillié was treated courteously. A patron adopted him and gave him a house, whose slaves brought him lamb-flavored couscous twice a day, and once, at the mosque—Caillié was careful to keep up his pious pretense—an elderly Tuareg gave him a little gift: "[He] stepped up to me gravely, and without saying a word slipped a handful of cowries into the pocket of my coussabe. He withdrew immediately, without giving me time to thank him."

Caillié's notes estimate the population of the city at ten or twelve thousand permanent residents, most of whom were then entirely dependent on the salt trade, since the flow of gold from Ghana had dried up. The gold was going elsewhere. A good part of it was being diverted south to the Ashanti, whose own supply didn't seem quite enough; the rest was making its way up the coast in barques to the countinghouses of Europe and the Maghreb. Despite his initial disappointment, he remarked that "there is something imposing in the aspect of a great city raised in the midst of sands, and the difficulties surmounted by its founders cannot fail to excite admiration."[24]

In the two volumes of his memoirs, Caillié comes across as an engaging traveler, self-deprecating in a very modern way. He was frank about his shortcomings and amusing about, for example, his squeamishness when confronted with the horrific deformities and diseases that he saw on a daily basis (for, like most outsiders, he was presumed on thin evidence to be a skilled healer). His solution to his lack of medicinal skills was inventive and usually involved the advice that whatever remedy he prescribed would not work for about twenty days, after which time he devoutly hoped to be far away from recrimination and reprisal. When confronted, for example, with a man complaining of impotence, "as ginger grew in the environs, I advised him to eat plenty."

One thing still troubled him: how to silence the naysayers and doubters who would greet his return? If he went back up the Niger to its source and thence overland to Gambia or Sierra Leone, where was the proof that he'd ever been to Timbuktu? They could say he'd merely cribbed notes from others, rewritten Leo Africanus and tales of Mande travelers, and made the whole thing up; the tale of the fair-skinned Arab would itself read rather like an engaging fiction. So he decided he'd take the hard route home: across the Tanezrouft to the Atlas, across 620 miles of perilous desert where, as he himself admitted with a thrill of trepidation, "caravans hundreds strong had disappeared without a trace." Of course, he also knew that caravans had been making the same crossing for centuries, and that there were men in Timbuktu itself who were, if not exactly commuters, at least experienced hands at trans-Saharan navigation.

The journey was grim, as he had expected. It got off to an inauspicious start when the caravan, bound for Fez, paused at the spot where Laing had been murdered, which occasioned a good deal of mirth and satisfied smirking; for his part, Caillié succeeded in masking his dismay. The caravanners paused for a week in Arawan to rest and fill their waterskins; then they set forth into the void. He soon became obsessed, as Saharan travelers do, with water. The idea of water filled his mind with craving. He mumbled constantly, no longer afraid of being found out. Oceans, lakes, rivers, streams, wells, ponds of water. He saw waterfalls, lakes shimmering before him, vanishing and reappearing, a constant torment as they plodded on. The sun scorched like hellfire; the heat rose through the nostrils into the brain, burning the blood. The wind came up, a searing heat, and sand enveloped them, filling every cavity and drying the mouth until it felt like the desert floor itself. Even the camels faltered and stumbled. When the wells finally appeared in sight, in reality and not in mirage, Caillié flung himself to the ground among the crazed camels and sucked at the thin black mud he found there.

At the salt mines of Taoudenni they paused again. It was as bad as Ibn Battuta had described, so many centuries before, nothing but sand and salt and searing heat, nothing to eat but the desiccated flesh of camels that had perished along the way. When the sun went down serpents came out from wherever they hid in the day, and slithered across the bones that everywhere littered the pathway; Caillié watched their progress in terrified delirium. The Tuareg of the city called him Christian and threw garbage at him; he was roughed up and spat upon. He simply endured.

Six weeks after setting out, at Tafilelt, they saw the first palms since the Niger. He also found in the Maghreb, among its educated and well-traveled people, a well-founded suspicion of his Arab credentials. Still, he persisted in his story and made his laborious way to Rabat, where he was met with suspicion and contempt not from the Arabs but from the French consul there, who refused to believe this ragged creature could be a Frenchman. "Clinging to the back of an overburdened donkey," he made his further way to Tangier, where he was, again, greeted with skeptical contempt. Again he persisted, and the consul in Tangier finally secured him a passage home. At the beginning of October, he landed in Toulon.

The British, jealous of their place in African exploration, doubted his tale to the end, but he was fêted in France and duly picked up his award from the Geographical Society of Paris. For the rest of his brief life, he plotted to get back to Africa but never succeeded. He died, presumably of exhaustion, in La Badiere, France, at the age of thirty-eight.

∾

HEINRICH BARTH, WHO followed Caillié to Timbuktu and went many places besides—he spent more than six years wandering around the Sahara and the Sahel—was an academic, and something of a pedant (some of his lectures in the School of Archaeology at the University of Berlin had to be canceled because so few students showed up), but he was a first-rate explorer, unfairly underestimated in his time and for long afterward. He had always yearned to travel, and to explore other cultures, and he had many attributes that perfectly suited him to exploration: he was immensely strong, for one thing; he was thorough and meticulous (his maps were models of their kind); he was a skilled linguist (fluent in Arabic, he later published vocabularies of eight African languages including Tamashek and Hausa, and learned enough Hausa on a single journey from Ghat to Agadez to be able to converse freely); and, far from least, he was a person of great curiosity who had a knack for getting on with people. For a man of his time, he was astonishingly unjudgmental; not for him the pious snobberies of Ibn Battuta or the cheerful racism of the English.

He prepared for his travels in a typically thorough way, by spending several years in Cairo studying Arabic. In 1849 he published the first volume of his *Wanderings Around the Mediterranean*, a record of several years he spent traveling "in that state of society where the camel is man's daily companion and the culture of the date tree his chief occupation."[25] In Tripoli he had met, as had many other explorers, Colonel Warrington, Laing's father-in-law, who promised him support if he ever wanted to attempt a desert crossing.

When Barth was apprised that the British government was outfitting an expedition to the interior and wanted a man of science to go with it, he volunteered immediately, putting up the two hundred pounds demanded to cover his expenses.

The expedition was put together with mixed motives. The foreign office intended to open up trans-Saharan trade to British advantage, but the expedition was initiated for other reasons entirely. James Richardson, its leader, was a zealot of the antislavery society, and after an early trip to Murzuq and Ghat, had persuaded himself that he could not only rescue the interior from slavery but also convert its inhabitants to Christianity by persuading them to reject what he called "the false prophet"—a perilous judgment that would get him into plenty of trouble later on. Lord Palmerston, the foreign minister, approved of both these objectives and outfitted the group accordingly. Richardson's society supplied the Bibles, but Palmerston supplied the guns and ammunition and, bizarrely, a disassembled boat, called of course the *Lord Palmerston*, which, as Barth put it, "was carried throughout the difficult and circuitous road by Murzuq, Ghat, Aïr and Zinder, exciting the wonder and astonishment of all the tribes in the interior, ultimately reaching its destination [it was launched on Lake Chad] though the director of the expedition had himself in the mean while unfortunately succumbed."[26] The British apparently saw nothing peculiar in the notion of carrying a full-scale boat, albeit in pieces, across the burning Sahara; the incongruity was, on the other hand, a fertile cause of ridicule in the desert, as Barth himself was to note.

After Richardson's death Barth was appointed leader. In the preface to his enormous journal of his travels (three volumes of over six hundred pages each) he felt obliged to say that he had tried to abolish slavery along the way, but felt constrained to apologize in advance for not succeeding. In fact, he noted ruefully, in order to survive he had at one point placed himself "under the protection of an expeditionary army, whose object it was to subdue another tribe, and eventually to carry away a large proportion of the conquered into slavery." The foreign slave trade, he observed, could be abolished; it would not be so easy to get rid of domestic slavery. Unlike many of the other African explorers, Barth made no attempt to pass himself off as an Arab, though he had darkened his skin with indigo, wore native dress and called himself Abd' el-Kerim. Except, he said, "I was once obliged, for about a month, in order to carry out my project of reaching Timbuktu, to assume the character of a Muslim. Had I not resorted to this expedient, it would have been absolutely impossible to achieve such a project, since I was then under the protection of no chief whatever, and had to pass through the country of the fanatic and barbarous hordes of the Tawarek (Tuareg)."[27]

Barth's first sight of the Niger roused him to new heights of orotund prose, but he nevertheless loaded up his descriptions with fact, as was his wont: "In a noble unbroken stream, though here, where it has been contracted, only about 700 yards broad, hemmed in on this side by a rocky bank of some twenty to thirty feet in elevation, the great river of West Africa (whose name, under whatever form it may appear, whether Dhiuliba, Mayo, Eghirreu, I'sa, Kwara or Baki-n-ruwa, means nothing but 'the river' and which therefore may well continue to be called the Niger) was gliding along, in a NNE and SSW direction, with a moderate current of about three miles an hour." He was transported across the river in ferry boats "of a good size, about forty feet in length and from four to five feet in width in the middle, consisting of two trunks of trees hollowed out and sewn together in the center." The largest, he reported, could carry three of his camels. He was the last to embark and was "filled with delight when floating on the waters of this celebrated stream, the exploration of which had cost so many noble lives."[28]

He headed west, from the riverside town of Dore, "along the last, and most dangerous, part of my journey." Dangerous not because of the topography but because it was infested with robbers. And on leaving Dore, indeed, an armed band attached themselves to his small cavalcade, "and their conduct was so suspicious we had to send them about their business, for the inhabitants of this place had, not long before, robbed and killed in a similar manner a wealthy *sharif*, whom they pretended to escort." In the village of Wulu, they found the place in an uproar because a Tuareg chief was said to be planning a raid upon it.

In the province of Dalla, adjoining Timbuktu, he for the first and last time took on the guise of an Arab, for the Fulani jihadists who then ruled it would permit no Christians within their borders. He crossed Tuareg territory by moving from one petty chieftain to another, and by guile and smooth talking, along with a good many small gifts. At Sarayamo, the chief persons of the town paid him a visit to solicit his aid in obtaining rain. "After a long conversation about the rainy season," Barth reported, "I felt obliged to say before them the *fat-ha*, or opening prayer of the Qur'an, and to their great amusement and delight concluded the Arabic prayer with a form in their own language, '*alla hokki ndiam,*' 'God may give water.' It so happened that the ensuing night a heavy thunderstorm gathered from the east, bringing with it considerable quantity of rain."[29]

Barth, like Laing, found himself embroiled in the bitter politics of Timbuktu; the Fulani and the Tuareg were constantly maneuvering for an edge over the other, the rule of the city uncertain and changeable. Barth, posing as an Arab for the general populace, had confessed to his host, the Tuareg Sidi Ahmed al-Bakay, that he was really a Christian but had the protection of the sultan of Constantinople himself, a claim that wore thin when it became apparent he possessed no documentation at all for so extraordinary a claim. Nevertheless, al-Bakay insisted on protecting him. His Fulani opponents, egged on by Fezzan merchants who resented what they saw as incipient competition, intrigued against him. They didn't have enough political muscle at the time to go directly against Barth's protectors, and contented themselves with a petulant exercise of religious puritanism, putting in irons those around him who had neglected their prayers. The threats mounted, as Barth took refuge in a tent outside the city, entering only with an escort at selected times. He nevertheless managed to deliver a detailed report of the city (correcting some of René Caillié's more eccentric townscapes, and, a great coup, was able to read a copy of Ahmed Baba's *History of Songhai* and to make extensive notes).

His protector, al-Bakay, assured him that he could travel home in safety, choosing his own route, either through the country of the Tuareg (northward), through the "country of the Fulbe" (westward), or by boat downriver to Gao and so back to Bornu. But it would be eight months before the countryside settled down enough for him to risk setting off again.

The politics of the region continued to be unstable. Not only were the Fulani still warring with the Tuareg tribes, but the Tuareg of the north, who guarded the roads to Morocco, fell into civil war, essentially a vendetta gone awry. On a more personal note, Hamed Weled Abeda, the Tuareg who had killed Gordon Laing, bound himself by oath to put Barth to death.

In the end, Barth returned via Gao and the Niger back to Kano, and thence to Lake Chad.

He closed his massive travel journals in a self-congratulatory tone, entirely deserved under the circumstances: "I had embarked on this undertaking as a volunteer, under the most unfavorable circumstances for myself . . . [and] after its leader had succumbed in his arduous task, instead of giving way to despair,

I had continued in my career, and when the leadership of the expedition was . . . entrusted to me . . . I resolved upon undertaking, with a very limited supply of means, a journey to the far west, in order to reach Timbuktu, and to explore that part of the Niger which, through the untimely fate of Mungo Park, had remained unknown to the scientific world."[30]

Barth died young, like most African explorers. He got to be received at Downing Street, he published his monumental books (poor reviews, fewer than two thousand copies sold) and died at the age of forty-four.

☙

SO TIMBUKTU AND its hinterlands were now "known," but still in so many ways unknown.

At first, the African Association had shared the dream of Moulay al-Mansur so many years earlier, with its visions of endless depositories of gold. After a while, though, that dream was transmuted into another, also shared with al-Mansur: the desire for territory. Like the Golden One, they wanted to control as much territory as possible, spreading their influence across the known and soon-to-be-known world, to the aggrandizement of king and country. The scramble for Africa was under way, as al-Mansur had scrambled for land in his turn.

After Napoleon was sent to an ungracious exile on barren St. Helena, Britain had the interior of Africa pretty much to itself, although the kaiser, cousin to Victoria, was wandering around various parts of the south. But British control of the interior wasn't to last; among the French, Anglophobia and dreams of empire were too strong.

Already by 1830, the French had captured Algiers, and army units were pushing out into the Sahara from the north, just as other units advanced snail-like up the Senegal River from the west. This leisurely conquest was interrupted several times—first by a Tuareg revolt led by Abd el-Kadar, then by the jihad of Umar Tal and finally by the Franco-Prussian War on their own borders—and only in the 1870s did their attention finally turn back to the trans-Saharan territories. Their desires were bundled with all the bombast of a newly confident metropolitan power bent on the *rayonnement* of French culture and civilization worldwide. By 1879, the governor of Senegal, Brière de l'Isle, had pushed well up the Senegal River, egged on by Admiral Bernard Jauréguiberry, the minister in charge of the colonies. Someone—even after all these years, it is still not clear who—conceived a mad scheme to construct a railway from the Mediterranean coast across 1,400 miles of trackless desert to the Niger, where, as one of its sponsors boasted, it would help "create a vast colonial empire . . . a French India rivaling its British counterpart in wealth and prosperity; to open up unlimited markets for trade and industry, [and] give free reign to our civilizing impulses." Of course, these riches had already amply been proved illusory, and the "civilizing impulses" was a bit rich even for the time, but that didn't stop the politicians from dreaming. Maurice Rouvier, a French government adviser, was even more effusive: "There lie vast regions watered by great rivers and great lakes, regions of unbelievable fertility inhabited by 200 million people. Shall not these regions provide unlimited opportunities for our trade?" The Chamber of Deputies apparently thought so and by 1879 voted the money (800,000 francs) to pay for a thorough survey of the route.[31] Who started it may be unclear, but its sponsors were two powerful French ministers: Jauréguiberry, then the minister of marine, and Charles de Freycinet, the minister of public works.

The survey mission, under Paul François Xavier Flatters, was a disaster. Flatters was massacred with most of his party by their Tuareg guides, hacked to pieces by swords. "And so the legend grows," the official French report said, abandoning at the end its otherwise matter-of-fact tone, "of the devilish Sahara, land of thirst and fear."[32]

For a few years conspiracy theories swirled about France, some of them with an eerily modern ring. Surely, the Tuareg must have known they would provoke the whole power of metropolitan France, and so the attack must have been deliberately set off, planned by some unnamed high official, perhaps the French government itself, as an excuse for further action, Flatters just the sacrificial lamb, his death actually desired by the empire builders, the perfect excuse for war. And surely France's civilizing mission would be recognized, even by those benighted barbarians? As a government adviser put it, "despite their rejection of strangers, surely the Tuareg can't doubt the progress that will ensue when they understand our technology, our methods, our pacific intentions and the well-being that we bring among them?"[33]

In any case, the French push into the desert remained steady and relentless. They never really abandoned their plan to link Algeria with the Sudan, and in 1890 a military expedition captured Ségou on the Upper Niger and put down a Bambara revolt there; three years later they defeated the southern Tuareg and rolled into Timbuktu.

One more time, occupiers from afar.

CHAPTER TWENTY-TWO

☙

And Now?

THE RAILWAY LINE from Algeria to the Niger remained unbuilt, and Timbuktu remained isolated. All through the French interregnum, the Tuareg resisted, essentially ungoverned and ungovernable, but the ancient trading towns of Mali and Songhai, Djenné and Timbuktu and Gao continued their awful decay—their raisons d'être vanished, their trade gone, their academies closed, their populations static or shrinking. To the imperial power in faraway Paris, Mali, Niger and Chad were of such fundamental unimportance that nearly half of all civil service positions were empty at any given time. Indeed, French officials were often assigned there as a punishment.

☙

WHEN THE ROMANTIC Frenchman Félix Dubois reached the city in the early 1900s, he was even more discouraged than Caillié had been. Entering the crumbling town, he saw mostly ruins. One, larger than the others, was "a lamentable wreck . . . no ordinary house, however . . . for the man who dwelt there was known all over Europe, all over the world, he had corresponded with the Queen of England . . . a man whom the learned and the explorers of every country held in pious memory, Barth's host and protector, Sheikh al-Bakay. Its crumbling walls have no other roof than the sky. The family of one of his servants vegetates in a little corner of the courtyard . . . that's all that remains of the brilliant life that held sway there. From one extremity of the city to the other the same story is repeated of roads ill and dying. You sink in their sands as though you were in the midst of the desert. A city in deliquescence, such is the town which the sun had shown from afar as majestically great."[1]

Independence from the European colonizers came to the Sahara as it did to the rest of Africa, after the chaos of World War II and the rebirth (or in some cases birth) of nationalism. Libya became an independent state in 1951; Morocco and Tunisia in 1956. Egypt became formally independent in 1952, Sudan in 1956. In 1960 a new country, Mauritania, was created to the south of Morocco and west of Mali, and given its independence a year later; and in 1962 Algeria achieved independence in a bloody insurrection in which several million were killed. The French departed from the Sahel in 1960, and all three Sahelian countries—Mali, Niger and Chad—gained their independence that year.

Timbuktu barely noticed. One set of uncaring masters replaced by another, of what moment? The new masters had no money, in any case, and could do nothing for the city even if they cared. The new republic of Mali was one of the poorest in the world; traders came no longer, the gold trade had vanished, slaving was now forbidden (though continuing in the deeper oases), and the only people who crossed the desert with any regularity were smugglers or refugees from one of the many wars to the south, heading for the old Maghreb and thence, if they were lucky, Europe. The salt caravans still came in from Taoudenni as they had for centuries, though much reduced in scale, because people need salt and so do animals, and they could still compete, just, with the bags of salt barged in from Bamako, provenance of the Caribbean.

Money is still a massive problem, as the Tuareg had been warning for decades. Partly because of its absence, partly because money corrupts. Development projects seldom work because the Big Men demand their share of the money off the top—the big men who live in big mansions in Bamako, a world away from Timbuktu; the presidential palace in the capital occupies the summit of a whole hill, like a castle looming over a medieval village, nicely separated from the peasants below, a symbol of what money has wrought. A Hollander who works for the Aga Khan Foundation, which is restoring the city's medieval mosques as well as the famous mud mosque of Mopti, said constant vigilance was needed to fend off the predatory powerful who wanted to skim off the funds before they were used. "Fortunately," he said, "this is essentially private money and we don't have to be the flavor of the month"—meaning that the Aga Khan can't be guilted into letting the Big Men run things by accusations of paternalism.

Profligacy and waste and missed opportunities are everywhere. Timbuktu generates electricity by diesel fuel brought in from Bamako; in a city where the sun shines more than 320 days a year, there isn't a single solar cell anywhere. Meanwhile, one doctor is left to look after Timbuktu's health, one for thirty-five thousand people, and a brand-new hospital built by the African Development Bank is left empty and unattended because there is no one to run it. Malaria and dengue fever are endemic; the roads are lined with public-spirited posters warning against AIDS, polio and other diseases. Neither garbage collection nor (yet) a sewage system exists in Timbuktu. Notoriously, the director of one of the international agencies designed to help children has the money to build himself a mansion in Timbuktu and another in the capital; but children with limbs missing are hardly noticed in the city because they are legion, too common to really be seen; children play in the sewage and are reduced to eating green dates off a few scrawny trees to assuage their hunger. Even UNESCO is not immune; one official spent ten million francs ($25,000) hiring a plane for a few days' work in Timbuktu, apparently too impatient to trust the commercial airline, which is notoriously erratic.

There's no help from Bamako. Foreign aid is now a quarter of the national budget, but poverty gets worse as the population explodes, the result of a high birthrate (a 3 percent population increase a year, with an average of seven children per mother) and a flood of refugees from the Ivory Coast and Liberia, driven out by decades of civil war. Bamako's population is closing in on a million, up from a mere 120,000 in 1965. It's almost a truism among NGOs that aid perpetuates corruption while achieving little or nothing. This seems merely obvious in Timbuktu.

ം

WHEN YOU LOOK back at Timbuktu from the air as you depart, it can hardly be seen, scarcely different in hue and texture from the surrounding desert. You can make out the grid pattern of the newer sections south and southwest of the city, but the streets are the color of the desert, and so are the houses. The old medina is an undifferentiated mass of beige, nothing much more than a stain of brown on a background of dun, and the mosques can't be seen at all. To the north, it is hard even to tell where the city ends and the Great Thirstland begins; the "road" to Taoudenni, Taghaza and Morocco, the route of caravans and their panniers of gold and slabs of salt and convoys of wretched stumbling slaves for just about a millennium, is quite invisible; neither a track nor a rut mars the caramel of the dunes. It's easy to think of this near invisibility as a metaphor for Timbuktu's place in the modern world: there it is, dozing under the desert sun, its glorious history and ancient learning and scholarship only tenuously preserved in the precious libraries so cherished by the great families, the Aqit, the Haïdara, the Baghayogho, the Kati. The spires of gold have vanished into legend; only the remoteness is left.

The judgment is tempting but too easy, for the city's spirit is more resilient than that. As we left the fading city, our minds kept returning to the central concern of so many we had met along the way, a concern that we came to see as the main thread of the long cord that was the story of fabled Timbuktu. Those precious repositories of learning may be vulnerable, but the miracle is the tenacity of their existence, not their vulnerability. In so many of those houses so invisible from the air, families have preserved little stores of knowledge from the elder days; preserving them through war and famine and invasion and now through the debilitating grind of seemingly endless poverty.

The public spaces of Timbuktu might be decrepit, but in the meticulously kept private houses (and tents) the spirit is still very much alive. We wanted to have one more conversation with Sidi Salem Ould Elhadj about this, but there was really no need. We knew what he would say. Timbuktu is not living off its history; it is not living in the past; it simply encapsulates that history and is what it is. You don't have to have *things* to be rich, he would say. You in the affluent West should know this better than anyone, that mere possessions don't mean real wealth or bring happiness. Over our long centuries we in Timbuktu have developed a fullness of living, a way of maintaining ourselves in the world, a tolerance for others. Walking through our streets and noticing the lack of material things won't show you any of that. *You have to know our people. We are our history. We are a metropolis of the mind.* He said something very like that, once. It wasn't defensive; it was just a fact. It is a mistake, he insisted, to think of Timbuktu as sad. Grindingly poor, yes, but never sad. "Poverty does not mean misery," Shindouk told us, saying the same thing in another way.

Foreign money is helping, in a modest way, to preserve Timbuktu's literary heritage—but why not do more, much more? Not just help with preservation or take on the scanning of umpteen thousands of documents. Why not reconstitute the University of Sankoré as a center of learning at the intersection of politics and religion, as it was before? Is this not the most demanding political issue of our time, this intersection? Why not do in fact what the dreamers who set up the Ahmed Baba Center had conceived, which is to make of Timbuktu *the* center for African history, once again an intellectual magnet for scholars from afar? Its trade has gone, but its intellectual resources are still there, waiting to be tapped. All it needs is money, and will. Lots of money, yes, and focused will, but what a cause, to restore a certain fabulousness to the fabled city.

In the mosques that can't be seen any longer from the air, the imams have preserved the traditions they inherited from the great *qadis* of the past, and those traditions include not only piety and charity but a resistance to the seductive ideas of fanaticism. They have not been at all deterred through the centuries by successive waves of jihadists, by all those pogroms and purges, all those invasions, treacheries and betrayals; nor have they yet been chased out by more militant mullahs imported from afar. They're still preaching that there are many possible paths to paradise, more than one way to truth, and that there is no need for constriction of vision; if all you can see is a path as narrow as a rifle barrel, they say, you will inevitably miss the glorious diversity of God's given landscape. The Conflict Resolution Group that Sidi Haïdara and his colleagues set up a few years ago is drawing on this long tradition of tolerance and accommodation. Their point is a simple one: in this world where the demons of intolerance seem once again to have been freed, in which suicidal killers can be called martyrs and in which the deadly technology of Western arms can be unleashed in cycles of atrocity and reprisal, Timbuktu still has lessons to teach.

Appendix 1: Commonly Used Titles

Amenekal. Tuareg leader.

Askia. Royal title used in the Songhai Empire.

Caliph. Successor or community leader; head of an Islamic state. Originally vice-regent of God, then leaders of the *umma*, or Muslim world, after the death of Muhammad.

Emir/Amir. Prince, also military commander; a general; an independent ruler or chieftain.

Imam. Prayer leader; elder of a mosque. With a lowercase *i*, it implies no special spiritual training beyond sufficient education to lead a congregation in prayers or deliver a sermon on Fridays; with an uppercase *I*, a direct descendant of Fatima and Ali in the Shiite tradition.

Khalif. Special representative, especially of a religious order.

Mansa. Royal title used in the Malian Empire.

Moulay. Respectful form of address for a leader.

Qadi. Judge in a sharia court; title for a male member of the sultan's council; a Muslim jurist.

Sharif (also spelled sherif). Direct descendant of the prophet Muhammad.

Sheikh. Leader of a religious brotherhood; leader of an Arab village or family; a venerable patriarch.

Sidi. Respectful title for a male, up from mister but a little down from sir; also a saint. It is an informal version of the word *sayyidi*, which literally means "my master." It can be used with a first name, a last name, or both, or can be used alone.

Sultan. Ruler of a Muslim country, especially the former Ottoman Empire; several historic meanings.

Uléma. Holy men or just learned men, a collective term.

❧

Appendix 2: Lineages

The Lineage of the Mansas, of the Empire of Mali, Rulers of Timbuktu in the Thirteenth and Fourteenth Centuries

Sundiata (aka Sogolon Djata, Mari-Djata), reigned 1230–55
Mansa **Wali (Uli)**, son of Sundiata
Mansa **Khalifa**, son of Sundiata
Mansa **Abu Bakr**, grandson of Sundiata by collateral line
Sankura, outsider and usurper
Mansa **Qu**, son of Wali
Mansa **Muhammad**
Mansa **Abu Bakr II**, the voyager king
Mansa **Musa**, reigned 1312–32
Mansa **Magha**, son of Musa
Mansa **Sulaiman**, brother of Musa
Mansa **Qasa**, son of Sulaiman
Mansa **Mari-Djata**, son of Magha
Mansa **Musa II**, son of Mari-Djata
Sandaki, a slave
Mansa **Mahmoud**, descendant of Qu, who took the name Mansa **Magha III** in 1390

The Lineage of the Askias of Songhai, Rulers of Timbuktu in the Sixteenth Century

Askia **al-hajj Mohamed**, overthrew Sonni Ali Ber to establish the dynasty, reigned 1493–1528
Askia **Musa**, his son, who deposed him in 1528 and was assassinated in 1531
Askia **Mohamed II Benkan Toraï (Bonkana)**, nephew of Mohamed I, deposed by Ismail in 1537
Askia **Ismail**, son of Askia al-hajj Mohamed, reigned 1537–39
Askia **Ishaq I**, brother of Ismail, reigned 1539–49
Askia **Daoud**, son of Mohamed I, reigned 1549–83
Askia **Mohamed al-hajj II** (sometimes known as **Mohamed III**), son of Daoud, reigned 1583–86

Askia **Bani**, son of Daoud, reign lasted less than a year, died in 1588

Askia **Mohamed IV**, son of Daoud, pretender and rival, "reigned" from Timbuktu, along with Bani in Gao, 1586–88

Askia **Ishaq II**, son of Daoud, succeeded Bani, defeated Mohamed IV, deposed by Moroccans in 1591

Askia **Mohamed Gao**, son of Daoud, treacherously killed by invaders, reigned only a few weeks

Askia **Nuh**, son of Daoud, last of the line, came to power in 1591, defeated and disappeared in 1595

❧

Appendix 3: Glossary of Tribes and Cultures

Note: in the old sources the terms *Berber, Sanhaja, Massufa, Lamtuna* and *Tuareg* are often used interchangeably.

Ashanti. Tribe in modern Ghana near the Volta and Akan goldfields.

Bella. The slave (or servant) class of the Tuareg and others, of unknown origins.

Benin. Vigorous West African culture renowned for their brasswork and art.

Bérabiche. Tuareg nomads whose language is a mix of Berber and Arabic called Bérabiche or Hassaniya. The Bérabiche were the nomads of the open desert and the operators of the great salt caravans; the Imagcharen Tuareg, who converted later to Islam, found their homes in the mountain fastnesses of the central Sahara. *See also* **Tuareg**.

Berbers (Zanata and Sanhaja; among the Sanhaja are the **Lamtuna** and the **Massufa**). Original inhabitants of North Africa and the northern desert, often displaced by Arab invaders. Ancestors of the Tuareg.

Bozo. Tribe along the Middle Niger, renowned for their boat building.

Dogon. Centered on the Bandiagara cliffs of southern Mali, ethnic cousins to the Bozo.

Dyula. May not be a tribe at all but the trading class of the Mande.

Fulani (Peul, Fulbe). Now distributed across the Sahel, origins seem to have been in Senegal or Guinea.

Garamantes. Libyan-based ancient culture, probably Berber in origin.

Hausa. Entrepreneurial traders and city builders from northern Nigeria, now found throughout the Sahara.

Ife. Powerful trading and artistic culture on the Lower Niger.

Mande. Tribe of many branches, including the Soninke, Malinke, Bambara, Cissé and others.

Mossi. Centered on modern Burkina Faso, always a troublesome enemy for the Central Niger empires.

Songhai. Tribe and empire centered on Gao, of uncertain origins.

Tuareg. The legendary nomads of the Sahara, known as the Blue Men of the Desert. Their language is called Tamashek. *See also* **Bérabiche**.

Tichitt (the Tichitt Tradition). Early inhabitants of the Tichitt escarpment in Mauritania.

Tukolor. Kin to the Fulani, the name a corruption of Tekrur.

Wolof. Tribe along the Atlantic coast south of Mauritania, related to the Fulani and Tukolor.

∾

Appendix 4: Who Was Who

Abu Bakr II (Mansa). Malian ruler, predecessor of Mansa Musa.

Africanus, Leo (El-Hasan ibn Muhammed el-Wazzan-az-Zayyati). Born 1485, visited Timbuktu in the reign of Askia al-hajj Mohamed.

Akil Ag-Amalwal. *Amenekal* (leader) of the Tuareg, briefly ruler of Timbuktu from 1433.

Alfarouk. Genie protector of Timbuktu.

Ali Ber (Sonni Ali Ber). The eighteenth of the Sonni dynasty, who overthrew the power of the Malian kings.

Aqit, Mohamed. Founder of the illustrious Aqit family of Timbuktu, arrived in town in 1440.

Baba, Ahmed al-Sudani. Timbuktu's greatest scholar, exiled by the Moroccans in 1600.

Baghayogho family. Prominent merchant and scholarly family of Timbuktu. **Mohamed Baghayogho** was the first of the family to settle in Timbuktu. He came from Djenné.

Bakay (Sheikh Ahmed al-Bakay). Ruler of Timbuktu who protected Heinrich Barth.

Bakri (Abu Abdullah 'Ubayd al-Bakri). Geographer from Cordoba, writing in middle of eleventh century.

Barth, Heinrich. German (and British) explorer, reached Timbuktu in the 1850s.

Battuta (Ibn Battuta, or Muhammad ibn Abdullah ibn Muhammad ibn Ibrahim ibn Muhammad ibn Ibrahim ibn Yusuf). Born 1304, renowned traveler and major source for information on Mali.

Buktu (Bouctou). Probably mythical founder of Timbuktu.

Caillié, René. French explorer who returned safely from Timbuktu.

Clapperton, Hugh. British explorer, first European to see Lake Chad.

Daoud, Askia. Son of Askia al-hajj Mohamed. Ruler of Songhai from 1549 to 1583, a time of great prosperity and peace in Timbuktu.

Dinar (Abu al-Muhajir Dinar). Arab general who completed the North African conquest before being succeeded by Nusayr.

Gharnati (Abu l'Hasan Ali ibn Said al-Gharnati). Thirteenth-century geographer.

Haïdara family. Prominent political and merchant family. The Mamma Haïdara Library is owned by the family. Its current custodian is Abd al-Qadir (Abdel Kader) Haïdara.

Idris Alawma. Ruler of Kanem-Bornu, who allied himself with Morocco before the invasion of Songhai.

Idrisi (Abu Abd' Allah Muhammad al-Idrisi). Twelfth-century geographer.

Jawdar, Pasha. Leader of the Moroccan invasion force in 1590.

Kandiago, Omar. Askia al-hajj Mohamed's brother, who was *Tombouctoukoï*.

Kati family. Prominent Timbuktu scholarly family; the renowned Kati family library was collected by and is still owned by the family. **Mahmoud Kati** and his grandson, also Mahmoud, wrote the *Tariq al-Fettach* just before 1600. The Katis came from Toledo; the first African Kati was Ali ibn Ziyad al-Quti.

Khaldun (Ibn Khaldun). Fourteenth-century Berber historian.

Kumzaghu, Omar. Askia al-hajj Mohamed's brother, governor of Tindirma Province.

Laing, Alexander Gordon. British explorer who reached Timbuktu but was murdered on the way home.

Maghili (Mohamed bin Abd al-Karim al-Maghili). Zealot who briefly had the ear of Askia al-hajj Mohamed.

Mahmoud ibn Zargoum, Pasha. Jawdar's successor, perpetrator of the Massacre of the Intellectuals.

Mansur, al- (Moulay Ahmad al-Mansur al-Dahabi, or Abu Yusuf Ya'qub al-Mansur). Sultan of Morocco who invaded Timbuktu in 1590.

Mohamed, Askia al-hajj (Mohamed ibn Abu Bakr Sylla). Founding ruler of the Askia dynasty of Songhai.

Musa (Mansa Musa). Greatest of the emperors (mansas) of Mali.

Naddi, Mohammed. Respected governor of Timbuktu under the Tuareg.

Nuh (Askia Nuh). Last of the Songhai rulers, defeated by the Moroccans.

Nusayr (Musa ibn Nusayr). Last commander of the Arab armies that invaded North Africa in the seventh century.

Park, Mungo. Scottish explorer who reached the Niger in 1795.

Sa'adi (Abd al-Rahman al-Sa'adi). Author of the *Tarikh al-Sudan*.

Shabeni, Asid al-hajj Abd-Salam. Arab traveler who visited Timbuktu and left a full description in the eighteenth century.

Sonni Ali Ber. *See* **Ali Ber.**

Sulaiman (Mansa). Mansa Musa's brother and (after a brief interval) successor.

Sundiata. Founding ruler of Mali, in legend a magician king.

Tachfin. *See* **Umar** (Abu Bakr ibn Umar).

Tadelsi (Sidi Yahiya el-Tadelsi ibn Abd al-Rahim al-Tha'alibi). Sufi sheikh who claimed Sharifian descent, and for whom the Sidi Yahiya mosque was built in 1440.

Tal (Al-Hajj Umar Tal). Tukolor cleric and jihadist.

Turjut (Yaya ibn Turjut). Lamtuna Berber, patron of **Yasin** (q.v.).

Umar (Abu Bakr ibn Umar), and **Yusuf ibn Tachfin**, his cousin. Almoravid generals and founders of Marrakech.

Umar (Abu Hafs Umar). *Qadi* of Timbuktu at the time of the Moroccan invasion.

Umar (Aqib ibn Umar). *Qadi* of Timbuktu under Askia Daoud.

Umar (Mahmoud ibn Umar). *Qadi* of Timbuktu under Askia al-hajj Mohamed and author of numerous texts, including one on medicine, that have survived.

Usman dan Fodio. Fulani holy man, originator of nineteenth-century jihad.

Yahiya, Sidi. *See* **Tadelsi.**

Yasin (Abd Allah ibn Yasin). Founder of the Almoravid movement.

☙

Notes

1. Dreaming Spires of Gold, Under the Desert Sun

1. Gardner, p. 4.
2. From an Arab manuscript dated 1686, quoted in Stanley, *In Darkest Africa*, p. 490.
3. Herodotus, book 2, p. 63.
4. Norris, p. 27.
5. Ibid., p. 54.
6. Burton, p. 468.
7. Bassani and Fagg, p. 173.
8. Adapted from Sattin, p. 4.
9. Ibn Battuta, vol. 1, p. 24 and vol. 2, p. 282.

2. The Founder, the Founding and the Legends

The legends of Timbuktu, one of which is recounted in this chapter, come from the Timbuktu scholar Sidi Salem Ould Elhadj and were either recounted to us in person or are contained in unpublished pamphlets he gave us.

1. That so much is known about Timbuktu and especially the Songhai Empire is mostly because of the two surviving chronicles of the time. The first is al-Sa'adi's *Tarikh al-Sudan*, written around 1656, translated into French around the turn of the twentieth century and in the last few years rendered into English, with copious notes, by John Hunwick. The other, the *Tarikh al-Fettach*, written by several members of the Kati family around 1650, exists in several French translations. The principal author was Mahmoud Kati, who died in 1593, but most of it was produced by another Mahmoud, his grandfather, and edited by his grandson. The first Mahmoud was a friend (and a relative by marriage) of Askia al-hajj Mohamed, while the second was close to Askia Daoud, who reigned from 1549 to 1583.
2. *Tarikh al-Sudan*/Houdas. The *Tarikh al-Sudan* is hereafter cited as *Tarikh*.
3. Bovill, *The Golden Trade of the Moors*, p. 43.
4. Nicolaisen and Nicolaisen, p. 539.

3. The City, Its Site and Its Neighborhood

1. Caillié, vol. 2, p. 107.
2. Leo Africanus, p. 497.

4. The Niger's Course and Meaning

1. Pamphlet, *La legende du Wagadu*, by Tereba Togola, head of archaeology, Institute of Human Sciences, Bamako.
2. Barth, vol. 3, p. 278.
3. Ibid.
4. Samuel Sidibe, director of the National Museum of Mali.
5. Park, p. LXXIV.
6. Ibn Battuta, vol. 4, p. 955.
7. Jackson, p. 8.
8. Ibid.
9. Quoted in Heseltine, p. 163.

5. The People of the Region

1. Quoted in Nicolaisen and Nicolaisen, p. 534.
2. Davidson, *Africa in History*, p. 101.
3. Ajayi and Crowder, p. 142.
4. Translation by Ulli Beier, in *African Poetry*.

6. Precursors: The Empires of the Sun

1. McIntosh et al.
2. This chronology is from the historian George Brooks, in *Cahiers d'Etudes Africaines* 26: 43–62, and the McIntoshes (S. K. and R. J), in the *Journal of African History* 27: 413–42.
3. Some of these details are from Kea.
4. UNESCO report, undated.
5. Quoted in Kea, p. 753.
6. Ibid., p. 744.
7. Ibid., p. 766.
8. Ibid.
9. Ibid., pp. 747–53.
10. Ibid., p. 746.
11. Al-Bakri's writings no longer exist except for fragments, but his account of Ghana has been published in many places. This version is adapted from Ajayi and Crowder (p. 132) and several Islamic Web sites.
12. Frobenius, p. 495.
13. Kea, p. 734.
14. Norris, p. 9.
15. Newman, p. 113.

7. The Coming of the Arabs

1. Cloudsley-Thompson, p. 313.
2. One of the four schools of Islamic jurisprudence named after its eighth-century founder,

Malik ibn Anas; to the noninitiate, the distinctions between Maliki and the other schools are minute to the point of invisibility, but rely on the notion that the practices of the people of Medina sometimes supersede the hadith of Muhammad himself, because the prophet lived and died there.

3. Quoted in Hrbek, *General History of Africa*, vol. 3, p. 118.
4. Lagardère, via http://bewley.virtualave.net/index.html, p. 8.
5. Ibid.
6. Hrbek, *General History of Africa*, vol. 3, p. 181.
7. *Tarikh*/Houdas.

8. Mansa Musa and the First Golden Age of Timbuktu

1. Sundiata legends are recounted in many places. This is from Frobenius, pp. 451–66.
2. Davidson, *Africa in History*, p. 99.
3. This story is recounted in many places, including Davidson, *Old Africa Rediscovered* and Jean-Yves Loude, *Le roi d'Afrique et la reine mer*.
4. Leo Africanus, vol. 3, p. 823.
5. Niane, *General History of Africa*, vol. 4, pp. 197–200.
6. Tayler, p. 215.
7. *Tarikh*/Hunwick, p. 9.
8. Ibn Battuta, vol. 4, p. 969.
9. Ibid.
10. Barth, vol. 3, p. 291.
11. Ibn Battuta, vol. 4, p. 948.
12. The account of Ibn Battuta's travels to Mali (this and subsequent quotations) is in ibid., pp. 950 ff.
13. *Tarikh*/Houdas.
14. Comtes et Récits de Tombouctou.
15. Ibn Battuta, vol. 4, p. 963.

9. The First Tuareg Interregnum

1. By 2004 ATT was back in power, duly elected.
2. Ajayi and Crowder, p. 134.
3. *Tarikh*/Houdas.
4. Ibid.
5. Sekéné Mody Cissoko, quoted by Sidi Salem Ould Elhadj.
6. *Tarikh*/Sidi Salem Ould Elhadj.
7. Ibid.

10. The Coming of the Songhai

1. Quoted in Kea, p. 787.
2. Quoted in ibid.
3. Quoted in ibid., pp. 789–90.
4. *Tarikh*/Hunwick, p. 6.
5. *Tarikh*/Houdas.
6. This quote and the story of Sonni ali Ber's accession are from Sidi Salem Ould Elhadj.
7. *Tarikh*/Houdas.
8. Ibid.

9. Ibid.
10. *Tarikh al-Fettach*/Sidi Salem Ould Elhadj.
11. *Tarikh*/Houdas.
12. Ibid.
13. Sekéné Mody Cissoko, quoted by Sidi Salem Ould Elhadj.
14. *Tarikh*/Hunwick, pp. 20–21.
15. *Tarikh*/Sidi Salem Ould Elhadj.
16. Ibid.
17. *Journal of African History* 34 (1993): 65–91.

11. The Rise of Askia al-hajj Mohamed and the Second Golden Age

1. Ahmed Baba, quoted by Sidi Salem Ould Elhadj.
2. For an interesting discussion on this point, see Blum and Fisher's article.
3. The provinces of the Songhai Empire were: Hombori, south of the Niger between Gao and Timbuktu; Gurma, an arid province southeast of Hombori and southwest of Dendi; Kukiya, on the left bank of the Niger upstream from Gao; Dendi, on the left bank of the Niger downstream from Gao; Dirma (or Tindirma), on the left bank of the Niger just upstream from Timbuktu; Masina, southwest of Timbuktu beyond Tindirma, on both banks of the Niger; and Mema, west of Masina.
4. *Tarikh*/Houdas.
5. *Tarikh*/Hunwick, p. 103.
6. Barth, vol. 3, p. 286.
7. *Tarikh*/Hunwick, pp. 106–7.
8. Barth, vol. 3, p. 667.
9. Blum and Fisher, p. 72.
10. *Tarikh*/Hunwick, p. 104.
11. Barth, vol. 3, p. 286.
12. Quoted in Benjaminsen, p. 102.
13. Both *Tarikhs*/Sidi Salem Ould Elhadj.
14. Barth, vol. 3, p. 666.

12. The Underpinnings of Wealth

1. Ibn Battuta, vol. 4, p. 947.
2. Quoted in Bovill, *The Golden Trade of the Moors*, pp. 68–69.
3. Jan Vansina in Africa Forum on H-Net (http://www.h-net.msu/edu/~africa).
4. Quoted in Sattin, p. 112.
5. J. J. Scarisbrick and P. L. Carter, *Ghana Notes and Queries* #1, 1961, Accra.
6. Leo Africanus, vol. 3, p. 825.

13. Travelers' Tales

1. Hall, p. 34.
2. Mills, p. 115.
3. Haywood, p. 5.
4. Chatwin, p. 167.
5. Tayler, p. 206.
6. Jackson, p. 8 ff.

7. Ibn Battuta, vol. 4, p. 948.
8. Quoted in Porch, p. 53.
9. Leo Africanus, vol. 3, p. 801.
10. Fage, *Cambridge History of Africa*, vol. 3, p. 267.
11. Ibn Battuta, vol. 4, p. 944.

14. Life and Learning in the City of Gold

1. Jackson, p. 10.
2. Kati and Baba, quoted by Sidi Salem Ould Elhadj.
3. *Tarikh*/Houdas.
4. Leo Africanus, vol. 3, p. 824.
5. Jackson, p. 28 ff.
6. Leo Africanus, vol. 3, p. 824.
7. Ibid.
8. Jackson, p. 42.
9. Sidi Salem Ould Elhadj provided a French version of this tale, which we translated into English.
10. Fitzgerald, p. 136.
11. Leo Africanus, vol. 3.
12. *Tarikh*/Houdas.
13. Jackson, p. 32.
14. Dubois, pp 273–74.
15. Jackson, pp. 37 ff.
16. Fisher, p. 192.
17. Ibn Battuta, vol. 4, pp. 965 ff.
18. Jackson, p. 19 ff.
19. Ibid., p. 31.
20. *Tarikh*/Houdas.
21. Saad, p. 22.
22. Quoted in Zouber, p. 457.

15. The Second Golden Age and the Intellectual Tradition

1. Bloom, pp. 112–13, quoted by Mary Minicka.
2. *Science* 308 (June 3, 2005): 1416.
3. Mary Minicka, talking to the Library and Information Association of South Africa: Winter Colloquium, June 15, 2006.
4. Leo Africanus, vol. 3, p. 825.
5. Quoted in a paper, "The Islamic Manuscript Heritage of Timbuktu," by John Hunwick at Northwestern University, Evanston, Illinois. Accessed via University of Oslo Centre for Development, http://www.sum.uio.no/.
6. Ibid.
7. Ibid.
8. Ford Foundation report, undated.
9. Bloom, quoted by Mary Minicka.
10. Christopher Reardon, in undated Ford Foundation report on Timbuktu's manuscript heritage.
11. Quoted in ibid.

12. Hunwick, "Islamic Manuscript Heritage."
13. In an interview with Karen Kostyal, in *National Geographic*, September 2006, p. 33.

16. The End of the Askias

1. Barth, vol. 3, p. 293.
2. Ahmed Baba, quoted in ibid., p. 670.
3. *Tarikh*/Hunwick, p. 149.
4. Ibid., p. 135.
5. *Tarikh*/Houdas.
6. *Tarikh al-Fettach*/Sidi Salem Ould Elhadj.
7. Ibid.
8. *Tarikh*/Hunwick, p. 124.
9. Ibid., p. 135.
10. The dialogue is from *Tarikh*/Hunwick. Hunwick comments that the Arabic adjective means "to push, pierce, penetrate a woman sexually," and suggests that the innuendo might be "you libidinous slave" (pp. 156–57).
11. *Tarikh*/Houdas.
12. *Tarikh*/Hunwick, p. 160.
13. Barth, vol. 3, p. 294, presumably quoting Ahmed Baba, though this is unclear.
14. Sidi Salem Ould Elhadj.
15. *Tarikh*/Hunwick, p. 166.
16. *Tarikh al-Fettach*/Sidi Salem Ould Elhadj.
17. *Tarikh*/Hunwick, p. 169.
18. Ibid., p. 174.
19. Adapted from *Tarikh*/Sidi Salem Ould Elhadj.

17. The Coming of the Moroccans

1. *Nozhet el Hadi*, cited in Ahmed En Naciri, *Kitab El istiqca*, vol. 5 (Paris, 1936).
2. Adapted from Ajayi and Crowder, pp. 203, 211–12.
3. This is in a note from *Tarikh*/Hunwick, pp. 187–88.
4. Quoted in Davidson, *Old Africa*, p. 198.
5. *L'Afrique Noire dans les relations internationales au XVI ème siècle*, an analysis of the crisis between Morocco and the Sudan, by Dr. Zakari Dramani Issifou, p. 141.

18. The Long March and the Pasha's Conquest of Timbuktu

1. Haïdara, quoted by Sidi Salem Ould Elhadj.
2. Haïdara, unpaginated.
3. *Tarikh*/Hunwick, note 3, p. 188.
4. Abitbol, *Tombouctou et les Arma*, unpaginated.
5. These passages adapted from Beraud-Vilars, pp. 130 ff. The original document was discovered by Marcos Jimenez de la Espada in the Academy of History in Madrid, in 1877. It was first rendered into French by Henri de Castries, in the *Revue Hespéris* (1923): 461–62, and then translated into English by John Hunwick (pp. 318 ff).
6. *Tarikh*/Hunwick, p. 320.
7. Beraud-Vilars, p. 134.
8. *Tarikh*/Houdas.

9. Ibid.
10. Ibid.

19. The Long Decline

1. Sidi Salem Ould Elhadj, "Le Pachalik arma de Tombouctou, 1591–1826."
2. Much of this reasoning was from the same Spanish agent of Philip II. See note 5 for chapter 18.
3. Sidi Salem Ould Elhadj, "Le Pachalik arma de Tombouctou, 1591–1826."
4. Both quotations are adapted from the *Tarikh*/Houdas and Hunwick, p. 207.
5. *Tarikh al-Fettach*/Sidi Salem Ould Elhadj.
6. Ibid.
7. *Tarikh*/Houdas.
8. Ibid.
9. Sidi Salem Ould Elhadj, "Le Pachalik arma de Tombouctou, 1591–1826."
10. Barth, vol. 3, p. 298.

20. The Coming of Jihad

1. Barth, vol. 3, p. 298.
2. We used one by members of the Special Conflict Resolution Research Group in Mali, Dr. Mahmoud Zouber, Sidi Haïdara, Mamadou Diallo and Stephanie Diakité, which was set up with the aim of "managing community and government conflict, in perpetuating a culture of peace, in the promotion of good by the banishment of evil, and in the application of methodologies and processes of conciliation between people."
3. Recounted here from a document produced by the Special Conflict Resolution Research Group in Timbuktu, a prominent member of which is Sidi Haïdara.
4. Quoted in Benjaminsen, p. 102.

21. Finally, the Europeans

1. Park, p. 185.
2. Quoted in Davidson, *Old Africa*, p. 78.
3. Quoted in Mountfield, p. 67.
4. Quoted in Sattin, p. 20.
5. Ibid., p. 74.
6. Jackson, p. 52.
7. Quoted in Sattin, p. 20.
8. Lonely Planet, *West Africa*, p. 512.
9. Mountfield, p. 68.
10. Park, p. 125.
11. Barth, vol. 3, p. 470.
12. Park, p. 165.
13. Ibid., p. 167.
14. Barth, vol. 3, p. 340.
15. Mountfield, p. 72.
16. The story of Gordon Laing comes from ibid., p. 77 ff.
17. Ibid., p. 78.
18. Barth, vol. 3, p. 471.
19. Ibid., p. 298.

20. Mountfield, p. 78.
21. Caillié, vol. 1, p. 1.
22. Ibid., p. 172.
23. Ibid., vol. 2, p. 49 ff.
24. Quoted in Mountfield, p. 87.
25. Barth, vol. 1, preface, p. vii.
26. Ibid., p. ix.
27. Ibid., p. xii.
28. Ibid., vol. 3, pp. 171, 266.
29. Ibid., p. 257.
30. Ibid., p. 630.
31. Pakenham, p. 167.
32. Quoted in Huré, p. 170.
33. Philebert, pp. 43–45.

22. And Now?

1. Dubois, p. 215.

Bibliography

Absent the translation—or even cataloging—of the historic manuscripts in the private collections of Timbuktu, the best extant sources for a proper history are the oral traditions—still very much alive in that curious city—and the two chronicles written in the mid-1600s. These are the *Tarikh al-Sudan* (Chronicle of the Land of the Blacks), written by Abd al-Rahman al-Sa'adi, himself a pupil of the prodigal son, Timbuktu's most famous scholar, Ahmed Baba; and Mahmoud Kati's *Tarikh al-Fettach* (Chronicle of These Who Seek Truth). Both of these histories are wonderfully informative, but as with all chronicles written for polemical purposes (in this case, pious instruction and the need to justify certain regimes), their information needs to be cautiously evaluated.

We used three versions of the *Tarikh al-Sudan*, the first translated into French from the original Arabic by O. Houdas in Paris at the end of the nineteenth century; the second an informal translation into French from the Arabic by our most generous informant in Timbuktu, Sidi Salem Ould Elhadj; and the third the recent English translation by John Hunwick. Where these three versions conflicted, or where the first two were obscure or uncertain, we tended to rely on Hunwick, and attribute the language to him.

Indeed, for anyone interested in the history of Timbuktu and the whole of Arabized North and West Africa, Hunwick, a professor emeritus at Northwestern University in Illinois, is the seminal figure. Almost everyone we met in Timbuktu who had an opinion, about almost anything, in the end dropped his name; and his works are listed in numberless bibliographies. For scholars in any language, he is the go-to authority. It helps that his own writing, for example, in his long and exemplary introduction to the *Tarikh* in his book, is admirably clear; and that in his speeches and papers, some of which can be hunted down on the Internet, he is articulate, passionate and committed. We are indebted to his scholarship.

For the other *Tarikh*, the *al-Fettach*, we relied on the French translation by O. Houdas and M. Delafosse, amplified by passages translated into French for us by Sidi Salem Ould Elhadj.

Sidi Salem, in addition, was a prime source for the tales and legends of Timbuktu, and for many wise observations about life as it was lived in his beloved city.

Abitbol, Michel, trans. *Tombouctou au milieu du XVIIIe siècle*. Paris: G.-P. Maisonneuve et Larose, 1982.

Abitbol, Michel. *Tombouctou et les Arma: De la conquête marocaine du Soudan nigérien en 1591 à l'hégémonie de l'empire peul du Maçina en 1853*. Paris: Maisonneuve et Larose, 1979.

Adams, Charles Hansford, ed. *The Narrative of Robert Adams a Barbary Captive*. Cambridge: Cambridge University Press, 2005.

Africanus, Leo (al-Hassan ibn-Mohammed al-Wezaz al-Fasi). *The History and Description of Africa and the Notable Things Therein Contained*. Translated by John Pory. 3 vols. London: Hakluyt Society, 1896.

Ajayi, J. F. A. *A Thousand Years of West African History*. Ibadan: 1965.

Ajayi, J. F. A., and Michael Crowder. *History of West Africa. Vol. 1*. New York: Columbia University Press, 1972.

Bakri, Abu Abdullah al-. *Kitâb al-Masâlik wa'l-Mamâlik* (Book of Highways and Kingdoms). Cordova, 1068. The book exists today only in fragmentary form.

Barth, Heinrich. *Travels and Discoveries in North and Central Africa, 1849–1855*. 3 vols. New York: Drallop, 1896.

Bassani, Ezio, and William B. Fagg, eds. *Africa and the Renaissance, Art in Ivory*. New York: Center for African Art and Prestel-Verlag, 1988.

Battuta (Ibn Battuta). *The Travels of Ibn Battuta, 1325–1354*. Translated by H. A. R. Gibb and C. F. Beckingham. 5 vols. London: Hakluyt Society, 1962.

Beier, Ulli, ed. *African Poetry*. Cambridge: Cambridge University Press, 1966.

Benjaminsen, Tor A. *Une histoire de Tombouctou*. Paris: Actes Sud, 2000.

Beraud-Vilars, J. *L'empire de Gao. Un état soudanais au XV et XVI siècles*. Paris: Editions Plon, 1942.

Bewley, Aisha. *The Preaching of Abdullah Ibn Yasin*. One of a series of essays. http://www.bewley.virtualave.net.

Bloom, J. M. *Paper before Print: The History and Impact of Paper on the Islamic World*. New Haven: Yale University Press, 2001.

Blum, Charlotte, and Humphrey Fisher. "Love for Three Oranges, Or, the Askiya's Dilemma: The Askiya, al-Maghili and Timbuktu, c. 1500 A.D." *Journal of African History* 34 (1993): 65–91.

Bovill, E. W. *Caravans of the Old Sahara, An Introduction to the History of the Western Sudan*. London: Oxford University Press, 1933.

———. *The Golden Trade of the Moors: West African Kingdoms in the Fourteenth Century*. Princeton: Marcus Wiener, 1958.

———, ed. *Missions to the Niger, 1: The Journal of Friedrich Hornemann's Travels and the Letters of Alexander Gordon Laing*. London: Hakluyt Society, 1964.

———, ed. *Missions to the Niger, III: The Bornu Mission, 1822–25, Part 2*. London: Hakluyt Society, 1965.

Brass, Mike, *The Antiquity of Man*. http://www.antiquityofman.com/complex_WA_EA.html.

Bruce-Lockhart, Jamie, ed. *Difficult and Dangerous Roads: Hugh Clapperton's Travels in Sahara and Fezzan, 1822–25*. London: Sickle Moon Books, 2000.

Burton, Sir Richard, trans. *The Arabian Nights (A Thousand and One Nights)*. New York: Random House, 2001.

Caillié, René. *Travels through Central Africa to Timbuktu and Across the Great Desert to Morocco, Performed in the Years 1824–28*. London: Henry Colborn, 1830.

Chatwin, Bruce, *Anatomy of Restlessness*. New York: Penguin 1997.

Cloudsley-Thompson, J. L. *Man and the Biology of Arid Zones*. London: Edward Arnold, 1977.

Davidson, Basil. *Africa in History*. New York: Collier Books/Macmillan, 1991.

———. *Old Africa Rediscovered. The Story of Africa's Forgotten Past*. London: Victor Gollancz, 1965.

Dayak, Mano. *Je suis né avec du sable dans les yeux*. Paris: Editions Fixot, 1996.

De Castries, Henri. "La conquête du Soudan par el-Mansour." *Hespéris* 3(1923): 433–88.

————. *Sources inédites pour l'histoire du Maroc de 1530 à 1845. Première série: Dynastie Saadienne (1530–1660)*. Paris: Paul Geuthner, 1925.

Djata, Sundiata A. *The Bamana Empire by the Niger: Kingdom, Jihad and Colonization, 1712–1920*. Princeton: Markus Wiener, 1997.

Dubois, Félix. *Tombouctou la Mystérieuse*. Paris: Flammarion, 1897; London: Heinemann, 1897.

Fage, J. D., ed. *The Cambridge History of Africa*. Vol 2, *500 BC to 1050 AD*. Cambridge: Cambridge University Press, 1978.

————. *The Cambridge History of Africa*. Vol 3, *1050 to 1600*. Cambridge: Cambridge University Press, 1977.

Fitzgerald, Mary Anne. *Nomad: Journeys from Samburu*. London: Sinclair-Stevenson, 1992.

Fisher, Angela. *Africa Adorned*. New York: Harry Abrams, 1994.

Frobenius, Leo. *The Voice of Africa*. New York: Benjamin Blom, 1968.

Gardner, Brian. *The Quest for Timbuktoo*. New York: Harcourt Brace and World, 1968.

Gomez, Michael A. "Timbuktu Under Imperial Songhay: A Reconsideration of Autonomy." *Journal of African History* 31(1990): 5–24.

Haïdara, Ismaël Diadié. *Jawdar Pasha et La Conquête Saâdienne du Songhay (1592–1599)*. Rabat: Publications de l'Institute des Etudes Africaines, 1966.

Hall, Leland. *Timbuctoo*. London, Cresset Press, 1934.

Haywood, Captain A. H. W. *Through Timbuktu and Across the Great Sahara*. London: Lippincott, 1912.

Herodotus. *Histories*. Books 1–6. Cambridge, Mass.: Harvard University Press, 1921.

Heseltine, Nigel. *From Libyan Sands to Chad*. London: Museum Press, 1995.

Hourani, Albert. *A History of the Arab Peoples*. Cambridge, Mass.: Belknap Press, 1991.

Hrbek, I., ed. *General History of Africa*. Vol. 3. Paris: UNESCO, 1992.

Hunwick, John. *Arabic Literature of Africa*. Vol 4, *The Writing of Western Sudanic Africa* (compilation). Leyden: Brill, 2003.

————. *Timbuktu and the Songhay Empire: Al-Sa'di's Ta'rikh al-Sudan Down to 1613 and Other Contemporary Documents*. Leyden: Brill, 1999.

Huré, Gen. R., et al. *l'Armée Française en Afrique, 1830–1962*, Paris: Charles-Lavauzelle, 1977.

Jackson, James Grey, ed. Contains *An Account of Timbuctoo and Hausa, Territories of the Interior of Africa, by El Hajj Abd Salam Shabeeny*. London: Longman Hurst Orme and Brown, 1820; reprint, Frank Cass, 1967.

Kake, Ibrahima Baba. *Djouder: La fin de l'empire Songhay*. Dakar: NFA, 1975.

Kati, Mahmoud. *Tarikh al-Fettach*. Translated into French by O. Houdas and M. Delafosse. Paris: A. Maisonneuve, 1913.

Kea, Ray A. "Expansions and Contractions: World-Historical Change and the Western Sudan World-System (1200/1000 BC–1200/1250 AD." *Journal of World-Systems Research* 10, no. 3 (2004): 723–816.

Keenan, Jeremy. *The Tuareg: People of the Ahaggar*. London: Sickle Moon Books, 1977.

Kennedy, Hugh. *The Court of the Caliphs: The Rise and Fall of Islam's Greatest Dynasty*. London: Weidenfeld and Nicolson, 2004.

Kryza, Frank T. *The Race for Timbuktu: In Search of Africa's City of Gold*. New York: HarperCollins, 2006.

Lagardère, Vincent. *Les Almoravides jusqu'au règne de Jusuf B Tasfin*. Morocco, n.d.

Laing, Alexander Gordon. *Travels in the Timannee, Kooranko and Soolima Countries in Western Africa*. London: John Murray, 1825.

Lonely Planet. *West Africa*. Lonely Planet Publications, 1995.

Loude, Jean-Yves, and Viviane Lièvre. *Le roi d'Afrique et la reine mer*. Arles: Actes Sud, 1994.

Marrozi, Justin. *South from Barbary: Along the Slave Routes of the Libyan Sahara*. New York: HarperCollins, 2001.

Mauny, R., et al. *Textes et Documents Relatifs a l'histoire de l'Afrique: Extraits des Voyages d'Ibn Battuta*. Université de Dakar, Faculté des Lettres et Sciences Humaines, Dakar, 1966.

McIntosh, Roderick J., Joseph A. Tainter, and Susan Keech McIntosh, eds. *The Way the Wind Blows: Climate History and Human Action*. Chapter 6, "Memories, Abstractions and Conceptualizations of Ecological Crisis in the Mande World," by Téréba Togola. Accessed via http://www.earthscape.org/r3/mcintosh/mcintosh6.html.

Mills, Lady Dorothy. *The Road to Timbuktu*. London: Duckworth, 1924.

Monod, Theodore. "A propos d'un document concernant la conquête du Soudan par le Pasha Djouder (1591)." *Bulletin des Séances* 4(1964): 770–91.

Mountfield, David. *A History of African Exploration*. London: Hamlyn, 1976.

Musée des Arts Décoratifs (Museum of Decorative Arts). *Peintures Préhistoriques du Sahara: Mission H. Lhote au Tassili*. Paris: Symposium proceedings at the museum, November 1957, based on the work of Henri Lhote.

Newman, James L. *The Peopling of Africa: A Geographic Interpretation*. New Haven: Yale University Press, 1995.

Niane, D. T., ed. *General History of Africa*. Vol. 4. Paris: UNESCO, 1992.

Nicolaisen, Johannes, and Ida Nicolaisen. *The Pastoral Tuareg*. Vols. 1 and 2. London: Thames and Hudson, 1997.

Norris, H. T. *Saharan Myth and Saga*. London: Oxford University Press, 1972.

Pakenham, Thomas. *The Scramble for Africa*. New York: Random House, 1991.

Park, Mungo. *Travels in the Interior Districts of Africa Performed under the Direction and Patronage of the African Association in the Years 1795, 1796, and 1797*. London: W. Bulmer, 1799.

Philebert, General, and Georges Rolland. *La France en Afrique et le Transsaharien*. Paris: Librairie Algérienne et coloniale, 1890.

Porch, Douglas. *The Conquest of the Sahara*. New York: International Publishing, 1986.

Saad, Elias. *Social History of Timbuktu: The Role of Muslim Scholars and Notables, 1400–1900*. Cambridge: Cambridge University Press, 1983.

Sa'adi, Abd al-Rahman b. Abd Allah al-. *Tarikh al-Sudan*. Translated by O. Houdas. Paris: École des langues orientales vivantes, 1898–1900. *See also* Hunwick, John.

Salak, Kira. *The Cruelest Journey: Six Hundred Miles to Timbuktu*. Washington, D.C.: National Geographic Society, 2005.

Salem Ould Elhadj. "L'âge d'or de la cité, ou Tombouctou es les Askia de Gao, 1493–1591." Timbuktu: unpublished pamphlet.

———. "Contes et récits de Tombouctou." Timbuktu: unpublished pamphlet.

———. "Le Pachalik arma de Tombouctou, 1591–1826." Timbuktu: unpublished pamphlet.

———. "Tombuctou: Coutumes et traditions." Timbuktu: unpublished pamphlet.

Sattin, Anthony. *The Gates of Africa: Death, Discovery, and the Search for Timbuktu*. New York: St. Martin's Press, 2003.

Shabeni. *See* Jackson, James Grey.

Smith, Richard. "What Happened to the Ancient Libyans: Chasing Sources across the Sahara from Herodotus to Ibn Khaldun." *Journal of World History* (University of Hawaii) 14, no. 4 (December 2003): 459–500.

Stanley, Henry M. *In Darkest Africa*. New York: Scribner's, 1890.

Sutton, John. *A Thousand Years of East Africa*. Nairobi: British Institute in Eastern Africa, 1990.

Tayler, Jeffrey. *Angry Wind: Through Muslim Black Africa by Truck, Bus, Boat, and Camel*. New York: Houghton Mifflin, 2005.

Tremearne, A. J. N. *The Niger and the West Sudan: The West African's Note Book*. London: Hodder and Stoughton, 1900.

Trofimov, Yaroslav. *Faith at War: A Journey from the Front Lines of Islam, from Baghdad to Timbuktu*. New York: Henry Holt, 2005.

Vrettos, Theodore. *Alexandria: City of the Western Mind*. New York: Free Press/Simon and Schuster, 2001.

Werner, Louis. *Libya's Forgotten Desert Kingdom*. Paper on the Garamantes written for Saudi Aramco World. http://www.saudiaramcoworld.com/issue/200403

Zouber, Mahmoud. *Ahmad Baba de Tombouctou (1556–1627): Sa vie et son œuvre*. Paris: Maisonneuve et Larose, 1977.

Index

౭ు

A Note on the Authors

Marq de Villiers and Sheila Hirtle have traveled widely and have written extensively about Africa, including *Into Africa: A Journey Through the Ancient Empires* and *Sahara: The Extraordinary History of the World's Largest Desert.* Their *Sable Island*, published in Canada under the title *A Dune Adrift*, won the Evelyn Richardson Award for Non-fiction in 2004. De Villiers's *Water: The Fate of Our Most Precious Resource* won the 1999 Governer General's Award for Non-fiction. Hirtle, former editor of *Toronto Life Homes*, is a researcher with a background in fine art and design. De Villiers and Hirtle live in Eagle Head, Nova Scotia.